199 CEMETERIES
TO SEE BEFORE
YOU DIE

❧

LOREN RHOADS

BLACK DOG
& LEVENTHAL
PUBLISHERS
NEW YORK

For the Association for Gravestone Studies,

likeminded souls who have inspired and educated me.

Black Dog & Leventhal Publishers
Hachette Book Group
1290 Avenue of the Americas
New York, NY 10104
www.hachettebookgroup.com
www.blackdogandleventhal.com

First Edition: October 2017

Black Dog & Leventhal Publishers is an imprint of Hachette Books, a division of Hachette Book Group.
The Black Dog & Leventhal Publishers name and logo are trademarks of Hachette Book Group, Inc.

The publisher is not responsible for websites (or their content) that are not owned by the publisher.

The Hachette Speakers Bureau provides a wide range of authors for speaking events. To find out more,
go to www.HachetteSpeakersBureau.com or call (866) 376-6591.

Additional photo credits information is on page 224.

Library of Congress Cataloging-in-Publication Data has been applied for.
ISBNs: 978-0-316-43843-8 (hardcover), 978-0-316-47379-8 (ebook)

Printed in China

1010

10 9 8 7 6 5 4 3 2 1

CONTENTS

United States: South

United States: Midwest

United States: West

United States: West Coast

Canada

Central and South America and the Caribbean

Europe

Eastern Europe

Middle East

Africa

Asia

Australia

STOPPING TO SMELL THE ROSES

When you stop to notice, you realize people are buried everywhere. Every tourist destination has a cemetery, from New York City to Hong Kong to the Isle of Iona. Some tourist destinations are tombs: the Great Pyramids of Egypt or the Taj Mahal or the Royal Mounds of Gamla Uppsala in Sweden, for instance. There are permanent residents in museums, houses of worship, ghost towns, battlegrounds…even in national parks. You may have already visited someone's grave without giving it a second thought, if you've been to Pompeii or Westminster Abbey or the *USS Arizona* Memorial at Pearl Harbor.

Why would anyone go out of the way to visit a graveyard intentionally? In addition to the fascinating stories they contain, cemeteries can be open-air sculpture parks full of one-of-a-kind artwork. They provide habitats for birds and wildlife, as well as arboretums and gardens of surprising beauty. Cemeteries appeal to art lovers, amateur sociologists, birdwatchers, master gardeners, historians, hikers, genealogists, picnickers, and anyone who just wants to stop and smell the roses. Our relationships with the places we visit can be deepened and enriched by learning the stories of those who came—and stayed—before us.

While 199 cemeteries may seem like a lot, that number really just scratches the surface of the possibilities of cemetery travel. I wanted to spotlight beautiful places, because I think we sometimes overlook beauty in our rush through our day-to-day lives. I also wanted to focus on historical sites, especially places where history has changed in the telling over the years. I wanted to look at familiar stories and to remember lesser-known people, knowing as I did that any list of gravesites is idiosyncratic and reflects the collector's fascinations and eccentricities.

I tried to include as wide a range of locations and cultures as possible, while being reminded that permanent grave markers are a luxury not

everyone can afford—and not every culture chooses to create permanent memorials to their forebears. Sometimes I couldn't find enough information about a site to write an entry. Other times, the graveyards were too fragile for visitors. This book is by no means the final word on funeral customs, because humans are so various in their traditions. Hopefully, your curiosity will be sparked and you'll use this book as a jumping-off place to learning more.

Rule number one about visiting cemeteries is to be respectful. Don't interrupt or impede mourners. Even cemeteries that are closed to new burials deserve to be treated like something precious and irreplaceable, because they are. Just as you would when visiting a pristine wilderness, take nothing but photographs. If you find a grave marker that's broken—or in danger of breaking—let the grounds crew or office staff know. Leave everything where you find it so the next visitor can enjoy it as much as you have.

Whether you take a tour or follow a guidebook or simply wander on your own, be aware of your surroundings. Most graveyards are safer than city streets, but if you feel unsafe, listen to your intuition. I've never had any problems on my cemetery travels, but I have seen rattlesnake skins shed in the grass and roamed alone to some pretty isolated spots. Stay alert.

There's nothing like visiting a cemetery to give you a little perspective, to remind you that every day aboveground is a good day. I hope you find some inspiration for your travels here. ⚜

UNITED STATES: NORTHEAST

Old Burying Ground

Pepperell Road, Kittery Point, Maine
http://www.kitterypointucc.org/
church-history.html

In the mid-1600s, the British claimed large stretches of Maine for timber to build ships. The town of Kittery was organized overlooking the Piscataqua River in 1647. Like many small European outposts, the village struggled to protect itself from local natives. For safety's sake, the region became part of Massachusetts in 1652. That arrangement required every town in Maine to provide a meeting house and a preacher.

Kittery's First Congregational Church was built in 1730. In addition to serving as a place of worship, the church provided a stronghold against Native American attacks, a weapons storehouse, and the site of the village's whipping post.

The graveyard stands across the street from the church. The congregation built the stone wall around it in 1733. The burying ground grew so popular that the congregation began to charge two dollars for a lot. Survivors were required to bring enough dirt to cover the coffin.

Starting with 18th-century slate stones, the Old Parish Burying Ground illustrates two and a half centuries' worth of gravestone trends. Iconography spans from winged death's heads to apple-cheeked angels leaning their heads together beneath a single crown. Later tombstones are decorated with weeping willows or urns. Most prevalent are Victorian-era marble tablets adorned with flowers. Twentieth-century graves are marked with polished granite blocks.

A black stone remembers the brig *Hattie Eaton*, lost March 21, 1876 with a "crew of eight, white and negro, and one stowaway." Six of the bodies went unclaimed, so the townsfolk buried them here. The gravestone is engraved with a storm-tossed ship.

The Old Parish Burying Ground is reckoned one of the prettiest cemeteries in Maine. It was added to the National Registry of Historic Places in 1997. ⚜

Overlooking the Piscataqua River, Kittery Point's Old Burying Ground illustrates 250 years' worth of gravestone trends.

Hope Cemetery

201 Maple Avenue, Barre, Vermont
http://vermonter.com/hope-cemetery

Granite is a relatively hard coarse-grained rock formed in ancient volcanoes. It varies in color from black to white to red. Light-colored granite is mostly quartz, mixed with feldspar and mica. It has been quarried in Vermont since early in the 19th century. Barre, Vermont calls itself the Granite Capital of the World.

Sixty-five-acre Hope Cemetery is a monument to granite produced in Vermont, a veritable open-air showroom of the craftsmanship of Barre's local stone carvers. Every monument in the graveyard is hewn from granite quarried and carved locally.

Its nearly 11,000 monuments range from angels and weepers to portrait sculpture

This one-of-a-kind monument was commissioned to honor a young man's hobby: auto racing.

(including a bust appearing from the smoke of the deceased's cigar). There are planes, cars, and pyramids, as well as an oversize soccer ball.

One touching monument features a young woman cradling a man slumping backward, his arms hanging limply. Stonecutter Louis Brusa died in 1937 of silicosis, an illness caused by the inhalation of granite dust. It's said he wanted to warn other stonecutters of the dangers.

Another stonecutter is remembered by a life-size statue carved by his fellow artisans. Elia Corti was accidentally shot at a riot provoked by local anarchists in 1903. His statue wears a suit and bow tie, staring pensively at the world with his chin in his hand. He leans against a broken column, symbol of a life ended too soon.

Another remarkable monument remembers Mr. and Mrs. Halvosa. A double portrait carved into an upright stone gives the impression that they are sitting up against their beds' shared headboard. Gently arched stones form counter-panes over their individual graves: like the old *I Love Lucy* episodes, where Lucy and Ricky slept in separate twin beds. The Halvosas are holding hands and gazing at each other, a beautiful tribute to love transcending death.

Hope Cemetery has become quite a tourist attraction, especially in the autumn when the leaves change color. ⚜

Old Dutch Burying Ground

430 North Broadway, Sleepy Hollow, New York
http://visitsleepyhollow.com/historic-sites/old-dutch-church

The Old Dutch Burying Ground is one of America's oldest cemeteries, last resting place of Dutch tenant farmers, Revolutionary War soldiers, and namesakes of characters in Washington Irving's *Legend of Sleepy Hollow*.

Frederick Philipse, first lord of the nearby manor, built this little church in 1685. The bricks were shipped from Holland. The burial ground, probably dating back to 1640, preceded its church by two generations. Dutch settlers' graves cluster close around it. Even though the words

This 17th-century church is surrounded by the gravestones of Dutch settlers and soldiers who fought in the Revolutionary War.

are Dutch, the epitaphs run in familiar patterns: "*Hier Leyt Begraven*" for "Here lies buried."

In the 19th century, Irving called the building "The Old Dutch Church" and the name stuck. His tale made use of names in the graveyard. Although some of the red sandstone grave markers have flaked and slivered until none of

Stonecutter
Elia Corti was
immortalized by his
brother sculptors
at Hope Cemetery
in Barre.

their inscriptions remain, there are Crane family graves. Catriena Van Tessel, the namesake of the farmer's daughter in Irving's *Legend*, died in November 1706.

Many of the graves have little metal signs placed by the Tarrytown DAR (Daughters of the American Revolution—descendants of Revolutionary soldiers). Only since the American centennial in 1876 have all soldiers of the Revolutionary War—even foot soldiers—been lionized as patriots worth remembering.

Even so, not all the figures in the graveyard have a connection to history. The sandstone marker belonging to James Barnerd is brightened by a cherub with sagging jowls. Above the cherub's head floats something like a lotus blossom, probably a tongue of divine fire. His epitaph indicates that he was a sailor: "The

This red sandstone headstone remembers a Dutch farmer. The winged and crowned face that adorns it is called a soul effigy.

Boisterous Winds and Neptuns Waves have Tost me too and fro. By Gods decree you Plainly See I am Harbourd here Below." Barnerd was 48 when he "departed this life" in 1768. ⚜

4   African Burial Ground National Monument

**Duane Street, between Broadway and African Burial Ground Way, New York, New York
https://www.nps.gov/afbg/index.htm**

The Dutch imported Africans to work as slaves in 17th-century New Amsterdam, now called Manhattan. Technically owned by the Dutch East India Company, these Africans could own property, be baptized, and marry.

When the British took over in 1664, slave laws became more restrictive. The British imported Africans from the present-day countries of Cameroon, Ghana, Madagascar, Mozambique, Nigeria, and Sierra Leone.

Originally located outside the city limits, the 6.6-acre "Negros Buriel Ground" dates from around 1697, when Trinity Church first forbade burial of Africans in its churchyard. This was the only graveyard for the African population until the late 1700s. The dead were wrapped in shrouds, placed in wooden coffins, and buried with their heads pointing toward the west, the direction of freedom. Some were buried with beads or coins on their eyes.

The final part of the African Burial Ground National Monument is architect Rodney Leon's 24-foot-tall *Ancestral Libation Chamber*.

During the Revolutionary War, the British used this space as a graveyard for prisoners. The burial ground closed officially in 1794. The following year, building lots were developed and sold. The burial ground was forgotten.

In 1991, when the United States General Services Administration broke ground here for a federal building, contractors discovered graves 16 to 25 feet below street level. Anthropologists estimated that as many as 20,000 Africans had been buried in an area now covered by five city blocks. Parts of 419 skeletons were sent to Howard University in Washington, DC for forensic analysis.

In October 2003, those remains were placed in coffins handmade in Ghana. They were accompanied to the monument site by dancers, singers, and priests, and reburied in a traditional African ceremony. President George W. Bush designated

the surviving fragment of the burial ground as a National Monument in February 2006.

Currently, the National Park Service mans an Interpretive Center in the Ted Weiss Federal Building, located at 290 Broadway. This small museum examines the history of Africans in the colonial era. While one wall displays archaeological photographs of the gravesites, everything tangible has been returned to the ground.

Behind the Federal Building lies the African Burial Ground National Monument itself. Seven small mounds cover vaults in which the remains were placed. The site includes "The Circle of the Diaspora," a spiral map of the world surrounded by African symbols and religious talismans from many faiths. The final part of the monument is the 24-foot black stone "Ancestral Libation Chamber" designed by architect Rodney Leon. ⚜

In this vintage illustration, the huge Gothic Revival archway greets visitors to Green-Wood Cemetery. Richard Upjohn, the entryway's architect, also designed Trinity Church in Lower Manhattan.

Green-Wood Cemetery

500 25th Street, Brooklyn, New York
http://www.green-wood.com

It is the ambition of the New Yorker to live upon Fifth Avenue, to take his airings in the Park, and to sleep with his fathers in Green-Wood.
—*New York Times*, 1866

In 1838, Brooklyn's Green-Wood Cemetery followed the garden cemetery movement pioneered in the United States by Cambridge's Mount Auburn. These burial grounds didn't belong to churches, but used the beauty of their landscaping to attract clientele. Sightseers took trains from Manhattan merely to walk Green-Wood's twenty miles of paths and admire its statuary, sit by its fountains, and gaze at its views. In 1860 alone, the cemetery pulled in half a million visitors: a tourist attraction second only to Niagara Falls in all of North America.

5

The mausoleum of Egyptologist Albert Ross Parsons is an Egyptian Revival pyramid fronted by statues of Christ carrying a lamb, the virgin and child, and an adoring sphinx.

Green-Wood Cemetery occupies the site of the first major skirmish of the Revolutionary War. Battle Hill, the highest point in Brooklyn, takes its name from the 1776 Battle of Long Island. At the crest of the hill, a statue of Minerva, Roman goddess of war, gazes across the harbor at the Statue of Liberty. Minerva was sculpted by Frederick Wellington Ruckstull, who also made the Soldiers' and Sailors' Monument in Queens.

When tourists came to see Green-Wood, they treated themselves to souvenirs. Among the mementos they took home were stereoview cards: stiff cardboard cards mounted with a pair of duplicate photographs. Slipped into a stereopticon viewer, the images magically became three-dimensional. Over a thousand different stereoview cards of Green-Wood Cemetery were produced.

Green-Wood's 478 acres contain the remains of more than 560,000 souls. Buried at Green-Wood are telegraph inventor Samuel Morse, sewing machine inventor Elias Howe, toy merchant FAO Schwarz, conductor Leonard Bernstein, painter Jean-Michel Basquiat, stained glass artist Louis Comfort Tiffany, Tammany Hall leader Boss Tweed, and Civil War generals, baseball legends, and more. Green-Wood offers walking and trolley tours, historical reenactments, and special events to draw attention to some of its lesser-known residents.

Until the 20th century, Green-Wood was the largest landscaped cemetery in the world. In 2006, the U.S. Department of the Interior named Green-Wood Cemetery a National Historic Landmark. It is only the fourth cemetery in the nation to receive this designation. ⚜

Minerva, Roman goddess of war, marks one of the sites of the Revolutionary War–era Battle of Long Island. She was sculpted by Frederick Wellington Ruckstull.

Mount Hope Cemetery

**1133 Mount Hope Avenue,
Rochester, New York
http://www.cityofrochester.gov/mounthope**

On October 3, 1838, the Reverend Pharcellus Church dedicated Mount Hope Cemetery with the words, "We have come to consecrate a home for the dead in which they may rest secure from the encroachments of industry and avarice till the last trumpet calls them to a judgment."

Many of the 5000 men from Rochester who fought in the Civil War are buried here. Their monument is inscribed with lines from Theodore O'Hara's poem *The Bivouac of the Dead*: "On Fame's eternal camping-ground, Their silent tents are spread, And Glory guards, with solemn round, The bivouac of the dead."

Mount Hope is also the final resting place of Frederick Douglass, who escaped slavery in 1838 and published an abolitionist newspaper in Rochester from 1847 to 1860. A tireless fighter for the rights of African-Americans, women, Native Americans, and immigrants, Douglass was the first African-American nominated for vice president of the United States in 1872. He authored three autobiographies.

When Susan B. Anthony began her crusade for women's rights in 1852, she was 33. Women had no legal custody of their children. They could not vote, inherit property, sign a contract, or be tried by a jury of their peers, since women were prohibited from serving on juries. Anthony was arrested in 1872 after voting in the presidential election. She died at the age of 86 in 1906. Women would not be granted the vote for 14 more years.

After the 2016 presidential election, women who voted for Hillary Clinton to become the first female president came to leave their "I Voted" stickers on Anthony's gravestone. Mount Hope stayed open late that night to welcome visitors honoring Anthony's legacy. ⚜

Voting stickers decorate Susan B. Anthony's gravestone.

7 Hartsdale Pet Cemetery

75 North Central Park Avenue, Hartsdale, New York
http://www.petcem.com

The War Dog memorial at Hartsdale was designed by Walter A. Buttendorf and sculpted by Robert Caterson to honor the dogs who served in World War I. It was unveiled in 1923 at a ceremony attended by representatives of every nation that fought in the Great War.

At the end of the 19th century, New York City banned burials of animals within its city limits. Since it was illegal to bury animals in human graveyards or public parks, the only option when a pet died was to put its body out with the trash.

In 1896, New York City veterinarian Dr. Samuel K. Johnson allowed a client to bury a dog in his apple orchard. Johnson eventually dedicated three acres of his land to a cemetery for people's best friends.

Johnson welcomed people to bring their deceased pets to his office on Manhattan's 25th Street, where they could purchase a zinc-lined casket. Then they would travel 25 miles by train to the quiet village of Hartsdale in Westchester County, where Johnson's apple orchard was filling with monuments.

Animals buried in the cemetery range from cats and dogs to horses, monkeys, rabbits, guinea pigs, goldfish, iguanas, snakes, and parakeets. Monuments vary from standard headstones to portrait sculptures, stone doghouses and cat baskets, and more. The oldest surviving monument dates to 1899.

The most exotic animal is the lion Goldfleck, "sincerely mourned by his mistress, Princess Lwoff-Parlaghy." She was a Hungarian artist who bought a lion cub from Ringling Brothers Circus. He lived with her at the Plaza Hotel until his death in 1912.

Although the practice of interring humans and animals together is illegal in the U.S., more than 700 pet owners have chosen to have their ashes interred with their companions. Several share gravestones with their pets.

During World War I, thousands of dogs were trained to locate wounded soldiers. Service dogs have a monument at Hartsdale: a ten-ton boulder of Barre granite, topped with a bronze statue of a kerchief-wearing dog with a dented helmet at his feet. Police, fire, and weapons-detection dogs are also buried at the cemetery. ⚜

8 Granary Burying Ground

Tremont Street, Boston, Massachusetts
http://www.cityofboston.gov/parks/hbgi/Granary.asp

Established in 1660 to alleviate crowding at King's Chapel Burying Ground, the Granary Burying Ground takes its name from a grain storehouse that once stood nearby.

Perhaps as many as 8000 skeletons lay inside this small patch of ground, which barely covers two acres. One source estimates that as many as twenty bodies lie beneath each tombstone. Unfortunately, few of the 2345 tombstones mark graves any longer. Around the dawn of the 20th century, groundskeepers realigned the gravestones to make it easier to mow between them.

The Granary Burying Ground is the final resting place of many of Boston's Revolutionary War patriots, including James Otis, who declared, "Taxation without representation is tyranny"; Robert Treat Paine, signer of the Declaration of Independence and first Massachusetts Attorney General; and victims of the Boston Massacre, including Crispus Attucks.

Visitors commonly line up to be photographed beside the monuments of Paul Revere and Samuel Adams. Also in the graveyard stands a monument to John Hancock. Legend says that grave robbers stole his hand first, either because they couldn't remove his rings or because a collector wanted the hand that signed the Declaration of Independence. Hancock's body may have vanished during the restoration of his gravesite.

In the Granary Burying Ground, ornamentation on gravestones runs from awkward death's heads to anatomically correct skulls to cherubs with portrait-like faces. These "soul effigies"

indicate a huge shift in Christian philosophy, from the Puritan belief that only the Elect will rise to Heaven to a general sense that all souls took flight toward Heaven upon the body's death.

Some of the gravestones can be traced to particular carvers, which demonstrates an advance in how people valued graveyards. When tombstones were acknowledged as works of art rather than a necessary evil, artists claimed their designs. Some carvers even autographed their stones.

The cemetery closed to new burials in 1879. ❦

The rediscovery of Roman-era tombs in Pompeii in 1748 inspired a fashion for urns as graveyard decorations. This gravestone is an early example.

Mount Auburn Cemetery

**580 Mount Auburn Street,
Cambridge, Massachusetts
http://www.mountauburn.org**

As the first garden cemetery in the United States, Mount Auburn represents a paradigm shift. Following fashion set by Père Lachaise in Paris and Highgate Cemetery in London, Mount Auburn Cemetery liberated the dead from the churchyard to rest in the beautiful arms of nature.

Dr. Jacob Bigelow, foremost botanist in New England, began the discussion of opening a country cemetery in 1825. In 1830, the Mount Auburn site—one mile from Harvard and four miles from Boston—was chosen for its beauty. It had hillocks and dells, valleys and promontories.

9

This 1914 stereoview image of Mount Auburn Cemetery shows one of the old ponds.

Mary Baker Eddy founded the Church of Christ, Scientist in 1879. Her Greek Revival memorial stands on the shores of Halcyon Lake at Mount Auburn Cemetery.

With Bigelow's assistance, the cemetery was carefully designed to give impressions of both space and privacy. Plantings were selected to turn the cemetery into an arboretum of unparalleled loveliness.

When it opened in 1831, 72-acre Mount Auburn Cemetery was the largest burial ground in the United States. Mount Auburn has now swelled to 175 acres.

A variety of maps and materials about the cemetery are available at the entrance gate. These include flyers that highlight a "Person of the Week," feature poetry by resident bards, or aid in locating state champion trees.

The Friends of Mount Auburn Cemetery offer guided walking tours, slide lectures, and special events at the cemetery. In addition to visiting the celebrities buried there, the

Friends explore the history, horticulture, art, and architecture of the cemetery. There are also birdwatching tours.

With so many other things to see and do at Mount Auburn, the graves serve as adornments, not distinguishing features. Still, Mount Auburn has been called the "Westminster Abbey of America." Its permanent residents include Oliver Wendell Holmes; poets Henry Wadsworth Longfellow and Amy Lowell, who won the Pulitzer Prize for poetry; John Bartlett, compiler of *Familiar Quotations*; publishers George H. Mifflin, Charles Little, and James Brown; as well as Dorothea Dix, who pioneered humane treatment for insanity; painter Winslow Homer; Julia Ward Howe, author of "The Battle Hymn of the Republic"; and Mary Baker Eddy, founder of Christian Science. ❖

Forest Hills Cemetery

**95 Forest Hills Avenue,
Boston, Massachusetts
http://www.foresthillscemetery.com**

Founded in 1848, 17 years after Mount Auburn Cemetery, Forest Hills Cemetery featured lovely artwork from the start. *Death and the Sculptor* by Daniel Chester French may be the most magnificent work of art ever designed for a graveyard. The large bronze combines relief work and statuary. Death is a stern-faced matron dressed in Grecian robes and a cowled cloak. She has wings, but doesn't carry a scythe or an hourglass. She merely reaches her shapely arm out to touch the sculptor's chisel. He's in the middle of carving a relief of the sphinx, a reference to Martin Milmore, for whom this monument was made. Milmore sculpted the Sphinx at Mount Auburn.

French, who sculpted the monumental figure seated inside the Lincoln Memorial in Washington, DC, has six sculptures at Forest Hills. His bronze *Angel of Peace* stands in a sun-struck meadow, her powerful wings raised behind her.

Statues of permanent mourners stand atop many of Forest Hills' graves. These drapery-clad graces pose in varying states of dishabille. One has her flowing hair wound in a partial bun, as if she'd been too distraught to fix it properly. Elsewhere, Faith turns blind eyes upward as she cups an anchor chain in her hands. Her gown, caressing every curve, slides dangerously low on both shoulders. Joyce Carol Oates, in her introduction to David Robinson's *Saving Graces*, notes that these mourning statues behave "as if grief were a form of erotic surrender."

The cemetery also serves as a lovely arboretum. The native trees tend toward pines and evergreens. In the spring, drifts of forsythia bloom in masses of sunny yellow. Flowering cherries and apples contrast dark gray shoulders of rock.

Forest Hills Cemetery is the final resting place of poets e e cummings and Anne Sexton, playwright Eugene O'Neill, Revolutionary War generals, suffragette doctors, as well as the Red Scare martyrs Sacco and Vanzetti. ✤

Daniel Chester French's *Death and the Sculptor* features a gentle female Death. She holds poppies, to symbolize sleep, in her right hand.

God's Little Acre

**Inside the Common Burying Ground,
Farewell Street, Newport, Rhode Island
http://www.colonialcemetery.com**

In 1639, Newport was founded as a port and shipbuilding center. Early in its history, Newport participated in the transatlantic slave trade. Thousands of Africans from the Gold and Ivory Coasts were transported to Newport, where they worked in the homes of merchants and rum distillers. During Colonial times, one in three families owned at least one servant. Slaves made up a full third of the population.

Newport had a large, diverse African-American community, including skilled professionals and artisans. Some of these highly skilled slaves became Free Africans and chose to remain in the area. They formed a benevolent society in 1780 to see to the burial of their fellows. Rhode Island abolished slavery in 1784.

The graveyard predates that, however. Inside the boundaries of the oldest public graveyard in Newport—the Common Burying Ground—stands God's Little Acre, a burial ground set aside for Colonial African-Americans. At one point, there were as many as 300 markers, but most have been stolen or vandalized. The earliest surviving stones have death's heads, later supplanted by

cherubs, some of whom have curly hair and African-American features. Some headstones use the words *Negro*, *black*, or *servant*, a euphemism of the period for "slave."

Many of the tombstones were carved by Pompe "Zingo" Stevens, servant of local stone-carver John Stevens. Zingo might possibly be the first African-American artist in the United States. Although he made stones for his wives, Philis, Elizabeth, and Violet, and his brother, Cufrie Gibbs, Zingo himself no longer has a monument of his own. ❧

The gravestone of Peg, a six-year-old slave who died in 1740.

Touro Jewish Cemetery

**Touro Street, Newport, Rhode Island
http://www.tourosynagogue.org/
history-learning/cemetery-literature**

When fifteen Jewish families arrived from Holland in 1658, they founded the first Jewish colony in America in Newport. The Touro Synagogue is the oldest Jewish place of worship in North America. It was designed by Peter Harrison, who also designed King's Chapel in Boston.

Land for the congregation's graveyard was purchased in 1677, which suggests an earlier

burial ground must have filled. This cemetery stands up the hill from the synagogue. Its Egyptian Revival gates were designed by Isaiah Rogers, who designed the identical gates at the Granary Burying Ground in Boston.

The Touro Cemetery has 100 known burials, but only 40 stones survive. The earliest stones still standing date to the 1700s. Throughout the graveyard, inscriptions vary from Portuguese and Spanish to Hebrew, Latin, and English.

Four obelisks mark the graves of the Touro family, from whom the cemetery takes its name. Patriarch Isaac was buried in Kingston, Jamaica, but his widow lies here, along with their son Abraham and daughter Rebecca and her husband, Joshua Lopez. Judah Touro has the tallest obelisk. He made a fortune in New Orleans, but donated

money for the upkeep of the cemetery, including paying for the fence and the Rogers gate to the tune of $12,000. When he died in 1854, his body was brought here to the family plot.

Henry Wadsworth Longfellow wrote "The Jewish Cemetery at Newport" the year of Judah Touro's death. His poem remarks on how the "Alvares and Rivera interchange with Abraham and Jacob."

Since the cemetery is fragile, it only opens to the public once a year, in August. Touro Synagogue offers a brochure designed for people who view the cemetery from outside its fence. ⚜

The Touro Jewish Cemetery's Egyptian Revival gate was designed by Isaiah Rogers, who had designed an identical gate for the Granary Burying Ground in Boston.

North Burial Ground

5 Branch Avenue, Providence, Rhode Island
**https://www.providenceri.com/parks-and-rec/
north-burial-ground**

In 1700, the town of Providence set this land apart for the burial of the dead. By 1848, when surviving records begin, 22 acres had already been filled.

Among those buried in the North Burial Ground are a number of Rhode Island governors, Providence city mayors, congressmen, senators, and a signer of the Declaration of Independence. Horace Mann, the champion of universal free public education, is buried here, as is Sarah Helen Whitman, a poet who inspired several of Edgar Allan Poe's poems. Maps of notable burials for a self-led walking tour are available from the office.

Many of the grave monuments illustrate Providence's shipping history by use of an anchor or windlass or images of ships at sea. Generally, anchors symbolize Christian faith as something that holds fast through the tempests of life.

Captain Joseph Tillinghast's monument bears this epitaph:

Tho' Borea's blast and Neptune's waves
have tossed me to and fro,
yet in spite of both by God's decree
I harbor here below.
And though at anchor now I ride
with many of our fleet,
yet away again I shall set sail
our Admiral Christ to meet.

Epitaphs—a phrase in memory of someone who died—began to be added to tombstones in the United States in the late 1700s. Before that, grave markers only listed names and sometimes dates, although the earliest stones seldom bore more than initials. That said, Captain Tillinghast's epitaph echoes (with liberties) the grave of Captain John Dunch, buried in Saint Dunstan's Church in Stepney, London, England in 1695. ⚜

During the first half of the 19th century, willows became acceptable stand-ins for mourners in gravestone iconography. Willows weep over urns on these gravestones in the North Burial Ground.

14 Swan Point Cemetery

**585 Blackstone Boulevard,
Providence, Rhode Island
http://swanpointcemetery.com**

Lovecraft received a gravestone of his own in 1977 after fans took up a collection. His epitaph is taken from one of his letters.

Founded in 1846, Rhode Island's Swan Point Cemetery absorbed people who had been previously buried in earlier graveyards around Providence. The oldest section of the cemetery, overlooking the Seekonk River, contains graves that date back as early as 1722.

In 1886, Chicago-based landscape architect H.W.S. Cleveland designed the wall of boulders that front Blackstone Boulevard for more than a mile. In 1903, the Butler Avenue trolley car extended to the cemetery, where a fieldstone shelter was constructed for riders. Many people came out just to walk the grounds.

Even now, Swan Point's chief draw is the beauty of its landscaping, which varies from lawn to forest to rhododendrons, azaleas, magnolias, and other flowering shrubs. In all, the cemetery contains more than 200 kinds of trees and shrubs, most of them labeled. In the spring, daffodils gild the section by the river.

Swan Point is also full of lovely Victorian statuary. Twenty-three former governors of Rhode Island are buried here, each under a suitably grand monument.

Among the better known people buried at Swan Point Cemetery is Major Sullivan Ballou, wounded in the First Battle of Bull Run, whose beautiful farewell letter to his wife is featured in Ken Burns's *Civil War* documentary.

Swan Point's most famous resident is Howard Phillips Lovecraft. His grave has a low gray granite marker with the epitaph "I am Providence," which is a line from one of his letters. Lovecraft's story "The Call of Cthulhu" appeared in *Weird Tales* magazine in 1928 and introduced the world to the Cthulhu mythos. ⚜

15 Grove Street Cemetery

**227 Grove Street, New Haven, Connecticut
http://www.grovestreetcemetery.org**

In New Haven, an 18th-century campaign to close the overcrowded churchyards led to a new type of burial place. Thirty-two wealthy men formed a private association to establish a burial ground—and created the first incorporated cemetery in America. Its 1797 charter said, "Any person or body politic, their heirs, successors, or signs, who shall be the proprietor or owner of a lot which now is, or hereafter shall be located or laid out in said burying ground, shall be a legal member of said corporation and entitled to one vote for every lot he or they shall own or possess." In other words, the lot holders owned the cemetery. That was revolutionary.

The 18-acre cemetery was laid out as a grid, a design considered innovative, just as the cemetery was considered huge. Also revolutionary: People could be buried with their families, rather than in the order in which they died. Families invested in large monuments with the family name—often an obelisk—as the centerpiece for their plots: celebrating kinship, rather than individual achievement. Lots were large enough to bury family members for generations.

The landscape design combined the aesthetic of 18th-century English gardens with the flowering orchards of Connecticut. Tall Lombardy poplars emphasized the geometric design of the grounds and underlined the stability of the institution. Weeping willows, recently accepted as metaphors for grief, added movement and color to the grounds.

A heavy brownstone Egyptian Revival Gate greets visitors. It was unveiled in 1848, after the popularity of the smaller Egyptian gateway at Mount Auburn. Egyptiana became a worldwide fad after Napoleon's campaign in Egypt at the turn of the 19th century. Grove Street Cemetery's gateway was designed by architect Henry Austin, who is buried here.

Many other distinguished people are also buried here: Eli Whitney, inventor of the cotton gin; Noah Webster, lexicographer who standardized American spelling with his dictionary; Charles Goodyear, originator of rubber vulcanization; Theodore Winthrop, a novelist who was one of the first officers killed in the Civil War; paleontologist Othniel Marsh; Hiram Bingham, pioneer missionary to Hawaii; and Roger Sherman, the only man to sign all four fundamental documents on which the United States government is based: the Articles of Association, the Declaration of Independence, the Articles of Confederation, and the Constitution. ❧

Eli Whitney's cotton gin made it easy to pull seeds from cotton. After its invention, cotton became the primary crop in the American South and led to the Civil War.

Mountain Grove Cemetery

2675 North Avenue, Bridgeport, Connecticut
http://www.mountaingrovecemetery.org

Phineas Taylor Barnum was born on July 5, 1810 in Bethel, Connecticut. He was a vocal antislavery crusader and philanthropist, who founded the lovely Mountain Grove Cemetery with his associates in 1849. In 1881, Barnum partnered with James Bailey to create the first three-ring circus: Barnum and Bailey's, the Greatest Show on Earth.

Charles Sherwood Stratton was born on January 4, 1838, in Bridgeport, Connecticut. A normal size and weight at birth, he grew very slowly. At the age of 5, he met P. T. Barnum, who taught him to sing and dance and took him on an American tour as General Tom Thumb. In 1844, they went to Europe, where Charles charmed Queen Victoria.

At his tallest, Stratton grew to only 3 feet 4 inches. He married Lavinia Warren, who also worked for Barnum, at Grace Church in New York City in 1863. Twenty years later, Charles died suddenly from a stroke at the age of 45.

Barnum commissioned a column forty feet high crowned with a life-size statue of his friend. The marble shaft cracked and had to be lowered, then the statue was vandalized several times. A plaque on the monument details its restoration, funded by the Barnum Festival Society and the Mountain Grove Cemetery Association. Lavinia,

16

Circus ringmaster P. T. Barnum and his associates founded the lovely Mountain Grove Cemetery in 1849.

who was 32 inches tall in life, is buried beside Charles.

Barnum suffered a stroke in 1890 and died the following year in April. His granite monument is surprisingly restrained.

Among the 40,000 people buried at Mountain Grove are Fanny Crosby, a blind poet who composed 8000 hymns, one of the most prolific hymnists in history; author Robert Lawson, who won the Newbery medal for *Rabbit Hill*; and Vernon Dalhart, the first country music singer to record a million-selling hit. His version of "The Wreck of the Old 97," about a mail train derailing, sold 7 million copies in the 1920s. ⚜

17 Old Swedes Burial Ground

**606 North Church Street,
Wilmington, Delaware
http://www.oldswedes.org**

Old Swedes Burial Ground stands near the place where the first Swedish settlers landed in the Delaware Valley on the shores of the Christina River. The burial ground encompasses the graveyard of the original Fort Christina and may date back to the original landing in 1638.

Holy Trinity Church, popularly called Old Swedes Church, was built alongside the graveyard in 1698–99. They stand on slightly higher ground, out of reach of the river's floodwaters. The church was originally Swedish Lutheran, but when the congregation couldn't hire a Swedish priest, they converted to Episcopalian in 1845. A

In the foreground, a small child's grave looks like a crib. Notice also the urn atop the granite column closer to the church.

number of people are buried beneath the church's floor, especially around the altar, where priests and their family members were interred.

More than 1200 gravestones survive in the burial ground, although not all of them are still legible. Although as many as 10,000 people may have been buried here, the records were lost. Surviving tombstones range from simple fieldstone markers to marble obelisks.

Buried here are three generations of Bayards, who served as U.S. senators from the state of Delaware. James Asheton Bayard Jr. also served as U.S. Attorney for Delaware. His son Thomas

Francis Bayard Sr. was a three-term senator, who became Secretary of State for President Grover Cleveland. His son Thomas Francis Bayard Jr. was a senator from 1922 to 1929.

Civil War Major General James Harrison Wilson is buried here, too. He was promoted to field command of the cavalry and destroyed Nathan Bedford Forrest's confederate cavalry at the Battle of Selma.

Since the church and its cemetery date to the first permanent European settlement in Delaware, the church was declared a National Historic Landmark in 1961. ⚜

Thomas Edison National Historical Park

221 Main Street, West Orange, New Jersey
https://www.nps.gov/edis/index.htm

In August 1931, 84-year-old Thomas Alva Edison collapsed at home. He had already created more than a thousand inventions, from electric lights to moving pictures to mimeograph machines. He remained housebound at his

15-acre Glenmont estate until October 18, when he died from complications of diabetes. Sculptor James Earle Fraser, who had been working on a sculpture of Edison, made a death mask.

In the morning of October 19, Edison's body was moved to the library of his laboratory, where it lay in state in a casket topped with glass so visitors could see him in his string tie. An estimated 40,000 people came to pay their respects.

Edison's funeral took place on the anniversary of the perfection of the incandescent light. His friends Henry Ford and Harvey Firestone were there, along with first lady Lou Henry Hoover, who came on behalf of the president.

Thomas Edison died at home in October 1931. He lay in state in the library.

Edison's grave is covered with a ledger stone engraved with a pearl inside a scallop shell. In this case, the pearl symbolizes wisdom.

After the funeral, the body was transported to Rosedale Cemetery, where it was consigned to the ground with a simple service as the sun set. All over the world, communities dimmed their lights in his honor.

Six New Jersey state troopers guarded the gravesite for six days to prevent his body from being stolen.

When Edison's wife, Mina, died in 1947, she was buried at his side at Rosedale. Both were exhumed in 1963 and moved to the grounds of the Glenmont estate, which had come under the auspices of the National Park Service. The estate's name was changed to the Thomas Edison National Historical Park in 2009.

The two graves lie side by side behind the house. Simple gray granite ledger stones cover them. Edison's, on the left, has only his name, the years of his lifetime, and a pearl engraved inside a scallop shell. Mina's is engraved with a cross bearing an ornate crown. Neither has an epitaph. ❖

19 Congregation Mikveh Israel Cemetery

825 Spruce Street, Philadelphia, Pennsylvania
http://www.mikvehisrael.org/e2_cms_dis-play.php?p=past_cemeteries

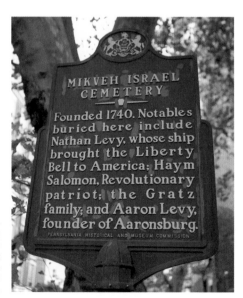

Pioneer fur trader Aaron Levy founded Aaronsburg, possibly the first settlement in the United States established by and named for a Jew.

When Nathan Levy's son died in 1738, no Jewish cemeteries existed in Philadelphia. Levy, whose ship would bring the Liberty Bell to America in 1752, spoke to Governor Thomas Penn. Penn sold Levy a wooded piece of land on the north side of Walnut Street between 8th and 9th Streets.

Scarcely a dozen Jews lived in Philadelphia at the time—most of them from Holland. Levy realized that the community would soon grow, which would require a larger permanent burial ground. A 30-foot-square piece of land on Spruce Street was purchased in 1740 and the bodies were moved from the Walnut Street graveyard. The new burial ground gained a little more land before it was enclosed with a brick wall in 1751. It's still very small.

Among those buried here are Nathan Levy himself, who died in 1753. His tomb has the oldest decipherable inscription in the cemetery. Haym Salomon, one of the primary financiers of the American Revolution, later ended up as a pauper. He was buried here in 1785 in an unmarked grave. A plaque on the wall remembers him now. Simon Gratz, who helped co-found the Pennsylvania Academy of Fine Arts—the first museum with an art school in

Haym Salomon was buried in an unmarked grave, but a plaque to his memory was placed by the Haym Salomon Lodge of Brith Sholom in 1976, to mark the bicentennial of the United States.

the United States—lies here, as does his sister Rebecca, the inspiration for her namesake in Sir Walter Scott's *Ivanhoe*. She founded educational institutions for women. Their brother Jacob, also here, served as a Pennsylvania state senator.

During the Revolutionary War, British soldiers occupying Philadelphia used the gravestones for target practice.

Jewish veterans of the War of 1812 rest here, alongside veterans of the Civil War. The cemetery closed to new burials in 1866.

Congregation Mikveh Israel Cemetery became part of Independence National Historical Park in 1956. It was added to the National Register of Historic Places in 1971. It's open only with a docent-led tour provided by the Mikveh Israel Synagogue. ⚜

Laurel Hill Cemetery

**3822 Ridge Avenue,
Philadelphia, Pennsylvania
https://thelaurelhillcemetery.org**

Founded in 1836, Laurel Hill Cemetery is the second oldest garden cemetery in the United States, after Cambridge's Mount Auburn. Architect John Notman designed Laurel Hill's maze of roads to wind amid terraces above the Schuykill River. His intention was to give the people of Philadelphia a park from which they could ponder their mortality and look forward to the glories of Heaven.

Within months of opening, Laurel Hill Cemetery became Philadelphia's most popular attraction, drawing more people than Independence Hall and the Liberty Bell. The cemetery was so popular that in 1860 it received over 140,000 visitors. The cemetery office issued admission tickets to control the flood.

Permanent residents include Sarah Josepha Hale (whom we have to thank for "Mary Had a Little Lamb"), portrait painter Thomas Sully, and Union General George Gordon Meade (who was victorious at Gettysburg) and thirty-nine other Civil War–era generals, both Union and Confederate. A signer of the Declaration of Independence is buried here, as well as a sailor who fought in the War of 1812. There are also six passengers of the *Titanic*.

20

The Angel of Death, as envisioned by Alexander Milne Calder, opens the Warner sarcophagus to release the soul trapped inside. Unfortunately, the angel's hands have been missing from this sculpture for decades.

The 78-acre cemetery is a sea of obelisks and grand mausoleums, with its own Angels Row. In fact, Laurel Hill contains more than 33,000 monuments and as many as 75,000 permanent residents. The most striking monument in the graveyard remembers the William Warner family. Designed by Alexander Milne Calder, the sculpture embodies the Angel of Death as a stern woman whose gown is slipping from her shoulder. She has opened the granite sarcophagus to release the soul trapped inside. A winged face rises from the open tomb in a flame of stone. ⚜

Soldiers' National Cemetery

Gettysburg National Military Park
1195 Baltimore Pike, Gettysburg, Pennsylvania
https://www.nps.gov/gett/planyourvisit/150th-anniversary-dedication-day-cemetery-history.htm

During the July 1863 battle in Gettysburg, Pennsylvania, there were 51,000 casualties. After losing 30 percent of his army, Confederate General Robert E. Lee withdrew on July 5th. Union General Meade, in charge of the Army of the Potomac, chose not to pursue. His men attempted to bury their own dead, but the job was too immense. When the Union Army finally withdrew from the field, thousands of corpses lay where they'd fallen, rotting in the humid Pennsylvanian summer. People could smell the battlefield as far away as York, 30 miles distant.

The sad state of the unburied dead drew the attention of Pennsylvania Governor Andrew Curtin. He championed a movement to buy land from the village to provide a cemetery where all Northern soldiers could lie with their comrades. Eventually, money was raised to purchase a "boot-shaped" piece of ground alongside the village's own Evergreen Cemetery. Reburials began in October 1863, four months after the battle ended.

These were the days before dog tags. Corpses at Gettysburg could be identified only by company insignia or marks of rank on their uniforms, or by the contents of their pockets, so long as they hadn't been robbed after death. Superintendent of Exhumation Samuel Weaver insisted that all temporary graves be opened in his presence,

so he could personally identify the corpses. As much as he was able, Weaver recorded hair color and height of the decomposing dead, to be compared with government service records for each man. Even so, stones labeled "Unknown" mark more than half of the graves inside Soldiers' National Cemetery.

A ceremony was planned for November 19, 1863, to dedicate the nation's first military cemetery. President Lincoln was invited to speak as an afterthought. Months after the battle, shallow graves still littered the surrounding countryside, but the war itself had moved south and once again Northerners could travel safely. Over 50,000 people descended on the shell-shocked village.

Lincoln traveled to the ceremony by train. Standing among new-made graves, he delivered the Gettysburg Address: "We have come to dedicate a portion of that field as a final resting place for those who here gave their lives that that nation might live….But in a larger sense, we cannot dedicate, we cannot consecrate, we cannot hallow this ground. The brave men, living and dead, who struggled here, have consecrated it far above our poor power to add or detract."

For the first time, a battlefield was seen as holy ground, consecrated not by the power of God but by the blood of men slain there. Soldiers became sanctified by the circumstances of their deaths. For the first time ever, bodies of common men were not treated as an inconvenient by-product of war, but venerated as its relics.

Soldiers' National Cemetery became a place of pilgrimage. Currently, 2 million people visit the national park at Gettysburg each year, making it one of the most popular historical destinations in the United States. ⚜

In this photo from 1913, graves at Gettysburg's Soldiers' National Cemetery are decorated with flags for Memorial Day. Although celebrated for more than a century, Memorial Day didn't become a federal holiday until 1971.

A spectacular
dogwood blooms
in Rock Creek
Cemetery.

UNITED STATES: SOUTH

Rock Creek Cemetery

201 Allison Street NW, Washington, DC
http://www.stpaulsrockcreek.org/cemetery

Saint Paul's Episcopal Church, Rock Creek Parish, began as a mission church in 1712. It is the only surviving Colonial church left in Washington, DC.

In September 1719, vestryman Colonel John Bradford donated 100 acres for the support of the church. Almost from the start, the area surrounding the church was used as a burial ground. Some of those old grave markers still exist.

In the 1830s, the church decided to expand the area it used for burials and convert its land from farming to a public graveyard. Inspired by the success of Mount Auburn Cemetery, they utilized the rolling landscape when they laid out the roads. An Act of Congress established Rock Creek Cemetery as a burial ground for the city of Washington.

The memorial that everyone comes to see belongs to Henry Brooks Adams, a grandson of John Quincy Adams (sixth president of the United States) and great-grandson of John Adams (the second president). Henry Brooks Adams himself was a professor of medieval history at Harvard. His autobiography won a Pulitzer Prize, but he considered *The History of the United States of America 1801 to 1817* to be his masterwork. After his wife Marian (called Clover) committed suicide by poisoning herself with photographic chemicals, he commissioned Augustus Saint-Gaudens to sculpt a monument to her. The statue is commonly referred to as *Grief*, but Saint-Gaudens called it *The Mystery of the Hereafter and the Peace of God That Passeth Understanding*.

In addition, the cemetery has a wealth of lovely sculpture, including *Rabboni* by Gutzon Borglum (sculptor of Mount Rushmore), *The Seven Ages of Memory* by William Ordway Partridge, and Brenda Putnam's statue of a child on Anna Simon's grave.

Famous burials include Upton Sinclair, author of *The Jungle*; Charles Francis Jenkins, the inventor of television; Abraham Baldwin, a signer of the Constitution; Charles Corby, creator of Wonder Bread; Gilbert H. Grosvenor, chairman of the National Geographic Society; two mayors of Washington; three Union Army generals; and four Supreme Court justices. ⚜

Congressional Cemetery

1801 E Street SE, Washington, DC
http://www.congressionalcemetery.org

The original plan for Washington, DC, made no provisions for a burial ground. In 1798, two squares on the borders of town were finally set aside as the eastern and western burial grounds. The eastern spot was prone to flooding, so residents of that part of town chose another piece of land—less than five square acres—and purchased it from the city for $200. Their intention was to sell grave plots for $2 each. Once the space was paid off, it would be overseen by Christ Church. Washington Parish Burial Ground, as it was named, banned "infidels" and people of color.

The first burial, in 1807, was William Swinton, a stonecutter for the Capitol Building. Three months later, Connecticut senator Uriah Tracy died. Benjamin Henry Latrobe, architect of the Capitol Building, was asked to design a monument to mark his grave along with the graves of any more congressmen who would follow him to the cemetery. The wide, heavy monuments are made

Benjamin Henry Latrobe, architect of the U.S. Capitol Building, designed a monument to honor members of Congress who died in office. Not all of the congressmen honored at the Congressional Cemetery are actually buried there.

of Aquia Creek sandstone to match the Capitol. Until 1877, whether buried there or not, every congressman who died in office had a monument in his name placed in the Congressional Cemetery.

Buried here are Civil War photographer Mathew Brady, the father of photojournalism; J. Edgar Hoover, the director of the FBI under eight presidents; John Philip Sousa, the most prolific composer of his time; and fifth vice president Elbridge Gerry, who gave his name to the term *gerrymandering*.

During the War of 1812, Choctaw Chief Pushmataha led his warriors into the Battle of New Orleans in support of Andrew Jackson. Afterward, Jackson granted the Choctaw Nation portions of Arkansas and Oklahoma in exchange for their land in Mississippi and Alabama. When President Monroe summoned Pushmataha to come to DC to break the treaties, he was poisoned. His monument was erected by his brother chiefs.

Belva Lockwood, a widow with a young daughter, attended the National University Law School, but was denied her diploma until she petitioned President Ulysses S. Grant personally. In 1879, she became the first woman to argue

before the Supreme Court, where she won $5 million in compensation for the Cherokee. In 1884, she was the first woman to run for president. She died in 1917, three years before women were given the vote. Her simple marble headstone bears no epitaph.

Leonard Matlovich received the Bronze Star for his service in the Air Force during the Vietnam War. After admitting he was gay, he was discharged. Matlovich designed his own headstone in black granite to match the Vietnam Veterans Memorial. His epitaph reads, "When I was in the military, they gave me a medal for killing two men—and a discharge for loving one." His gravesite is a rallying place for gay rights activists. ⚜

John Philip Sousa became the first American-born conductor of the U.S. Marine Corps Band in 1880. He remained with them for 12 years and led his farewell concert on the White House lawn.

24

Westminster Hall Burying Ground

519 West Fayette Street, Baltimore, Maryland
http://www.law.umaryland.edu/westminster/tours.html

This land originally belonged to John Eager Howard, a three-term governor of Maryland, who deeded the plot to the First

Presbyterian Church in the 1780s. A city ordinance in 1849 banished graveyards from inside Baltimore city limits, but this burial ground squeaked by because it was attached to a church.

Which is a story in itself: Most churchyards are built around an existing church. In this case, since the burial ground was established first, the Presbyterians built their red-brick church on piers, to raise it above the old graves in the 1840s. Eventually the piers were enclosed, creating catacombs.

Legend says the catacombs are haunted by Frank, a bodysnatcher who plundered these graves to supply Johns Hopkins University with cadavers for dissection. Doesn't that sound like an Edgar Allan Poe story?

In fact, the burying ground's best-loved resident lies just inside its gates. A large monument marks the graves of Edgar Allan Poe; his wife, Virginia; and her mother, Maria Clemm.

Poe was originally buried in his grandfather's plot, elsewhere in the churchyard. The poet's unkempt grave went unmarked for decades. Eventually, after his mother-in-law died in November 1875, his body was moved to this more prominent plot. It took 10 more years before his wife was exhumed from her grave in New York and reburied beside him.

For decades, a mysterious black-clad figure would toast Poe's grave with a bottle of cognac on Poe's birthday in January. A new Poe Toaster took up the mantle in 2016.

Also buried in the churchyard are one signer of the Constitution and 18 generals of the Revolution and War of 1812. ⚜

When Poe's mother-in-law died in 1875, his body was reburied in a more prominent spot beside his wife and her mother. This massive monument marks their graves.

Old Churchyard of Jamestowne

Colonial National Historical Park
1368 Colonial Parkway, Jamestown, Virginia
https://www.nps.gov/jame/index.htm

I n 1607, three small English ships arrived in Chesapeake Bay, carrying 108 poorly equipped settlers. They founded Jamestown in a mosquito-filled marsh along the James River, giving Britain its first permanent settlement in the New World. The men set about building a triangular fort. They thought they were in paradise: The river was full of fish, the forest was full of deer, and oysters were thick for the harvesting.

Three years later, they were starving. Graves were hastily dug inside the fort, hidden so that the Powhatan natives wouldn't see how few settlers were left. Archaeological exhumations uncovered evidence of cannibalism during those rough years.

Eventually, the settlers recovered their numbers. They began to grow tobacco, which they traded for supplies from England. As farms spread into the surrounding area, Jamestown served as Virginia's capital through the 17th century.

Beginning in 1617, successive churches were constructed outside the fort. Archaeological evidence hints that the area surrounding the church

The Jamestown Memorial Church was constructed on the site of the first Anglican church in America. Few of the graves in its churchyard continue to be marked.

was used as a burying ground prior to 1617, but the oldest recorded burial was Benjamin Harrison, who died between 1642 and 1649. The earliest known gravestone—now lost—dated from 1682.

Throughout the 17th and into the 18th centuries, most graves were marked with wooden planks that quickly rotted away. Tombstones were a rarity, since the local area possessed little natural stone. Headstones had to be imported, usually from England, as ballast in ships.

Of the possibly hundreds of burials in the churchyard, only 25 still have markers.

A fragmented stone marks the grave of Lady Frances, wife of William Berkeley, twice the colony's governor.

At least 20 early settlers were buried inside the church, their graves marked by stones set into the floor. One of these is Sir George Yeardley, who started leading Jamestown in 1609 and was governor of Virginia several times. Originally, his grave was decorated with inlaid brasses, unique in Colonial America, but they were stolen. Yeardley died at Jamestown in November 1627. ⚜

Washington's sarcophagus is visible inside the family's brick tomb. When ships pass Mount Vernon on the Potomac River, it's customary for the crews to stand at attention out of reverence for the first president.

26

George Washington's Tomb

3200 Mount Vernon Memorial Highway, Mount Vernon, Virginia
http://www.mountvernon.org

In 1797, George Washington happily retired from public life to Mount Vernon, his estate on the Potomac River in Virginia. In December 1799, he toured the estate in the sleet. Afterward, he developed a sore throat that led to complications. After a two-day illness, Washington died while checking his own pulse in his master bedchamber. He was 67.

Washington feared being buried alive, so he directed his secretary to keep his body around for three days after death. After that, Washington was buried in the simple family vault on his property. The rector of Christ Church in Alexandria, Virginia, read the Episcopal Order of Burial, followed by a Masonic funeral rite conducted by two of Washington's Lodge brothers.

In his will, Washington appointed a site for a new brick tomb to replace the original vault. The new tomb wasn't completed until 1831. His body was moved there, along with the remains of his wife, Martha (who died in 1802), and other family members. In 1837, the tomb was enlarged to accommodate two marble sarcophagi to hold the remains of General and Mrs. Washington.

A total of more than 80 million visitors have paid their respects since 1860, when the Mount Vernon Ladies Association bought the estate in order to preserve it. The nonprofit organization—the oldest national historical association in the country—continues to oversee the estate now.

Mount Vernon also has a slave burial ground, which contains graves of both slaves and free African-Americans who worked for Washington and his family. Because the graves are unmarked, the number and identities of those buried here are largely unknown. Among the unknowns lies William Lee, George Washington's personal servant during the Revolutionary War.

In 1983, a Slave Memorial was designed and built by architecture students from Howard University. ⚜

Hollywood Cemetery

412 South Cherry Street, Richmond, Virginia
http://www.hollywoodcemetery.org

Hollywood Cemetery, on the bluffs above the James River, was named after the holly trees on the property. Hollywood has the distinction of being one of only three graveyards where two presidents are buried. The others are Arlington and the crypt of the First Parish Church in Quincy, Massachusetts, where the Adamses lie at rest.

When James Monroe died in 1831, America's fifth president was originally buried in New York. In the 1850s, a movement arose to bring all the Virginian presidents home. Monroe was exhumed in 1858, attended by an honor guard. When the ship bearing his body ran aground in the James River, a grandson of Alexander Hamilton drowned.

Albert Lybrock designed the Monroe memorial. Through its mullions, you can see the marble sarcophagus covering his remains. Monroe's ornate tomb attracts thousands of visitors to the cemetery each year.

Also in the President's Circle is buried John Tyler, the tenth president, who took office after William Henry Harrison died from the pneumonia he caught at his own inauguration. During his presidency, Tyler opposed secession, but after the Civil War broke out, he served in the Confederate Congress. He died in Richmond in January 1862. In October 1915, the United States government finally forgave him and erected the tall square pillar, crowned with a shrouded urn, that marks his grave. It was the first monument for anyone who had joined the Confederacy to be paid for by the U.S. government.

Elsewhere in the graveyard is buried Jefferson Davis, sole president of the Confederacy. Davis was originally buried in New Orleans's Metairie Cemetery, but was reburied here on Memorial Day, 1893. He rests near his children. Daughter Winnie, known as the Angel of the Confederacy, died of grief after her father forbade her to marry the grandson of a Northern

A 90-foot-tall pyramid honors the 18,000 Confederate soldiers buried at Richmond's Hollywood Cemetery.

James Monroe, America's fifth president, is buried inside a confection of wrought iron that resembles a birdcage.

abolitionist. Davis's son Joseph died after falling from the porch of the Confederate Capitol. The boy's grave is marked by a broken column to symbolize a life cut short.

A pyramid marks the graves of 12,000 Confederate soldiers, many of whom were recovered from Gettysburg, where their bodies had been left after they'd fallen. Originally, the Confederate graves at Hollywood were laid out side by side and marked with wooden boards. Many of the bodies could not be identified. In 1869, the women of Richmond raised $26,000 to build a 90-foot-tall pyramid of undressed James River granite. It is dedicated to the 18,000 Confederate soldiers buried around the cemetery.

Also in the cemetery lie six Virginia governors, many of the founding fathers of Richmond, and 25 Confederate generals: more than any other cemetery in America. Among them are J. E. B. Stuart, who died in a battle called Yellow Tavern; and George Pickett, who ordered the suicidal charge on Cemetery Hill at Gettysburg. ⚜

28 Arlington National Cemetery

1 Memorial Avenue, Arlington, Virginia
http://www.arlingtoncemetery.mil

Founded on the commandeered grounds of Robert E. Lee's family home during the Civil War, Arlington National Cemetery currently spans 624 acres and encompasses more than 400,000 graves. It is the second largest national cemetery. Arlington was intended to be strictly a military cemetery, but that definition can be set aside by presidential directive to include anyone who served the United States.

Among the famous buried at Arlington lie Kennedy brothers John, Robert, and Edward; Supreme Court Justices Oliver Wendell Holmes Jr., Thurgood Marshall, and Harry Blackmun, author of *Roe v. Wade*; author Dashiell Hammett; explorers Richard Byrd and Robert Peary; the Brown Bomber, boxer Joe Louis; and several astronauts.

Major Glenn Miller, the big band leader, is remembered at Arlington with a cenotaph. A cenotaph often looks like a grave monument, but it honors someone whose remains were not

Magnolias bloom above the graves. More than 4 million people visit Arlington National Cemetery each year.

recovered. After Miller's plane vanished in World War II over France, his body was never found. The crew of the space shuttle *Challenger* also has a memorial cenotaph at Arlington.

Arlington is home to many other monuments, including the United States Marine Corps memorial (better known as the Iwo Jima Monument), the *USS Maine* Memorial, the Lockerbie Cairn in memory of the Pan Am flight brought down by Libyan bombers, and The Tomb of the Unknowns, where the remains of three unidentifiable soldiers symbolize all the anonymous dead of World Wars I and II and the Korean War. The unknown soldier from the Vietnam War has since been identified by his DNA. The crypt he occupied now stands empty.

Arlington's Visitors Center welcomes 4 million tourists each year. In addition to exhibits on the history of the graveyard, it contains a bookstore that offers maps and guidebooks. ⚜

Robert E. Lee's Arlington House stands atop the hill in the national cemetery, overlooking the graves of more than 400,000 people.

Hatfield Family Cemetery

Highway 44, Sarah Ann, West Virginia

Anderson "Devil Anse" Hatfield served two years in the Confederate Army as a captain. He left the army and came home to West Virginia to join a local Confederate militia called the Logan Wildcats. Simultaneously, Asa Harmon McCoy served in the Union Army. In 1865, he was wounded and came home to Kentucky to recuperate. When he was murdered and no one was charged, rumor blamed the Logan Wildcats.

Several legal cases between the Hatfields and the McCoys were settled through the courts.

29

The statue of Devil Anse Hatfield was carved in Italy from photographs provided by his children. It has stood in the cemetery since 1926.

Then in 1880, Johnson "Johnse" Hatfield, one of Devil Anse's sons, got Randall McCoy's teenage daughter Roseanna pregnant. Disowned, Roseanna ended up at her Aunt Betty's, where she delivered a daughter, who died of measles at 8 months old.

At an election day celebration in 1882, Devil Anse's brother Ellison got into a fight with three of Randall's sons. Ellison was stabbed 27 times before being shot in the back. Devil Anse's posse captured the responsible McCoys, who were then hauled across the river into Kentucky, tied to pawpaw trees, and shot to death. The governor of Kentucky attempted to extradite Devil Anse to stand trial, but the governor of West Virginia opposed him. Afterward, Devil Anse named his son Willis in the governor's honor.

Finally, in January 1888, some Hatfields set fire to Randall McCoy's home in Kentucky. Two children were killed and Randall's wife seriously injured. The Hatfields involved in the fire were sentenced to life in prison, except for Ellison Mounts, who was hanged. The feud finally ended.

Devil Anse died of pneumonia at the age of 82. He was buried in a $2000 solid steel coffin. His surviving children commissioned a life-size statue of their father from Italy. The statue is said to have cost between $3500 and $5000; a car in the 1920s cost $700. The bearded figure in Carrera marble has towered over this leafy cemetery since 1926.

The names of Anse's thirteen children are listed on the pedestal below his statue. Adjacent to his grave stands a square column topped by a draped urn, which marks Johnse's grave.

Also buried in the cemetery are Anse's wife, Levicy; physician Elliot R. Hatfield; and two more of Anse's sons, Detroit "Troy" and Elias, both killed in a gunfight protesting a competitor's liquor sales.

The cemetery, listed on the National Register of History Places, is still used by family members. ⚜

God's Acre, the Moravian Graveyard

**South Church Street,
Winston-Salem, North Carolina
http://www.salemcongregation.org/
salem-moravian-graveyard-gods-acre**

After Jan Hus was burned at the stake in 1467, his followers founded the Moravian Church. Historians consider it the first Protestant faith, predating Lutheranism by 50 years. The Moravian Church barely survived the Thirty Years' War, but rebounded in Saxony in 1722, before moving to the United States in 1741. Moravians founded the town of Salem (Shalom, meaning Peace) in North Carolina in 1765 on 100,000 acres of land purchased by Count Zinzendorf.

Even before the town was settled, God's Acre (from the German *Gottesacker*) appears on the proposed map. The graveyard was laid out on a gentle slope and planted with cedars. On June 7, 1771, tailor John Birkhead was the first to be buried there.

In Moravian graveyards—as in their churches—the dead are segregated by marital

Practically identical marble gravestones mark all the graves in the Moravian God's Acre. Married women are buried apart from married men, just as boys are buried separately from girls.

status, gender, and age into what are called choirs. People are buried in the appropriate choir in the order in which they die. Because of this, families are spread throughout the graveyard. All are considered one family under God. Since everyone is equal, everyone is buried under nearly identical markers. In 1778, the church board decreed that all markers would be labeled in English, to make them even more similar.

The Moravian faith believes that death is a transition one should look forward to. They are "called home" or "permitted to rest." Those left behind are expected not to grieve. More than 6000 people are buried in the Salem Moravian Graveyard.

On the Saturday before Easter, Salem Moravian congregations come to decorate graves with flowers until the graveyard looks like a large garden. The highlight of the cemetery's year is the sunrise service on Easter, when they sing hymns about resurrection. The ceremony was first observed here in 1772. ⚜

Lichens and moss grow on the old tombstones in Beaufort's 300-year-old Burying Ground.

Old Burying Ground

400 Ann Street, Beaufort, North Carolina
beauforthistoricsite.org/old-burying-ground

On the sea islands that form the Outer Banks of North Carolina stands Beaufort, the third oldest settlement in the state. Native Americans practically destroyed the town in 1715. The British captured it during the Revolution. After that shaky start, Beaufort flourished, shipping rice and cotton from local plantations.

This small patch of land may have been used as a graveyard as early as 1709, but it was deeded to the town in 1731 by Nathaniel Taylor. Since there is no native stone in the area, the earliest graves are unmarked. It's thought that settlers killed by the local Coree and Neusiok tribes lie in the northwestern corner.

The earliest legible marker dates to 1756. Pre–Revolutionary War records were lost when the Anglican rector who oversaw the graveyard fled to Canada. However, Colonel William Thomson, the highest-ranking officer from Beaufort to serve in the Revolution, lies here.

At the behest of the United States government, Captain Otway Burns preyed on British ships during the War of 1812, plundering from Nova Scotia to South America. After the war, he served as a member of the North Carolina

31

Legislature. His grave is marked by a cannon from his privateer ship, the *Snapdragon*.

Under more sedate markers lie several Civil War veterans. Captain Matthew Gooding ran the Northern blockade in his ship, the *Nashville*. Sergeant George Johnson served in the United States Colored Infantry (USCI), who fought for the Union. Several soldiers who seized Fort Macon the month before North Carolina seceded from the Union are also buried here.

The graveyard has several unusual burials, too. An anonymous British officer died aboard ship at the port and, per his request, was buried in his uniform standing up. After a local girl died on the voyage home from England, her father preserved her body in a keg of rum, in which she is buried here. ⚜

Magnolia Cemetery

**70 Cunnington Avenue,
Charleston, South Carolina
magnoliacemetery.net**

On the banks of the Cooper River, Magnolia Cemetery occupies 92 acres of a former rice plantation called Magnolia Umbra. In fact, the plantation house, which dates to 1805, serves as the superintendent's office.

Magnolia Cemetery is a lovely place, full of live oaks, ornate ironwork, and sculpture. The cemetery was planned by architect Edward C. Jones during the rural cemetery craze. He also designed the United States Custom House in Charleston. The National Register of Historic Places calls Magnolia Cemetery extensively landscaped, with excellent examples of late 19th-century architecture and sculpture. Its winding drives and paths encircle small ponds and a lake.

The cemetery's construction was hurried along when a yellow fever epidemic struck Charleston in the 1850s. Many of its victims were buried here.

Also buried here is a spectrum of society, from planters and politicians to bootleggers and whorehouse madams. The grounds also provide the final resting place for several former governors.

Like all Southern cemeteries of its era, Magnolia has a Civil War plot. This section, which holds 1700 Confederate soldiers, is the site of Charleston's Confederate Memorial Day celebrations.

Buried here more recently were the crew of the Confederate submarine *H.L. Hunley*. Although it was not fully submerged, the *Hunley* was the first submarine to successfully sink an enemy ship. Over the course of the Civil War, the *Hunley* killed 21 men in its own crews. The final crew

This photomechanical print of a live oak in Charleston's Magnolia Cemetery dates to around 1900. Rather than a color photo, the black-and-white photograph was colorized in the printing process.

was not recovered until August 2000. Those eight crewmen were buried here in 2004.

Separate from the White graves lies the historic African American Cemetery at Magnolia. These graves are grouped by association, such as the Humane Friendly Society. Grave markers range from finely carved marble to hand-lettered cement. Some plots are decorated with conch shells.

Magnolia Cemetery was a popular picnicking spot in the Victorian era, but modern picnickers are reminded that the cemetery explicitly prohibits feeding the alligators. ❧

The clock tower at the grand entrance to Cave Hill Cemetery is prone to lightning strikes.

Cave Hill Cemetery

701 Baxter Avenue, Louisville, Kentucky
cavehillcemetery.com

Louisville city fathers purchased the old Johnston family farm, Cave Hill, because it had good limestone for quarrying. The Louisville and Frankfort Railroad was supposed to run through the property, which should have made the quarry very profitable. When the railroad detoured, the old farmhouse was converted to the City Pest House, a sanitarium for patients with contagious diseases. This use necessitated a cemetery, added by the city in 1846.

Civil engineer Edmund Francis Lee decided that the site's promontories would become its primary burial sites, reached by gently serpentine roads. Low spots became ponds or groves of trees. In the mid-19th century, death was considered a transition full of hope and promise, not to be feared or shunned. Cave Hill Cemetery promoted the concept of being asleep in nature.

The most beautiful monument at Cave Hill is the Classical Revival Temple of Love commissioned by Dr. Preston Pope Satterwhite for his wife, Florence. Inspired by the incomplete Roman

Harland Sanders was 62 and facing bankruptcy when he began franchising his Kentucky Fried Chicken recipe. He died a millionaire at the age of 90.

Temple of Vesta at Tivoli, acanthus-topped Corinthian columns support the Satterwhite dome. One can look through the open monument to the lawn and trees beyond. In its center, Venus poses in a body-hugging gown.

The most recognizable person buried at Cave Hill Cemetery is Colonel Harland Sanders, founder and spokesman for KFC. Sanders is buried in the lawn in front of a classical colonnade surrounding a bronze bust of his familiar face with its goatee.

Boxing champion Muhammad Ali was buried in Cave Hill in 2016. His black granite monument bears the epitaph, "Service to others is the rent you pay for your room in heaven." ❧

The Kentucky Horse Park

**4089 Iron Works Parkway,
Lexington, Kentucky
kyhorsepark.com**

Horses were ritually buried in Shang-era China, Bronze Age Greece, and in late Iron Age Scandinavia. Remains of horses have been discovered alongside Viking ship burials, inside Scythian burial mounds in Russia, and beside a human grave at Sutton Hoo. Alexander the Great's warhorse Bucephalus received a state funeral before he was buried in what is now Pakistan.

In the United States, the practice of burying champion racehorses dates back almost a century and a half. More than a thousand champions are buried across the country, mostly in Kentucky, California, and Florida.

The most famous thoroughbred racehorse of the 20th century—Man o' War—lies buried beneath a life-size statue at the Kentucky Horse Park.

In his two years of racing, Man o' War won 20 of his 21 races. After his retirement, he was a prolific stud, siring 379 offspring. In 1947, his groom and friend, Will Harbut, died suddenly. Man o' War pined for Harbut and died less than a month later. The horse was embalmed and lay in state for three days at Faraway Farm, where he'd lived, before being buried in an enormous wooden box lined with his racing colors. More than 2000 mourners attended his funeral, which was broadcast on the radio.

American sculptor Herbert Haseltine created a sculpture of the big racing horse in 1948. It stood over Man o' War's original grave until 1977, when the oversize casket was exhumed and moved to the Kentucky Horse Park. The huge bronze statue came, too. It stands on a pedestal just inside the entrance at Kentucky Horse Park, which opened in 1978.

Buried around Man o' War are five of his descendants, including Triple Crown-winner War Admiral, who beat Seabiscuit in 1938.

Throughout the park lie several horse cemeteries, final resting places of 52 thoroughbreds, standardbreds, quarter horses, and saddlebred show horses. In addition to American horses, European steeplechaser Jay Trump and race mare Allez France are also buried at the park, as is jockey Isaac Burns Murphy. ❧

American sculptor Herbert Haseltine created the bronze portrait sculpture of Man o' War in 1948. It stands over the racehorse's grave at the Kentucky Horse Park.

Cades Cove Primitive Baptist Churchyard

Great Smoky Mountains National Park
Cades Cove Loop Road, Townsend, Tennessee
https://www.nps.gov/grsm/index.htm

For generations, the Cherokee hunted deer, elk, and bears in the Little Tennessee River valley of the Smoky Mountains. In fact, this area takes its name from Chief Kade.

In the early 1820s, settlers cleared land for farming. John and Lucretia Oliver brought the Baptist faith to the Cove in 1825. Initial meetings took place in various cabins, before William Tipton donated land for the first log church and its attendant cemetery in 1832. The current frame church dates to 1887.

When a member of the community perished, the church bell tolled to alert the neighbors. After a pause, the bell would ring out the years of the deceased's life. Men gathered to dig the grave and build the coffin, while women prepared the body. In the churchyard stand markers for the Olivers, Shields, and Cables: the pioneer families of Cades Cove.

In 1927, Tennessee began buying up land in the mountains to create a national park. Some of the community gladly sold out. Others signed life-leases that allowed them to stay in their homes. They received less money and were restricted in their hunting and timber cutting.

The National Park Service designated the surviving buildings of Cades Cove as a historical area in 1945. They restored the church and several log cabins, then opened them as a museum. Today the village of Cades Cove is one of the most visited areas of Smoky Mountains National Park.

Until 1960, 229 graves were marked in the churchyard. Over time, markers have gone missing and the cemetery deteriorated. The Cades Cove Preservation Association was organized in January 2001 to care for the graveyard and the 12 other burial areas in the Cades Cove vicinity.

The Cades Cove churchyard is still open to families who own plots or have negotiated with the National Park Service to be buried there. ⚜

36

The Meditation Garden at Graceland

3734 Elvis Presley Boulevard, Memphis, Tennessee
https://www.graceland.com

With the encouragement of his parents, 22-year-old Elvis Presley bought the 23-room Graceland Mansion in 1957. His wife Priscilla, daughter, Lisa Marie, both of Elvis's parents, his paternal grandmother, and an aunt all called the mansion home.

Elvis added the Meditation Garden to the Mansion grounds in 1964. Its centerpiece is a round 12-foot pool with six fountain jets, surrounded by a semicircular pergola on its south side. Beyond that stands a brick wall with arched stained glass windows.

After his sudden death from heart failure on August 16, 1977, Elvis was dressed in a white suit, packed into a 900-pound copper coffin, and driven down the street that bears his name to Memphis's Forest Hill Cemetery. Over a million people visited Presley's mausoleum in the first month after his death.

Late in August 1977, three men were jailed for criminally trespassing at Elvis's Forest Hill mausoleum. After that, his father Vernon petitioned the city to change its zoning laws so that Graceland could host a burial ground. The Meditation Garden became Elvis's final resting place. On October 3, 1977, he was reburied with

On the 35th anniversary of Elvis's death, an estimated 75,000 people took part in a candlelight vigil at Graceland. The 40th anniversary of Elvis's death in 2017 is expected to increase the number of visitors.

his mother, who had predeceased him. The Meditation Garden area opened to the public in 1978, four years before the mansion itself opened as a museum. Elvis's grave is now under 24-hour video surveillance.

In addition to Elvis's mother, Gladys, his father, Vernon, and his grandmother Minnie Mae, there's a cenotaph in the Meditation Garden to Jesse Garon Presley, Elvis's still-born twin, who remains buried in an unmarked grave in Tupelo, Mississippi.

Each year, 600,000 people visit the Graceland Mansion in all its exuberantly decorated glory and pay homage at the King's grave. ⚜

37

Bonaventure Cemetery

330 Bonaventure Road, Savannah, Georgia
http://www.bonaventurehistorical.org

In Colonial-era Georgia, John Mullryne and his son-in-law Josiah Tattnall owned 600 acres on Saint Augustine Creek, three miles outside Savannah. They built the family plantation Bonaventure—French for "good fortune"—overlooking a

bend in the Wilmington River.

Unfortunately, Mullryne and Tattnall, as British loyalists, were banished during the Revolutionary War. After the war, Bonaventure was sold at auction. Josiah Tattnall Jr. didn't regain it until 1788.

As most rural families did, the Mullrynes and Tattnalls set aside a small plot for a family burial ground. In 1802, Harriet Fenwick Tattnall was the first adult known to be interred there. The following year, Josiah was buried next to her. Of their nine children, six lie nearby.

In 1846, the Tattnall family sold the plantation to a Savannah hotelier named Wiltberger, with the provision that he care for the family plot. The following year, Wiltberger incorporated 70 acres as the Evergreen Cemetery of Bonaventure. Two years later, Wiltberger became one of its permanent residents.

When John Muir camped in the cemetery in September 1867, he fell in love with its wildlife, birds, and oaks draped with Spanish moss. The cemetery was, he wrote, "so beautiful that almost any sensible person would choose to dwell here with the dead."

The city of Savannah bought Evergreen Cemetery in 1907 and changed its name to Bonaventure Cemetery. The garden cemetery is one of the most beautiful and romantic burial grounds in the South. The best time to visit is at the end of March, when the azaleas bloom.

Confederate generals Claudius Charles Wilson and Hugh W. Mercer are buried here. Great-grandson Johnny Mercer, who crooned "Moon River," is also here, beside his mother, who was murdered by his father when Johnny was a child. Their plot has a curved white marble bench inscribed with his song lyrics. Also here is Conrad Aiken, a poet who wrote more than 50 books, but may be best known for introducing Emily Dickinson's poetry to the world.

The most widely recognized monument of Bonaventure was the Bird Girl, featured on the cover of the novel *Midnight in the Garden of Good and Evil*. The Bird Girl was part of a set of four bronze statues made by Sylvia Shaw Judson. After the novel's success, the statue drew so many visitors to the graveyard that tourists disturbed adjacent graves. The statue was moved to the Telfair Museum of Art for its own protection. ⚜

A pensive muse sits atop the grave of Thomas N. Theus, a Confederate soldier, and his wife Eliza. Bonaventure Cemetery is known for its lovely statuary and the Spanish moss that drapes its trees.

After serving as a brigadier general in the Civil War, Robert H. Anderson served as Savannah's chief of police until his death in 1888. He is buried at Bonaventure Cemetery under the bust on the left.

Behavior Cemetery

Sapelo Island, Georgia

The first European settlers reached Georgia in 1732. They had been condemned in England as debtors and sent to work off their sentences by supplying Britain with agricultural products. Prior to 1750, slavery was banned in Georgia. Once the antislavery laws were overturned, West Africans were imported as slaves, on the shaky justification that they could withstand the heat and humidity of the South.

Plantations on the Sea Islands grew rice. Africans from the Windward Coast (modern-day Senegal, Gambia, Sierra Leone, and Liberia) grew rice at home, so they were preferred to work on the islands. These Africans brought their winnowing baskets, burial practices, and especially their language with them.

One of Georgia's barrier islands, Sapelo Island is a seven-mile boat trip from the mainland. The village of Behavior was established

on Sapelo after Thomas Spalding purchased a 4000-acre tract there in 1802.

After the Civil War ended, land on the coastal islands was sold to newly freed slaves as part of the Reconstruction plan.

Fewer than 50 people remain on Sapelo, descendants of Africans brought here as slaves. They follow the traditions of Geechee culture, which is the longest surviving West African culture in the United States.

The Behavior Cemetery dates to 1805 or so. Traditionally, Geechee cemeteries were dug in unoccupied wooded areas. Markers in the cemetery range from modern granite cubes to cement markers lettered by hand.

Geechee people believe that spirits remain active after death and can become mischievous if disturbed. To keep spirits from roaming, personal objects are left on graves: cups, china plates, tobacco pipes that the deceased used in life, as well as clocks or other domestic items. Incorrectly dismissed as grave decorations, these offerings have been stolen from graves at Behavior as souvenirs—much to the horror of surviving families.

Cemetery records were destroyed in a fire in 1921. Because the cemetery has been in use for so long, it became increasingly common to disturb unmarked burials whenever a new grave was opened. At the request of Geechee residents, students from the University of Tennessee at Chattanooga did archaeological research in the graveyard in May 2010. Using ground penetrating radar, they looked for unmarked graves and headstones that might have sunken beneath the earth's surface. The students then mapped the cemetery to protect the ancestors buried there. ⚜

Still in use today, Behavior Cemetery first served as a burial ground for enslaved Africans from the Windward Coast. Descendants still practice customs passed down over the centuries.

The Martin Luther King Jr. Center for Nonviolent Social Change

449 Auburn Avenue NE, Atlanta, Georgia
http://thekingcenter.org

After his assassination in Memphis by James Earl Ray in April 1968, Dr. Martin Luther King Jr.'s body was brought home to Atlanta. A farm wagon, drawn by mules, carried his coffin to Atlanta's South-View Cemetery, where his parents would later be buried.

South-View Cemetery was founded in 1886 by nine former slaves after African-Americans were barred from Atlanta's Whites-only graveyards. In consequence, South-View Cemetery is the oldest African-American not-for-profit corporation in the United States. It serves as the final resting place for over 70,000 African-Americans and others, regardless of race or religion.

In June 1968, Coretta Scott King, King's widow, opened the Martin Luther King Jr. Center for Nonviolent Social Change in the basement of the couple's home. Two years later, she had Dr. King's body removed from the cemetery and placed in a new tomb on a lot near the Ebenezer Baptist Church. Eventually the King Center moved nearby.

The gravesite has evolved over time. Originally, it held only the white marble sarcophagus with an epitaph taken from King's *I Have a Dream* speech: "Free at last, free at last, thank God Almighty, I'm free at last." In 1976, a memorial park was built around the tomb. It consisted of a brick and concrete plaza ringed by an arcade. In time, the raked gravel around the grave was replaced by a reflecting pool, with King's sarcophagus on a raised pedestal in the center. An eternal flame was added in 1977.

Coretta Scott King died from a stroke and complications of ovarian cancer in January 2006. She was interred in a small white tomb near Dr. King's grave until a sarcophagus to match his could be constructed. Her epitaph comes from I Corinthians: "And now abide Faith, Hope, Love, these three; but the greatest of these is Love." ❧

To honor his Southern roots, Rev. King's tomb is faced with Georgia marble. Coretta Scott King, his wife, joined him in 2006.

Tuskegee University Campus Cemetery

Booker T. Washington Boulevard, Tuskegee, Alabama

Booker Taliaferro Washington, founder of Tuskegee Normal and Industrial Institute, was born enslaved in Virginia in 1856. Freed by the Civil War, he pursued an education at the Hampton Institute on the shores of Chesapeake Bay. After graduation, he wanted to open a college for African-American students farther south. Donations to the Tuskegee Institute came from Andrew Carnegie and John D. Rockefeller, among others.

In Missouri, George Washington Carver had also been born enslaved. He and his mother were kidnapped by slave stealers. Although he was reclaimed, she disappeared. After the Civil War, Carver graduated from the Iowa State College of Agriculture and Industrial Arts. He dreamed of becoming an artist. Instead, Washington invited Carver to join the faculty at Tuskegee. Carver taught there for the next 47 years.

While at Tuskegee, Carver invented a program of crop development and soil conservation. He revolutionized Southern agriculture by demonstrating that a single crop—peanuts, for instance—could be used in hundreds of different ways. Peanuts grew to be a $200-million industry by 1938, thanks to his experiments.

In 1915, Washington fell ill in New York and returned to Alabama to die. He was laid to rest on the campus he loved. His burial in the little campus cemetery elevated it to a shrine.

The university's unassuming, informal cemetery is located near the University Chapel. Within its confines lie all but one of the university's past presidents, including Frederick Douglas Patterson, who served as president for 25 years and founded the United Negro College Fund.

Also buried here is William Levi Dawson. His 1935 *Negro Folk Symphony* was the first symphony written by a Black composer. He also founded the Tuskegee Institute School of Music. ⚜

Born enslaved, Booker T. Washington founded the Tuskegee Institute (now University) in 1881. He wished to be buried in the campus cemetery near the chapel.

Maplewood Cemetery

1419 Maplewood Road, Harrison, Arkansas
**http://www.harrisonarkansas.org/
c_upe_view.php?id=25**

Over 700 sugar maple trees shade the grounds of this cemetery. The trees were originally planted in 1924 by the women of the Twentieth Century Club, who transplanted

them from the surrounding woodland. Some of the original trees still put on a show each year.

In summer, sugar maples cast dense shade over the granite markers below. In the fall, however, the deciduous trees explode into their full glory. As the weather grows colder, some turn crimson, others orange, still others sunny yellow. Maplewood Cemetery comes into its true glory between mid-October and early November.

The cemetery invites visitors to walk the grounds, photograph the trees, and absorb its sense of peace.

Buried at Maplewood is John Paul Hammerschmidt, the first Republican representative in Arkansas since the Reconstruction. He served in the United States House of Representatives from 1967 to 1993, narrowly defeating Bill Clinton for the seat in 1974. Hammerschmidt's father was a lumberman, so the congressman worked on behalf of conservation while in office. He died of heart disease in 2015. ⚜

Approximately 9,000 people rest in the shade of 700 sugar maple trees, from which the cemetery takes its name.

42

Natchez City Cemetery

2 Cemetery Road, Natchez, Mississippi
natchez.ms.us/150/Cemetery

The city of Natchez is located on the Mississippi River between Vicksburg and New Orleans. The Spanish founded it as the capital of the surrounding area around 1790. It was acquired by the United States as part of the Louisiana Purchase in 1803.

Natchez City Cemetery, established in 1822, contains reburials from a former graveyard located downtown. Markers with 18th-century dates of death still stand in the cemetery.

While the cemetery is enhanced by beautiful ironwork fences and benches, most visitors come to explore its legends.

The most famous statue in the Natchez City Cemetery is the Turning Angel. When headlights filter in from outside the cemetery gates, an optical illusion makes it seem as if the angel twists to watch passersby. The angel marks the mass grave of 12 employees killed in an explosion at the Natchez Drug Company in March 1908. The youngest victim was 12. The explosion put the company out of business, but the owner purchased the burial plot and the angel to mark their graves.

One of the well-known denizens of the Natchez City Cemetery is 10-year-old Florence Irene Ford, who had been afraid of storms. After she died of yellow fever, her mother had her buried in a vault constructed with a staircase down into the ground, so that she could sit with her baby whenever a storm came along. Clear glass used to look in at the head of Florence's coffin, but that was removed in the 1950s to prevent vandalism.

One curious headstone seems to have sunken into the sod so that all that's visible is "Louise. The Unfortunate." It's commonly believed that Louise was a mail-order bride who arrived on the dock at Natchez expecting to meet her fiancé. Sadly, her husband-to-be never claimed her. Louise started working as a seamstress and cook, but ended up as a prostitute. When she died, someone took pity on her. She's buried in a corner of the City Cemetery's Jewish section under a nice marble stone. ⚜

On a bluff overlooking the Mississippi River, the Natchez City Cemetery is full of angels and ironwork from the antebellum era. Notice the unusual iron mausoleum stained with rust.

43

Saint Louis Cemetery #1

425 Basin Street, New Orleans, Louisiana
http://www.saveourcemeteries.org/
st-louis-cemetery-no-1

Like the Cathedral in Jackson Square, this New Orleans graveyard is named for Louis IX, the 13th-century king of France. He crusaded to the Holy Land twice and was canonized in 1297.

While Saint Louis #1 is the oldest surviving cemetery in New Orleans, it is only a shadow of its former self. The Varney family pyramid, now near the Basin Street gate, once stood at the geographic center of the graveyard. Built circa 1810, the pyramid is one of the oldest tombs to survive. The earliest marked grave, adorned with a simple iron cross, remembers Antoine Bonabel, who died in February 1800.

One of the most unusual aspects of Saint Louis #1 are the so-called oven vaults that line its perimeter. These niches can be reused after a year and a day. The extreme heat and humidity in New Orleans reduces a corpse placed inside to bones within the span of a year, after which time a second coffin can be pushed inside. The back of the vault opens into a chamber called a caveau, where the

New Orleans's aboveground tombs hark back to the family tombs in France and Spain. An estimated 100,000 people have been buried in Saint Louis Cemetery #1.

bones of everyone buried in that niche reside, jumbled together.

The most famous resident of Saint Louis #1 may or may not be Marie Laveau, the Voodoo Queen. The Glapion tomb is inscribed (in French): "Here lies Marie Philome Glapion, deceased June 11, 1897, aged 62 years. She was a good mother, a good friend, and regretted by all who knew her." The death date of 1897 is not the famous Marie's, but closer to her daughter Marie's.

The "tradition" of breaking a brick off one of the neighboring tombs to scrawl XXX on the Glapion mausoleum began in the 1960s, promoted by unscrupulous tour guides. The surviving Glapions, the Archdiocese of New Orleans, and the city itself consider the ritual vandalism.

Other famous residents of Saint Louis #1 include Homer Plessy, plaintiff in the 1896 Supreme Court case that established the "separate but equal" doctrine, overturned by *Brown v. Board of Education* in 1954; land developer Bernard de Marigny, for whom New Orleans's Faubourg Marigny is named; Etienne de Bore, first to granulate sugar commercially, creating the local industry; Mayor Ernest "Dutch" Morial, New Orleans's first African-American mayor; and Paul Morphy, the first U.S. chess champion. In the city's earliest days, there was no division between Black and White in the graveyard or its caveaus. Segregation began after America made the Louisiana Purchase in 1803.

In 2015, the Archdiocese of New Orleans restricted access to the cemetery to registered tour groups and family members of the deceased. Luckily, there are many tours from which to choose. ⚜

Metairie Cemetery

**5100 Pontchartrain Boulevard,
New Orleans, Louisiana
http://www.saveourcemeteries.org/
metairie-cemetery**

Metairie Cemetery opened in 1872 on the grounds of the old Metairie Race Course. Legend holds that the Creole aristocracy had shunned the graveyard's owner, Charles T. Howard, as a crass American who'd made his fortune in the corrupt Louisiana State Lottery Company. At his first opportunity, Howard bought the land, closed the track, and charged the Creoles money to be buried there. Even though the story is not historically accurate, the oval shape of the track still dominates the cemetery.

Antique postcards show the grand entrance to the cemetery as an ivy-swathed archway. Unfortunately, since Louisiana chopped the Pontchartrain Expressway through the Metairie District, the former grand entrance now serves as a back exit.

44

An angel crowned with a star indicates that she has come from heaven. She is dropping blessings on the grave in the form of flowers in Metairie Cemetery.

Near the highway rises the 30-foot-high tumulus of the Louisiana Division of the Army of Tennessee. The tumulus, a manmade hill, is the most ancient form of grave monument. This burial mound belonged to a Benevolent Society that provided burial space to Civil War veterans. Inside the grass-blanketed tumulus lay 48 niches full of old soldiers, including Confederate General Pierre G. T. Beauregard, who ordered the first shot fired on Fort Sumter and later commanded the Army of Tennessee. The last Civil War veteran was interred in 1929.

The most famous person ever buried in Metairie Cemetery was Jefferson Davis, president of the Confederate States of America. He died in New Orleans in 1889 and was laid to rest beneath the 38-foot granite column marking the tomb of the Army of Northern Virginia. Davis's funeral was the largest New Orleans has yet seen. Even so, several years after his death, Davis's widow Varina allowed his remains to be removed to Hollywood Cemetery in Richmond.

One of the most fascinating monuments in Metairie belongs to the Egan family, who had it designed to look like a ruin. Its marble archway yawns open to the sky, just like the Gothic chapel on the Egan property in Ireland that inspired it. New marble blocks were distressed to appear cracked and broken. Even the family's nameplate looks as if it has been dropped.

The Brunswig tomb is a granite pyramid taller than wide. A Greek maiden raises her hand to knock on the tomb's door. Behind her stands a tall Roman urn with ornate handles and a marble eternal flame frozen in its mouth. Across the entryway crouches a sphinx whose broad shoulders dwarf her impassive face. The inspiration for the tomb is one that stands in the Cimitero Monumentale in Milan, Italy.

A final note: Since it occupies low ground close to Lake Pontchartrain, the Metairie District was completely inundated after Hurricane Katrina. The disaster underlines the fragility of old cemeteries. ⚜

From Egyptian Revival to Gothic to Romanesque, these tombs demonstrate the range of architectural styles in Metairie Cemetery.

Tolomato Cemetery

14 Cordova Street, Saint Augustine, Florida
http://www.tolomatocemetery.com

Saint Augustine was founded on September 8, 1565, which makes it the oldest continuously occupied settlement established by Europeans in the continental United States.

Citizens of Saint Augustine began to use this acre of land as a graveyard in 1777. In 1799, the parish priest Don Miguel O'Reilly claimed in a deposition that the land had been used "since time immemorial" as a burial ground. In fact, the Spanish used it to bury Native Americans converted to Christianity before the British took over the area.

The Spanish used this area to bury Christianized Indians before the British took over. The names on surviving tombstones combine Spanish and Irish surnames.

Names on the grave markers here are Spanish or Irish, or Spanish *and* Irish as in the case of Don Juan McQueen, who lies in an unmarked grave but is acknowledged by a historical marker. McQueen carried messages between George Washington and the Marquis de Lafayette during the Revolutionary War, but had to flee the United States to escape debtor's prison in Georgia. He worked for the Spanish governor in Florida before his death in 1807.

French-born Augustin Verot became the first bishop appointed to Florida in 1858. He was staunchly pro-Confederacy: the first time an American bishop took a political stance on a subject unrelated to the Church. Northerners called him the Rebel Bishop. He is buried in the mortuary chapel in the heart of the cemetery. A bust of him stands nearby.

The final burial recorded in the graveyard was Robert P. Sabate, who died in 1892. The cemetery was closed after that.

These days, the cemetery is open to the public one Saturday a month, thanks to the Tolomato Cemetery Preservation Society. ❧

Huguenot Cemetery

A1A Orange Street, Saint Augustine, Florida
http://www.memorialpcusa.org/
huguenot-cemetery

Although the cemetery is named for the French Protestant movement, it's unlikely there are any actual Huguenots here. During the Spanish colonial era, this half-acre piece of land across from Saint Augustine's city gates was used as a potter's field to bury criminals and other excommunicants. All non-Catholics would have been buried here. The oldest graves have no inscriptions, since the Spaniards felt it was better to erase the memory of people who died outside the Church.

After the United States took control of the Florida territory, Saint Augustine's oldest Protestant burial ground opened officially in September 1821. Shortly thereafter, a yellow fever epidemic gripped the city.

The land's owner, Reverend Thomas Alexander, deeded the cemetery to the Presbyterian Church in 1832. It was maintained by the Presbyterians until it closed in 1884.

Among the approximately 436 people buried here are U.S. Congressmen Gideon Barstow, who retired to Florida and died in 1852, and Charles Downing, who also served as a colonel in the Seminole War in 1836.

That isn't what draws most people to the old cemetery. By many accounts, it is the most haunted place in the ancient city. One of the ghost stories begins with the body of a 14-year-old girl left at the city gates during the yellow fever epidemic. Since no one claimed her, she was buried in the Huguenot Cemetery. It's said her ghost, clad in a flowing white dress, still wanders the cemetery after midnight. Sometimes she waves at visitors.

The most famous ghost has been identified as Judge John Stickney, who died in 1882. When his children had him exhumed years later, the gravediggers opened his coffin to find the judge reasonably well preserved. In the mob of people watching the exhumation was a thief who stole the judge's gold teeth right out of his skull. Although Stickney's body was moved to Washington, DC, the tall dark figure of the judge's ghost still prowls the cemetery, searching for his missing teeth. He's been seen day and night.

The fragile old cemetery is usually locked these days, but the Friends of the Huguenot Cemetery open it on the third Saturday of each month. ❧

The grave of Godfrey Foster is illustrated with two hands clasping. One wears a lacy feminine cuff, while the other cuff looks more businesslike and masculine. Probably it indicates that Foster was married, but it may signify his welcome to heaven.

This artificial reef off the coast of Key Biscayne is designed to accommodate cremated remains of divers and others who loved the sea.

Neptune Memorial Reef

**International waters off Key Biscayne, Florida
N 25° 42.036' W 80° 05.409'**
http://www.nmreef.com

Three and a quarter miles off the coast of Key Biscayne stands a one-of-a-kind cemetery. Inspired by sunken cities like Alexandria and Herakleion, the Neptune Memorial Reef is the world's most beautiful underwater graveyard.

As conceived by Key Largo artist Kim Brandell, the monuments are huge and heavy: 5-ton columns on 50-ton bases. Even smaller sculptures of shells weigh 10 pounds. Brandell considers his architecture futuristic rather than classical, but the broken columns, colonnades, and massive lion echo the mythical Atlantis.

Sponsored by the Neptune Society—one of the largest providers of cremation in the United States—the reef is designed as a repository for human cremains, the by-products of cremation. Families select one of Brandell's designs, add their loved one's cremains and small mementos like fishing lures to the concrete, and the monument is placed forty feet below the waves by divers. The Reef belongs to the Green Burial Council.

Shipwreck diver Bert Kilbride—immortalized in the Guinness World Records at the age of 90 as the world's oldest scuba diver—has a place of honor atop one of the columns at the Reef gate. Other monuments in the cemetery include benches, columns, and starfish. Future monuments may include dolphins and Neptune himself.

The largest manmade reef yet conceived is intended to transform more than 16 acres of barren ocean floor. Designed to welcome fish and promote the growth of corals, the reef meets the guidelines of the EPA, NOAA, Florida Fish and Wildlife, and the Army Corps of Engineers.

Since 2007, the reef has attracted 56 species of fish. Most common are bluehead wrasses, followed by sergeant majors, bar jacks, and tomtates. Long-spined sea urchins, green moray eels, and many species of crab have moved into the reef's crevices, while sponges colonize its vertical surfaces. Fourteen species of coral have settled in. All in all, the ecosystem is developing faster than expected.

The Neptune Memorial Reef welcomes recreational scuba divers, marine biologists, and researchers from all over the world. ⚜

UNITED STATES: MIDWEST

Mound Cemetery

5th Street at Scammel Street, Marietta, Ohio
http://genealogytrails.com/ohio/washington/
cemetery_mound.html

Archaeologists believe the 30-foot-tall Conus mound was built by the Adena people between 800 BC and 700 AD. Inside it lie their chiefs, who were laid to rest, then covered over with a layer of dirt carried from a nearby pit one basketful at a time. Each generation of chiefs was laid above their ancestors until the mound reached its current height.

In April 1788, General Rufus Putnam led a party of settlers to the area. Many of them were officers and soldiers who had fought in the Revolutionary War and were granted land in the Northwest Territory as thanks for their service.

Although Marietta bills itself as the first permanent White settlement in the Northwest Territory, it is predated by the French settlements in Green Bay and Detroit. Still, Marietta has one of the oldest surviving pioneer graveyards west of the Appalachian Mountains. General Putnam donated land surrounding this large Native American mound to be a graveyard in January 1801. He hoped to protect and preserve the mound.

The cemetery claims to have the highest concentration of Revolutionary War officers in the country. Colonel Robert Taylor was the first person buried here in October 1801, as noted on his headstone. Colonel Ebenezer Sproat served as Ohio's first sheriff for 14 years, before he was buried here. Abraham Whipple was the first American naval commander to fire on the British. He sank the first British ship during the Revolution.

Return Jonathan Meigs Jr., while too young to have served in the Revolution, was Ohio's fourth governor, a U.S. senator, and postmaster general. He's one of several congressmen buried here.

The cemetery is still in use. It was added to the National Register of Historic Places in 1973 and the mound can be climbed via a staircase. ⚜

The 30-foot-tall Conus mound was built by the Adena people between 800 BC and AD 700. The surrounding land became a graveyard for Ohio settlers in 1801.

Spring Grove Cemetery

4521 Spring Grove Avenue, Cincinnati, Ohio
http://www.springgrove.org

Guided by the Cincinnati Horticultural Society, Cincinnati's town elders hoped to create a large, nondenominational, nonprofit cemetery that could also serve as a public park. Future Supreme Court Justice Salmon P. Chase had helped to prepare the Spring Grove charter.

The cemetery trustees hired landscape designer Howard Daniels, whose innovative "lawn plan" design for Spring Grove Cemetery gave landscape precedence over monuments. The plan was carried out by German-born horticulturalist Adolph Strauch, who took over as superintendent in 1855, ten years after the cemetery opened. Strauch envisioned a cemetery with open vistas and large expanses of lawn. His intent was that the total effect would outshine individual monuments.

Strauch was a pioneer, in that he employed his own team of gardeners and maintenance workers, rather than trusting the cemetery's upkeep to individual lot holders. He rerouted roads to follow the terrain. He built lakes around islands, added footbridges, and populated the water with frogs and fishes in order to bring life

A rather chaste mourner places a wreath on a grave in Spring Grove Cemetery, the second-largest graveyard in the United States.

to the graveyard. He planted trees from around the world with an eye for color and texture. Under his supervision, the cemetery developed into a nationally regarded arboretum.

Bucking the trend for grand monuments, Strauch encouraged families to choose small markers for their large lots, lending a sense of

spaciousness. Strauch's ideas took a while to catch on: The Cincinnati papers condemned him repeatedly for removing fences and hedges and opening up the cemetery.

Justice Chase was buried here in the end. Other famous residents include Civil War General Joseph Hooker; Waite Hoyt, Hall of Fame pitcher for the New York Yankees; Bernard Kroger, founder of the grocery store chain; and both William

Procter and James Gamble. Kroger and Procter & Gamble continue to be among the largest employers in town.

The cemetery has long been a popular picnicking spot. One visitor remarked that it was a more magnificent park than any that exists for the living. That remarkable beauty inspired Spring Grove's addition to the National Register of Historic Places in 2007. ⚜

Tulips, redbud trees, and forsythia explode into bloom in Spring Grove to celebrate the end of winter.

Lake View Cemetery

12316 Euclid Avenue, Cleveland, Ohio
https://lakeviewcemetery.com

Cleveland's Lake View Cemetery is a large, lovely rural garden cemetery that climbs a ridge east of town and provides a spectacular view of Lake Erie.

Inside the Euclid Gate, an angel encircles children with her arms. This poignant monument remembers the 175 victims of the Collinwood School fire. An unexplained fire struck the relatively new building in March 1908. Teachers saved half their charges, but some children fell, blocking the stairwell so that others couldn't

escape. The tragedy brought national attention to the issue of school safety for the first time.

One of Lake View's treasures is the chapel named for Jeptha H. Wade. His namesake grandson hired Louis Comfort Tiffany to design the chapel, which is unusual among cemetery buildings because it contains no remains. Tiffany

The Angel of Death Victorious was sculpted by Herman Matzen to mark the grave of Francis Haserot, who made his fortune canning vegetables. The way the bronze has discolored looks like tears running down her face.

designed the breathtaking Resurrection window, the room's focal point, in addition to the biblical murals lining its walls. Because Tiffany refused to allow soot to sully his artwork, his friend Thomas Edison wired the chapel for electric lights, making it the first electrified building in Cleveland.

The cemetery's showpiece is its monument to assassinated President James A. Garfield. Garfield was born in a log cabin in Ohio's Cuyahoga County. He was elected to the Ohio Senate, a post he left to serve as a major general in the

Civil War. He was elected to the U.S. House of Representatives, then the U.S. Senate, but received the Republican nomination for president before taking office. He served four months of his presidential term, then a deranged fan shot him in the back on July 2, 1881. One of the bullets lodged in his spine. Garfield lingered for 80 days, before infection killed him.

Nine years after his death, the president was laid to rest inside this monument. It has been called the first true mausoleum in America, since it serves both as tomb and a tribute to his memory. The structure combines Romanesque, Gothic, and Byzantine architecture in a tower, domed interior, and crypt. A statue of Garfield looks as if he's just stepped out of his chair, a roll of parchment in his hand.

Garfield's coffin lies in the crypt, alongside his wife, Lucretia. Their daughter, Molly, who was 14 at the time of the assassination, and her husband, Joseph Stanley-Brown, Garfield's private secretary, are inurned nearby. ⚜

51 Elmwood Cemetery

1200 Elmwood Avenue, Detroit, Michigan
http://elmwoodhistoriccemetery.org

The hilly terrain at Elmwood Cemetery is similar to what the French explorer Cadillac saw in 1701 when he founded Detroit at the straits of Lake Huron.

During the French and Indian War, Chief Pontiac's troops defeated the British at Parents Creek on July 31, 1763. British blood stained the water until the creek became known as Bloody Run. It still flows through Elmwood Cemetery.

Six prominent Detroiters purchased a rural cemetery, which opened in 1846. Almost 50 years later, Frederick Law Olmsted (designer of Central Park) landscaped Elmwood Cemetery. His plans included the roads that swoop over and around the 86 acres of rolling hills. He also planted groves of trees where squirrels, pheasants, and other wildlife now live.

Not far from the Renaissance Center and the Ambassador Bridge into Canada, Elmwood Cemetery is the oldest continually used non-denominational cemetery in Detroit. It holds 6 Michigan governors, 11 U.S. senators, 28 Detroit mayors, as well as inventors, explorers, artists, abolitionists, and former slaves.

Among the notables lie Detroit's legendary first African-American mayor, Tuskegee Airman Coleman Young; the Michigan Territory's first governor, Lewis Cass; Canadian Club whiskey founder Hiram Walker; and guitarist Fred "Sonic" Smith of the MC5. Michigan's first African-American schoolteacher is buried here, along with the state's first African-American lawyer, legislator, newspaper owner, and radio station owner. The State of Michigan purchased a lot for veterans of the Civil War, which includes 15 members of the 102nd U.S. Colored Troops regiment.

In consequence, Elmwood Cemetery offers Black History tours. It also partners with local schools to give kids a chance to work in the graveyard on gardening and restoration projects. ⚜

This Gothic Revival gateway welcomes visitors to Detroit's Elmwood Cemetery, which was landscaped by Frederick Law Olmsted.

J. Seward Johnson's *Crack the Whip* is only one of the realistic bronze sculptures that greet visitors to Sunset Hills.

Sunset Hills Cemetery

G-4413 Flushing Road, Flint, Michigan
http://www.sunsethills.com

Sunset Hills Cemetery lies near the Flint River, between the former automotive capital of Flint and the former farming village of Flushing, Michigan. It's a lovely combination of lawn cemetery, with bronze monuments lying flush with the sod, and garden cemetery, full of gorgeous old trees, winding roadways, and peaceful views. What makes it worth visiting is its amazing collection of life-size figurative sculpture.

The first piece stands just inside the gate. *The Provider* is an older gentleman, in bronze. He raises a tin can to fill a real bird feeder. The statue wears striped rubber boots, slacks with a belt, and a button-down shirt. *The Provider* was sculpted by Derek Wernher in the likeness of Albert Koegel, patriarch of the Koegel's hot dog empire.

Tucked under the trees is *The Generation Bridge* by J. Seward Johnson. A grandfather in a tweed suit offers a broken Hershey bar to a little girl in a quilted pale blue outfit. Beside him on the wooden bench sits her dolly. More than one visitor has mistaken the enameled bronze figures for real people.

The centerpiece of the Sunset Hills sculpture collection is Johnson's *Crack the Whip*: eight children with linked hands running in a semicircle as if playing the game. *Crack the Whip*, the first of Sunset Hills' sculptures, was dedicated in 1983. It was donated by an anonymous Flint-area resident whose family lies here.

The sculpture is composed of two African-American kids, a Native American, four White kids, and an Asian American girl who lost her Birkenstock sandal, which lies nearby in the grass.

Johnson's *The Gardener* is a crouching man dressed in blue denim overalls with a handkerchief dangling from his back pocket. In one hand, he holds a spade. The other holds a small flowerpot, sometimes filled with living flowers. He appears real enough that people probably ask him for directions.

The final sculpture is Derek Wernher's *The Flag Raiser*. The bronze statue stands beside the cemetery's flagpole and reaches up as if raising the American flag. He wears a large ring of keys clipped at his hip, modeled on Charles Smith, grounds supervisor for over 39 years. ⚜

52

Almost a million visitors come each year to pay their respects at the tomb of President Abraham Lincoln. Oak Ridge Cemetery is the second most visited cemetery in the United States.

Oak Ridge Cemetery

1441 Monument Avenue, Springfield, Illinois
http://www.oakridgecemetery.org

When the Civil War ended on April 9, 1865, many refused to accept peace. Five days after the Confederacy surrendered, John Wilkes Booth shot President Lincoln in the back of the head. Lincoln died the following morning without regaining consciousness.

Lincoln was the first president to die from an assassin's bullet. Mourning gripped the Northern states. A funeral carriage delivered Lincoln's body to the White House, where doctors performed an autopsy and undertakers embalmed his body. He was dressed in the same black suit he had worn to his inauguration.

Mary Lincoln would have preferred to have her husband buried in the unused vault prepared for George Washington in the Capitol Building, but Springfield's businessmen banded together to offer a monument to their hometown hero. Mary had visited Oak Ridge Cemetery's dedication ceremony in 1860, while Lincoln ran for his initial term as president. She remembered that her husband asked to be buried somewhere quiet. The rural cemetery seemed like the ideal place.

The 117-foot tomb, designed by sculptor Larkin Mead, was constructed of brick faced with granite from Quincy, Massachusetts. Two sets of stairs lead to a terrace crowned with an obelisk. At the corners of the tower stand four bronze sculptures representing the four Civil War services: infantry, artillery, cavalry, and navy. The obelisk's south side features a bronze statue of Lincoln. A bronze reproduction of Gutzon Borglum's marble head of Lincoln in the U.S. Capitol stands at the tomb's entrance. The interior is highly polished marble trimmed with bronze.

In 1876, thugs from Chicago broke open the white marble sarcophagus in which the president lay, attempting to steal his body. They couldn't move his 500-pound iron coffin. Pinkerton officers arrested them after they fled the scene.

In 1901, Lincoln's coffin was sealed in an iron cage, then sunk into concrete in a vault ten feet below the marble floor of the burial chamber. A massive red granite cenotaph in the shape of a sarcophagus marks the gravesite. Crypts in the chamber's south wall hold the remains of Lincoln's wife Mary and three of their four sons: Edward, William (who had died at the White House), and Thomas. Robert, the eldest son, was buried in Arlington National Cemetery.

The 365-acre Oak Ridge Cemetery is the final resting place of 70 other notable historic figures, including labor leaders, poets, four Illinois governors, and Lincoln's law partner.

Oak Ridge is the second most visited cemetery in America, hosting almost a million visitors each year. ❧

Graceland Cemetery

4001 North Clark Street, Chicago, Illinois
http://gracelandcemetery.org

This area of Chicago was practically wilderness in 1860 when real estate developer Thomas B. Bryan bought 80 acres to create a cemetery. Bryan received a perpetual charter from Illinois the following year and hired landscape architect H.W.S. Cleveland—considered second only to Frederick Law Olmsted—to plan a parklike burial ground.

Architect Ossian Cole Simonds was so inspired by Graceland that he gravitated toward landscape design. He came on board when the cemetery expanded to 119 acres in 1883 and used native plants to create a pastoral landscape. Plots were sodded uniformly and fences and curbs removed. Wealthy Chicagoans were encouraged to purchase "landscape rooms" for their final disposition.

The cemetery's gates were designed by Holabird & Roche, who went on to design the administration building and the cemetery's chapel. The chapel contains the city's first crematorium, built in 1893.

The Getty mausoleum, designed by Louis Henri Sullivan, has been designated a Chicago landmark. The limestone cube with its delicate

Lorado Taft's *Eternal Silence* is one of many bronze statues in the Midwest to have inspired ghostly urban legends.

geometric ornamentation is regarded as the origin of modern architecture in America. Frank Lloyd Wright commented, "Outside the realm of music, what finer requiem?"

Sculptor Lorado Taft made the *Crusader*, who stands over the grave of *Chicago Daily News* publisher Victor Lawson. Taft also is responsible for Graceland's most photographed monument. Named *Eternal Silence*, the shrouded bronze figure is more popularly known as *The Statue of Death*. It marks the family plot of Dexter Graves,

Architect Louis Henri Sullivan, called the father of the American skyscraper, is buried beneath a boulder adorned with this medallion in Chicago's Graceland Cemetery.

hotelier and early settler, who died in 1844 and was moved to Graceland after the fact. Urban legend claims that staring into its unflinching eyes will reveal a vision of the afterworld.

Another remarkable sculpture marks the grave of Marshall Field, pioneer in the concept of department stores. It was sculpted by Daniel Chester French. The thoughtful bronze female figure called *Memory* sits in an oversize granite throne and gazes at an oak branch in her hand.

George Pullman, who perfected sleeping cars for trains, was buried encased in concrete in order to foil disgruntled ex-employees. Above his grave stands an enormous Corinthian column with exedra—curved stone benches—designed by Solon Beman, architect of the company town named for Pullman.

Graceland is the final resting place of a host of other famous people, including Allan Pinkerton, founder of the detective agency; Cyrus McCormick, who revolutionized farming with his harvesting machine; and Jack Johnson, the first African-American world heavyweight champion in boxing. ⚜

Saint Casimir
Catholic
Cemetery

4401 West 111th Street, Chicago, Illinois
catholiccemeterieschicago.org/
locations.php?cem=23

Southernmost of Europe's Baltic states, Lithuania is surrounded by Belarus, Latvia, and Poland. It has been independent from the Soviet Union since 1990. In 1871, many Lithuanians

emigrated to Chicago after the Great Fire to work in the factories, steel mills, and stockyards. By the turn of the century, about 5000 Lithuanians lived in Chicago. They established their own cemetery in 1903 and named it the Saint Casimir Lithuanian Cemetery, after the patron saint of Lithuania.

Originally, the cemetery's simple monuments looked generically American. When a new wave of immigrants fled the Soviets in 1949, the tombstones became emblazoned with tulips, stalks of wheat, and other symbols of home. Crucifixes, rosaries, and images of the Blessed Virgin of Vilnius or Saints George and Joseph appeared on gravestones.

Ramojus Mozoliauskas was one of the Lithuanians who escaped the Soviets. He studied sculpting in West Germany before coming to Chicago, where he worked as a stonecutter. After he opened his own shop, he created more than a hundred monuments in Saint Casimir's Cemetery. Often Mozoliauskas carved figures emerging from the granite: Christ with wrists bound or a worried Jesus with his head in hand. His art translated to plate steel, polished aluminum, and stained glass as well. Mozoliauskas was buried beneath one of his own sculptures in 2010. ⚜

Very modern statuary mixes with more classic monuments in this cemetery founded to serve Lithuanian immigrants to Chicago.

Oakland
Cemetery

1000 Brown Street, Iowa City, Iowa
https://www.icgov.org/city-government/
departments-and-divisions/oakland-cemetery

Oakland Cemetery is known for the eight-and-a-half-foot-tall Black Angel standing over the Feldevert grave.

Teresa Dolezal was born in Bohemia in 1836, where she worked as a physician. She moved to Iowa City with her son Eddie and found work as a midwife. In 1891, 18-year-old Eddie died of meningitis. Teresa buried him in Oakland Cemetery under a tree stump monument, to symbolize a life cut off in its prime.

Teresa moved to Eugene, Oregon, where she married Nicholas Feldevert. After he died in 1911, she returned to Iowa City to bury her husband's ashes near her son. She hired Mario

Korbel, a Bohemian artist in Chicago, to design a bronze angel to mark their graves.

The angel arrived by railroad in November 1912. Teresa purchased a larger plot in the cemetery, had Eddie's remains transferred, and installed her husband's ashes under the angel. Eddie's tree stump monument was also moved to the new plot.

Twelve years later, Teresa succumbed to cancer. Her ashes were also buried near the angel.

Then the story goes from sad to strange. At some point—which varies, depending on the storyteller—the bronze angel oxidized black. Some say the angel was struck by lightning the night after Teresa's burial. Some say Teresa had vowed to remain faithful to her husband and the angel's color revealed her infidelity. Teresa was a witch, others claim. Her son didn't die of meningitis: Teresa murdered him. And so on.

Urban legends surround the Black Angel: If you kiss the statue, you'll be struck dead. Pregnant women must stay out of the angel's shadow or risk miscarriage. If ever a virgin is kissed in

front of the statue, the angel will return to its original color and its curse will be broken.

Colin Dickey, author of *Ghostland: An American History in Haunted Places*, says that ghost stories and curses often spring up around women who were unusual in their time, say, women doctors in the 19th century: "In my research, I found repeated evidence that ghost stories often originate with an individual or family who—one way or another—doesn't conform to cultural and societal expectations: women who live alone or choose not to marry, for example. Ghost stories seem to be one way in which we both explain this 'abnormal' behavior, while simultaneously keeping that person or her story at a remove."

Which may explain why Teresa is blamed for the oxidation of her monument. In fact, another black angel stands in the Fairview Cemetery in Council Bluffs. It marks the grave of Ruth Anne Dodge, spiritualist wife of General Grenville M.

Dodge, a Civil War veteran who became the chief engineer of the Transcontinental Railroad. That angel, sculpted by Daniel Chester French, was created as a fountain, spilling the water of life from a basin in her hand. Rumors of a curse surround her as well.

The weather in Iowa is hard on bronze angels. ⚜

57 Walnut Hill Cemetery

1805 East Street, Baraboo, Wisconsin
http://www.walnuthillcemetery.com

High atop the bluffs in Baraboo lies Walnut Hill Cemetery, a nondenominational cemetery founded in 1855. After it opened, burials from three other cemeteries in Baraboo were consolidated on Walnut Hill's initial ten acres.

The most famous resident of Walnut Hill is C. August Albrecht Ringling, known as Al. (complete with the period), eldest of seven Ringling brothers.

Al., born in 1852, was trained by his father to be a carriage finisher, but his real love was juggling. In 1882, Al. and brothers Charles, Otto, Alfred, and John started a traveling vaudeville show. They spent their first $300 buying tuxedoes.

The following year, Al. married Lou, who performed in the show as a snake charmer. By 1884, the vaudeville show blossomed into a circus, which toured 114 towns in its first summer, traveling by wagon pulled by a rented horse.

By 1900, the Ringling Circus started absorbing other circuses. When they acquired James Bailey's show, the Ringlings owned the largest circus in North America: the Ringling Brothers and Barnum & Bailey Circus.

When Al. died in 1915, he was interred in a surprisingly sedate mausoleum, constructed of Vermont granite. Its ornamentation runs to palm leaves and wreaths.

Of the five Ringling Brothers who started the circus in Baraboo, only Al. and Otto are buried in Walnut Hill. Otto's family plot is marked by a heavy granite sarcophagus decorated with whimsical flowers. A simple gravestone marks his place in the ground.

Although the Ringling Brothers Circus closed in March 2017, Circus World Museum in Baraboo keeps the magic alive. ⚜

Glorious in the autumn, tree-filled Forest Hill Cemetery preserves several very unusual Native American effigy mounds.

Forest Hill Cemetery

1 Speedway Road, Madison, Wisconsin
https://www.cityofmadison.com/parks/
find-a-park/cemetery

Alice Whiting Waterman cared for the Confederate Rest section of Forest Hill Cemetery and is buried there now. The graves are decorated with flags for Memorial Day.

Between 500 and 1000 AD, Native Americans called the Effigy Moundbuilders used this high point, with its view of the lakes, to build several burial mounds. Because people were already buried here, this site was chosen as a cemetery in 1858.

Unfortunately, the goose mound was decapitated in the 1880s when the Illinois Central Railroad cut through the edge of the cemetery. What's left of it and two intact panther mounds survive, thanks to archaeologist Charles E. Brown, buried in Section 1. The sinuous panther mounds are now surrounded by veterans from the Spanish-American and more recent wars. All three surviving mounds are listed on the National Register of Historic Places.

The trees have grown up, obscuring the views, but the rural-style cemetery retains its winding roads and rolling hills. Buried in the cemetery are eight Wisconsin state governors, a Nobel Prize winner, and many faculty members of the University of Wisconsin. Harry Steenbock, a professor of biochemistry, discovered vitamins A, B, and D. A Classical Revival monument remembers Moses Stephen Slaughter, professor of Latin

at the university, and his wife, Gertrude Elizabeth Taylor Slaughter, author of books about Paris, Shakespeare, and Saladin.

Confederate soldiers captured on Island #10 in the Mississippi River were imprisoned in Madison at Camp Randall in 1862. POWs who died there were buried in Forest Hill's Confederate Rest plot. No one cared for the graves until a widow from Louisiana named Alice Waterman moved to town. She maintained the plot at her own expense until her death in 1897. She is buried in the plot now.

Among the Union soldiers buried in Forest Hill is Theodore Read, the last Union general to die in the war. On April 6, 1865, he fought a saber duel with Confederate General Dearing, which delayed the retreat of Lee's army and contributed to the surrender at Appomattox on April 9. Also here is Henry Harden, brigadier general in command of the unit that captured Jefferson Davis after the war's end. More soldiers are buried in the Union Soldier's Lot, along with eight children who died at Madison's Soldiers' Orphans' Home. ⚜

Inspired by the Hagia Sophia in Istanbul, the Lakewood Mortuary Chapel is a spectacular example of Byzantine Revival mosaic.

Lakewood Cemetery

**3600 Hennepin Avenue,
Minneapolis, Minnesota
http://www.lakewoodcemetery.com**

On the edge of the cemetery, above Lake Calhoun, stands a 40-foot obelisk in memory of the victims of the Washburn "A" Mill disaster. In 1878, the mill was one of the country's largest when a dust explosion, caused by flour particles in the air, killed 18 people: 14 Washburn millworkers, 3 workers at mills nearby, and a bystander. The white granite monument, quarried at Barre, Vermont, features a millstone, a sheaf of wheat, and a broken gear to symbolize the lives lost.

The Lakewood Mortuary Chapel, dedicated in 1910, is a spectacular example of Byzantine Revival architecture. It was designed by local architect Harry Wild Jones, who modeled it after the Hagia Sophia in Istanbul. Its breathtaking interior is adorned with hand-laid mosaic tiles as small as fingernails.

Lakewood Cemetery is the final resting place of Vice President Hubert Humphrey and several Minnesota governors, including three-term governor John S. Pillsbury. Governor Rudy Perpich's grave is marked with a soaring modernist stainless steel sculpture that represents the governor and his wife supporting each other. Senator Paul Wellstone's monument is a granite boulder.

Former owners of the Minnesota Twins and the Minnesota Timberwolves are both buried here, as is Herbert B. Khaury, the entertainer known as Tiny Tim, and H. David Dalquist, whose Nordic Ware company invented the pan for baking bundt cakes. Franklin Mars, creator of the Milky Way candy bar, is buried here in the Mars mausoleum. Also here is Charles Alfred Pillsbury, founder of the Pillsbury Company. A statue of Hope clutching a wreath stands atop his family monument. ⚜

Bellefontaine Cemetery

**4947 West Florissant Avenue,
St. Louis, Missouri
http://bellefontainecemetery.org**

Bellefontaine Cemetery began as a family plot. Its earliest monument belongs to Stephen Hempstead, a Revolutionary War veteran who died in 1817 and was buried on his own farmstead. Near him lies Manuel Lisa, one of the founders of the Missouri Fur Company, who died in 1820. Lisa had been buried in the Catholic Cemetery closer to town, but was moved to the Hempstead farm in 1830.

Nearly two decades later, a rural cemetery committee—headed by a prominent banker and a lawyer who had been mayor—predicted the growth of Saint Louis, perched alongside the Mississippi River on the edge of the West. They purchased 138 acres of the Hempstead farm for a rural cemetery in 1849. The lovely name *Bellefontaine* came from a fort that stood up the road.

Before the cemetery had been properly planned, a cholera epidemic swept upriver from New Orleans. By mid-August 1849, the population of Saint Louis had been literally decimated—and Bellefontaine was in common use.

Perhaps the most famous person buried here is General William Clark, half of the Lewis and Clark Expedition. Clark had served as governor of the Missouri territory. He lies with his family beside a granite obelisk unveiled during the 1904 World's Fair.

Also buried here is Adolphus Busch, the beer baron, and his father-in-law, Eberhard Anheuser. Other notables include Henry Taylor Blow, the abolitionist who set Dred Scott free; his daughter Susan, who founded the first kindergarten in the United States; and poet Sara Teasdale, who won the first Pulitzer Prize given to a woman for her book *Love Songs*.

More recently, William S. Burroughs, Beat Generation writer and author of *Naked Lunch*, was buried in Bellefontaine in his family's plot. Burroughs's namesake father founded the Burroughs Corporation after inventing an adding machine.

In addition to being an arboretum with over 180 species of trees and shrubs, Bellefontaine holds 100 acres of undeveloped land, some of which has been returned to prairie. The cemetery provides habitat for foxes, bats, waterfowl, wild turkeys, and many migratory birds. ⚜

The tomb of Adolphus Busch, cofounder of the Anheuser-Busch Brewing Company, was designed in the Bavarian Gothic style, complete with ornate bronze spire.

Mount Olivet Cemetery

101 Missouri 92, Kearney, Missouri

Jesse James was 16 when he followed his brother Frank into the Civil War. After their side lost, Jesse, Frank, and several other veterans spent 20 years robbing banks.

On April 3, 1882, Jesse was shot dead in his home in Saint Joseph, Missouri (now a museum). Surviving members of the gang, including Frank, packed his body in ice and brought it back to his childhood home in Excelsior Springs (now called Kearney). His mother Zerelda had Jesse buried near the house, where she could keep an eye on his grave. She feared grave robbers would display his remains in a traveling show, as was common in those days.

Still, Zerelda wasn't above making a little money off her son's notoriety herself. She sold rocks from his grave for 25 cents each.

After two decades in the grave outside his mother's farmhouse, Jesse James's body was exhumed and reburied in the family plot in Mount Olivet Cemetery in 1902. His wife, Zee (short for Zerelda—she was a first cousin named for his mother), had died in November 1900 and was already buried in the plot. Jesse's half-brother, Archie Payton Samuel, is also buried there. He was killed by a Pinkerton bomb that cost Mother Zerelda a hand.

Zerelda herself died in 1911 and was buried with her boys.

Jesse's original tall marble tombstone has been replaced by a government-issued military headstone. It details the outfits with which Jesse fought in the Civil War. A large granite marker, flush with the ground, names Jesse and Zerelda.

In 1995, forensic experts proved that Jesse's remains were, in fact, in his grave. *Rest in Pieces: The Curious Fates of Famous Corpses* gives a pretty good rundown of the exhumation and analysis. All those men who claimed to be Jesse James, escaped and grown old peacefully, were proved to be imposters. ⚜

Jesse James shares a modern gravestone with his wife Zerelda, a first cousin named in honor of his mother.

Boot Hill Cemetery

500 West Wyatt Earp Boulevard, Dodge City, Kansas
http://boothill.org

Soon after the Civil War ended, Fort Dodge was founded near the Arkansas River in the young state of Kansas. Fort Dodge's mission was to protect westward-moving settlers from Native American attacks.

In 1871, H. J. Sitler built a sod house nearby and opened the area's first bar. Other settlers soon recognized that the steady stream of pioneers on the Santa Fe Trail would make for good business. A town grew up.

In its early days, Dodge City was a rough, lawless place. Its graveyard was the original Boot Hill, so-called because the men buried there "died with their boots on," either in a gunfight or from being hanged, as opposed to expiring quietly in their beds of illness or old age. From Dodge City, the term *boot hill* came to be used for any Western burial ground dating to the post–Civil War era in the last third of the 1800s.

Approximately 34 persons were interred on the site. Wolves often disturbed their unmarked graves. In 1879, the city council ordered that the bodies be removed. A modern sign calls the people who had been buried here "drifters, troublemakers, and unknowns," although actress Dora Hand was laid to rest here after being shot by someone with a grudge against the judge in whose bed she was sleeping at the time of her death. Newspaper accounts consider her a legitimate actress and point out that the judge was not sleeping at home at the time of the attack, on account of an illness.

A modern marker incised with a buffalo skull says, "A buffalo hunter named McGill amused himself by shooting into every house he passed. He won't pass this way again."

Another grave marker remembers "George Hoyt, shot July 26, 1878. One night he took a pot shot at Wyatt Earp. Buried on Boot Hill August 21, 1878. Let his faults, if he had any, be hidden in the grave." George Hoyt was among the drunken cowboys who fired their guns in the Comique Theater. In response, Assistant Marshal Wyatt Earp and Marshal James Masterson, along with several other citizens, returned fire. Hoyt received a gunshot to the arm and fled. He died from gangrene. While some historians doubt that Earp actually shot Hoyt, the assistant marshal took the credit.

The *Marion County* (Kansas) *Record* reported on March 29, 1873: "an unmitigated scoundrel and desperado named McGill was shot and killed at Dodge City."

Boot Hill Cemetery is now located in the heart of present-day Dodge City, Kansas. It is part of the Boot Hill Museum, which displays more than 60,000 objects, photographs, and documents from the last half of the 19th century. As part of the museum, Front Street's businesses have been re-created, including the Long Branch Saloon and the Tonsorial Parlor. ⚜

Ogallala Boot Hill

West 10th and Parkhill Drive, Ogallala, Nebraska

Ogallala was a sleepy 10-year-old town when the Union Pacific Railroad constructed pens for livestock just west of the main street. Longhorn cattle roaming the open ranges of Texas were rounded up, herded up the Western Trail to Ogallala (a journey of more than 700 miles), then loaded onto rail cars for markets in the East.

Overnight, Ogallala became a booming cow town. In his book *Log of a Cowboy*, trail driver Andy Adams called the town "the Gomorrah of the cattle trail." Saloons, dance halls, and gambling houses lined its streets, ready to separate cowboys from their pay. Those cowboys who didn't make it out of Ogallala alive ended up on a hill outside of town.

Townsfolk didn't waste wood on coffins for ne'er-do-wells. Instead, bodies were placed in canvas sacks and buried in shallow graves marked only with wooden headboards. Among those buried in Ogallala's Boot Hill is "Rattlesnake Ed," shot down over a $9 bet at the Cowboy's Rest Saloon.

To be fair, not everyone buried in the cemetery was a reprobate. The first burials in Boot Hill were a mother and her child. In fact, many of the respectable folk buried originally at Boot Hill were exhumed by their families and moved after Ogallala's new cemetery opened in 1886.

Millions of cattle made the trip between 1870 and 1885, when the trail closed down. Now the old graveyard drowses on the hill, surrounded by a subdivision.

Alongside the graves stands the bronze statue of a horse and rider called *The Trail Boss*. Embodying a weary cattle drover, the statue looks over the graves and past town back down the trail to Texas. The statue, made by Robert Summers, is a duplicate of one standing at the other end of the trail in Dallas. ⚜

Robert Summers's *The Trail Boss* marks the end of the Western Trail in Ogallala's Boot Hill.

Mount Moriah Cemetery

**10 Mount Moriah Drive,
Deadwood, South Dakota
http://www.cityofdeadwood.com/index.
asp?SEC=A0DB4AD3-F0E9-4EAC-8E22-
995D27A3329B&**

James Butler Hickok, known as Wild Bill, was a Civil War veteran, cavalry scout, stagecoach driver, and deputy marshal in the roughest towns in Kansas, before he became a showman in Buffalo Bill's Wild West Show. The "Prince of the Pistoleers" had a reputation as the fastest gunslinger in the West. Estimates of the number of men he'd killed range from seven to over a hundred. There were 36 notches on his gun.

Wild Bill came to Deadwood in July 1876, looking for gold. Less than a month later, while playing poker in a saloon, he was shot in the back of the head. He died holding two black aces and two black eights: the dead man's hand. His assailant, who'd lost a poker game to Hickok the night before, was sentenced to death by hanging.

In a dark suit with his rifle by his side, Hickok was buried in a pine coffin on the outskirts of

64

Moriah is the name of the mountain on which Abraham was commanded to sacrifice Isaac in the biblical book of Genesis.

The markers on Wild Bill Hickok's grave have been replaced many times after souvenir hunters have whittled them away.

Deadwood. Three years later, his remains were exhumed and reburied at Mount Moriah Cemetery, named for the mountain in the biblical book of Genesis on which Abraham was ordered to sacrifice his son Isaac.

Martha Jane Cannary Burke, called Calamity Jane, was illiterate, orphaned at an early age, and claimed to have worked through 12 husbands in the course of her life. She drank and swore, sometimes dressed in men's clothing, and settled in Deadwood to take up with Wild Bill in 1876.

After his murder, she wandered off, finding work where she could get it. Eventually, she washed up in Deadwood again, was photographed leaning against the fence around Bill's grave, and died the day before the 27th anniversary of his death in 1903. Her dying request was to be buried beside Bill.

Originally Bill's grave was marked by a whitewashed board with the epitaph, "Pard we will meet again in the Happy Hunting ground to part no more. Goodbye. Colorado Charlie C.H. Utter."

At some point, Bill and Calamity's graves were covered with boulders mortared together to discourage souvenir hunters. Granite stones with their real names beneath their sobriquets now mark their graves. ⚜

UNITED STATES: WEST

Apache Prisoners-of-War Cemeteries

The East Ridge at Fort Sill, Lawton, Oklahoma
http://www.ftsillindianagencycemetery.com/
references/other-indian-cemeteries

G oyahkla was born in the early part of the 19th century in what is now Clifton, Arizona. Mexican soldiers, impressed by his skill, gave him the name *Geronimo*. No one knows exactly why, but it's theorized that the name comes from Saint Jerome, the patron of translators. Goyahkla's band of Apaches took Geronimo up as their battle cry.

Geronimo and his warriors were hunted down by the U.S. Cavalry in 1886. They were sent off to Alabama and Florida, where many died of malaria. In 1894, the government relented and sent the

Apaches west again, although not back to their homes in Arizona. Instead, they were brought to Fort Sill on the plains of southwestern Oklahoma. They lived in 12 villages around the fort. Over the next 19 years, they built houses, raised cattle, farmed crops, and fenced the entire military compound.

Geronimo worked as an Indian scout, delivering government rations around the reservation. Aside from travels with Pawnee Bill's Wild West Show, he remained a prisoner of war until his death from pneumonia in February 1909. He had asked his wife to tie his horse to a tree, so that he could come to retrieve it after he spent three days in the grave. Instead she buried his riding whip and blanket with him.

Buried near Geronimo are his wife, two daughters, and a son. Some of the military-issue stones designate the men around him as "Apache warrior with Geronimo."

Fort Sill is dotted with Prisoners-of-War Cemeteries. The earliest is the Post Cemetery, established west of the original post in 1869. Its highest

Paratroopers from the 501st Airborne built the pyramid of stones that marks Chief Geronimo's grave.

point is Chiefs Knoll because chiefs of the Southern Plains tribes, including signatories of the Medicine Lodge Peace Treaty, are buried here. It was added to the National Register of Historic Places in 1978. The largest cemetery, where Geronimo was buried, was established in 1894. It was added to the National Register of Historic Places in 1977. The Otipoby Comanche Cemetery lies on the East Range of the fort, northeast of the Apache cemeteries.

Nine years after Geronimo's death, a member of Yale's Skull and Bones Society broke into a tomb with metal doors to steal the warrior's skull, femurs, and a horse's bit and saddle horn. One of the secret society's rituals involves kissing the skull of "Geronimo the Terrible."

In *Rest in Pieces: The Curious Fates of Famous Corpses*, Bess Lovejoy points out that not only was Geronimo buried in the ground, but his grave was also unmarked in 1918, so there were no metal doors to pry apart. However, Chief Kicking Bird was buried on Chiefs Knoll at the time, in an aboveground tomb with metal doors. It's possible his skull was the one stolen.

In the early days of World War II, paratroopers from the 501st Airborne took *Geronimo* as the motto of their brigade, with the permission of Geronimo's descendants. The paratroopers built the eagle-topped pyramid of stones that marks Geronimo's grave. ⚜

Old brick tombs stand beside marble monuments in Galveston's Old City Cemetery, which dates to 1839.

66

Old City Cemetery

Broadway and 40th Street, Galveston, Galveston Island, Texas
http://www.galvestontx.gov/528/ Galveston-Cemeteries

In 1839, as part of Galveston's charter, city fathers donated four square blocks for a public burial ground. The cemetery stood a respectable distance outside the city limits. Good thing, too, since the city was prone to yellow fever epidemics.

The City Cemetery is now the easternmost of seven historic graveyards between 40th and 43rd Streets along Broadway. The Potter's Field was renamed Oleander Cemetery on its centenary in 1939. Both Trinity Episcopal and the Old Catholic cemeteries were founded in 1844. New City Cemetery was established in 1867, followed the next year by the Hebrew Benevolent Society burial ground, and New Cahill Cemetery in 1900. Collectively, the cemeteries hold more than 6000 visibly marked burials within a six-block area. The Broadway Cemetery Historic District was added to the

National Register of Historic Places as recently as 2014.

Ships coming from Europe carried marble in their holds for ballast. When they unloaded at Galveston's docks, the stone sold more cheaply than American marble. Because of this, many beautiful monuments stand in the Broadway cemeteries. The oldest surviving grave marker in Old City Cemetery belongs to Ira Day, an inspector at the port. He died in October 1839.

Veteran of the War of 1812 Captain Aaron Burns served with the U.S. gunboat flotilla. He delivered cannons to Sam Houston during the Texas Revolution. He's buried under a simple marble stone beside his wife, Rebecca.

Also buried in Old City Cemetery is Noah Noble John, who survived three shipboard disasters: the *Brownsville*'s sinking, the *Star State*'s burning and the *Farmer*'s explosion, where the steamship burst her boiler while racing another ship in March 1853. Between 30 and 40 people died. Several of them ended up in Old City Cemetery.

In the aftermath of the Battle of Galveston on New Year's Day 1863, both Union and Confederate soldiers were buried in the Broadway cemeteries. Also buried here is Captain Joseph Archibald Robertson, a Confederate veteran who survived Gettysburg.

In 1900, a hurricane struck Galveston, killing 8000 people. Among them were the wife and three children of Herman F. Kleinecke, a first-generation American who fought in the Battle of Galveston and owned a butcher stall in the central market for 22 years. They are buried under a granite column with an unusual square urn on top. ⚜

Texas State Cemetery

909 Navasota Street, Austin, Texas
http://www.cemetery.state.tx.us

On December 28, 1851, General Edward Burleson was buried on private property in Austin. Burleson had been senior colonel for Stephen F. Austin, a veteran of the Battle of San Jacinto, vice president of the Republic of Texas, then a state senator. Burleson's death inspired his fellow senators to create a cemetery to celebrate "the great and glorious past of the Republic of Texas." The Texas State Cemetery opened in 1854.

Although he died in 1836, a dispute with Stephen Austin's family prevented his reburial here until 1911. Pompeo Coppini created a life-size bronze likeness for Austin's grave. Coppini also sculpted Joanna Troutman, designer of an early version of the Lone Star Flag, who is buried here.

Austin sculptor Elisabet Ney created a reclining figure in marble to mark the grave of Albert Sidney Johnston, a Confederate general who died at Shiloh. A high-peaked Gothic structure covers the sculpture now.

Among the more than 3500 who rest in these 18 acres are 11 former governors, including Ann Richards; Texas authors Chris Kyle (*American Sniper*), James Michener (*Tales of the South Pacific*), J. Frank Dobie (called the Storyteller of the Southwest), and Fred Gipson (*Old Yeller*); and Texas historian Walter Prescott Webb. U.S. Congresswoman Barbara Jordan sat on the House Judiciary Committee for President Nixon's Watergate Impeachment. Her grave is marked with a massive granite column labeled "Patriot."

Astronaut Gene Cernan, the last man to walk on the moon, was buried here in January 2017.

The site fell into disrepair for a number of years, before a renovation in 1994. A new visitor center welcomes guests while interpretive paths pass points of interest. ⚜

67

Italian-born Pompeo Coppini sculpted the bronze figure of Stephen Austin with his arm upraised to show off the city that bears his name, but the statue was moved to mark Austin's grave instead.

Albert Sidney Johnston served as secretary of war for the Republic of Texas, fought in the Mexican American War, escorted Mormons to Salt Lake City, and more, before becoming a brigadier general for the Confederacy. He died leading his troops at the Battle of Shiloh.

Founded in 1629, the Spanish mission church of San Esteban del Rey overlooks the graveyard at Acoma Pueblo in this vintage postcard from the author's collection.

San Esteban del Rey Mission Churchyard

Acoma Pueblo, Cibola County, New Mexico
https://www.nps.gov/nr/travel/American_
latino_heritage/San_Estevan_del_Rey_
Mission_Church.html

Seventy miles west of Albuquerque stands the Acoma Pueblo, the oldest continuously occupied site in the Western Hemisphere. Archaeologists have dated initial occupation to 1150.

The Acoma Mesa rises 360 feet above the plain, to an elevation of 6600 feet above sea level. It stood high enough that Hernando de Alvarado of the Coronado expedition in 1540 called it one of the strongest pueblos he'd ever seen. Not until January 12, 1599 did the Spanish attack in force, killing 800 Acomans and enslaving the survivors.

Between 1629 and 1640, the Spanish built a mission church called San Esteban del Rey on the mesa. The church was difficult to complete because its building materials—even the dirt and water to make its adobe walls—had to be carried up from the valley floor. Acomans moved an estimated 20,000 tons of earth and stone to build the church and its graveyard.

With the imposition of Catholicism came the ritual of burial. Since the mesa top was barren rock, earth to fill the cemetery had to be carried up in woven baskets. The tradition of carrying dirt continued until the road up the mesa was finally built. Now earth is carried up in the beds of pickup trucks. Five layers of graves fill the cemetery, which is surrounded by a retaining wall that measures nearly 50 feet high on the outside.

The current level of graves will be the last. Space in the cemetery is reserved for tribal elders and those who live in the pueblo year-round. Most other Acomans choose to be buried elsewhere in the reservation.

In front of the church stands a memorial to the unknown ancestors buried here in unmarked graves. The walls around the cemetery contain sculpted faces. These are the guardians of the dead. One wall is pierced by a hole, to allow spirits of the deceased an exit into the afterlife.

Kit Carson Cemetery

Kit Carson Park
Dragoon Lane, Taos, New Mexico
http://www.taosgov.com/recreation/
kit-carson.php

Kit Carson was born in Kentucky in 1809. He worked as a fur trapper and Indian interpreter before guiding John C. Fremont to California and participating in the Bear Flag Revolt to liberate California from Mexican control in 1846. Carson served the Union as a brevet brigadier general, then took part in the Indian Wars, where he forced 8000 Diné to relocate to

Many early traders, merchants, and members of old Spanish, French, and American families are buried here alongside Indian scout Kit Carson and his family.

KIT CARSON - "HE LED THE WAY"

Fort Sumter. He died at age 59 of an aneurysm in his throat.

Carson was originally buried in Boggsville, Colorado, beside his wife Josefa, who had died in childbirth the previous month. The following year, their bodies were transported to Taos, New Mexico, as Carson had stipulated in his will, and reburied two blocks from Josefa's adobe home.

The cemetery, originally called El Cemeterio Militar, had been established in 1847 as a burial place for those killed in the Taos Rebellion. Its name changed to the American Cemetery

in 1852. It was the only burial place in Taos for non-Catholics. Its name changed to the Kit Carson Cemetery in 1869. Currently, there's a movement to change its name again to something more peaceful.

The simple iron fence that surrounds Kit and Josefa's graves was erected by the Masonic Grand Lodge of New Mexico in 1908. The Masons also own the Carson home and run it as a museum.

Some of Carson's children, grandchildren, and other relatives are buried in the cemetery. In their 26 years of marriage, Kit and Josefa had eight children of their own, as well as adopting several Native American children. The priest who married them—Father Antonio José Martinez—is also buried here. He spent 40 years in Taos, fighting for the rights of Spanish-speaking Americans.

Soldiers in this cemetery served in the Mexican War, the Indian Campaigns, the Civil War, the Spanish-American War, and both World Wars. Old Taoseño families—Spanish, French, and American—are buried here as well.

In the corner of this graveyard is buried Mabel Dodge Luhan, the art collector who established Taos's reputation as an art community. She befriended many authors and artists, including D. H. Lawrence. ⚜

Boothill

408 North Highway 80, Tombstone, Arizona
http://www.boothillgraves.com

I n 1877, prospector Ed Schieffelin discovered silver and named his mine Tombstone. Gunslingers, gamblers, Chinese laborers, and fancy ladies flocked to the town that sprang up. For a while, Tombstone was the fastest-growing city between St. Louis and San Francisco. Population peaked at an estimated 20,000.

Shortly after the mine opened, a slight hill northwest of town was chosen for a graveyard. It didn't have a name in its earliest days. Tombstone's pioneer cemetery was used only until 1884, when the New Tombstone City Cemetery opened on Allen Street. That cemetery continues in use today.

While Tombstone's early history was mirrored by boomtowns across the West, the Gunfight at the OK Corral echoes through the folklore of the West. On October 26, 1881, U.S. Marshals Virgil Earp and his brothers, Wyatt and Morgan, joined by the newly deputized Doc Holliday, faced down the Clantons and the McLaurys. Half a minute and thirty shots later, Billy Clanton and the McLaury brothers were ready for their journey to Boothill.

One of the best known of all epitaphs comes from a grave marker in Tombstone. Lester Moore was an agent for the Wells-Fargo Stagecoach. He and another man disputed over a package. Both men died in the gun battle that followed. Moore's marker reads, "Here lies Lester Moore. Four slugs from a .44. No Les no more."

George Johnson's epitaph approaches poetry: "Here lies George Johnson, hanged by mistake. He was right. We was wrong. We strung

Tombstone's "Old Cemetery" was renamed Boothill in the 1920s as a way of drawing tourists. It was in use from 1878 until 1884.

him up and now he's gone." Johnson was hanged for stealing a horse he'd legally purchased.

The graveyard was neglected for many years. Vandals stole the original wooden grave markers and the desert reclaimed the hill. The locals referred to the area as the "Old Cemetery" until the late 1920s, when it was renamed in hopes of drawing tourists.

The graves on Boothill were originally heaped with stones "to keep the varmints from stealing the bones." Those heaps of stones helped when it came time to make new grave markers, but a number of the pioneers resting here went to their final rewards anonymously. Their names and stories may never be known. ⚜

On October 26, 1881, U.S. Marshal Virgil Earp and his brothers Wyatt and Morgan, joined by Doc Holliday, faced the Clantons and the McLaurys outside the OK Corral.

Grand Canyon Pioneer Cemetery

Grand Canyon National Park,
Grand Canyon Village, Arizona
http://grandcanyonhistory.clas.asu.edu/
sites_southrim_cemetery.html

Although beautiful, the Grand Canyon Pioneer Cemetery can be difficult to stumble across since it doesn't lie on—or in view of—the Canyon Rim. Its entrance is flanked by two native stone columns supporting a huge tree trunk as a lintel.

The grave markers—made of wood, cement, brick, and granite—range from handmade to professionally carved. Many are native boulders labeled with bronze plaques.

Tale-spinner John Hance was the first person

buried in this grove of ponderosa pines in 1919. He is considered the first White settler on the canyon rim. Little can be confirmed about his life, but in the 1890s, he was the first to lead tours into the Grand Canyon. His tall tales were so popular that even Theodore Roosevelt hired him as a guide.

Pete Berry came to the canyon as a miner, but stayed to open its first hotel. When the Santa Fe railroad wanted a monopoly on the tourist trade, it cut off water rights to Berry's hotel and put him out of business. He's buried here with his wife and son.

Ralph Henry Cameron served as the territorial delegate from Arizona to the U.S. House of Representatives at the time of statehood. He surmised correctly that the National Park would invalidate his mining claims. In 1920, he got elected to the U.S. Senate, but he was so vindictive against the Department of the Interior that he served only one term.

One of the most historically significant sites at the Grand Canyon—full of pioneers, park rangers, and paleontologists—is the least known.

In 1956, two commercial jetliners collided after their pilots detoured over the canyon to show their passengers the view. Of the 128 people who died, only 29 could be identified enough to go home to their families. Four coffins of body parts were buried in a mass grave in the Pioneer Cemetery.

Emery Kolb worked as a photographer on the canyon's rim for decades. He shot many of the iconic photos of the canyon and sold them at his studio, now a museum. He was buried in the cemetery in 1976. Also buried here are park superintendents, rangers, geologists, archaeologists, paleontologists, concession workers, potter Inger Garrison, and painter Gunnar Widforss. ⚜

Riverside Cemetery

5201 Brighton Boulevard, Denver, Colorado
http://friendsofriversidecemetery.org

In 1876, the year Colorado became a state, Riverside Cemetery opened downstream from Denver on the South Platte River. It was meant to be a true rural cemetery, with winding carriage roads, tree-lined walking paths, and a mausoleum row that overlooked the river. Civil engineer H. C. Lowrie constructed an irrigation system—the first in Colorado—to allow the cemetery to counteract the dryness of the climate by piping in river water. They planted trees, shrubs, and flowers.

Riverside did not segregate by race, religion, or nationality. Anyone could be buried in any plot they could afford. Miguel Antonio Otero, a three-term Congressman from New Mexico, is buried under a very large granite obelisk.

African-American Lewis Price owned the *Denver Star*, the first Black newspaper west of the Missouri River. Both are buried in the most prestigious center section of the cemetery.

Dr. John Evans was one of the first to theorize that cholera was contagious. He lobbied Congress for a quarantine system. It's possible Evans suggested emancipation to President Lincoln. Lincoln personally asked Evans to become the territorial governor of Colorado in 1862. In that capacity, Evans brought the railroads to Colorado.

Clara Brown, who had been born a slave, worked as a laundress for miners during Colorado's gold rush. At the end of the Civil War, she returned east to search for her daughter. Clara spent all the money she'd saved helping other former slaves. She was the first African-American woman to be inducted into the Society of Colorado Pioneers.

A life-size horse stands over the grave of Addison E. Baker, who provided the first water service in Denver by hauling barrels of spring

72

Obelisks of differing heights stand in Riverside Cemetery. The obelisk is an ancient Egyptian construction, symbolizing a permanently captured ray of light.

water into town. The horse was sculpted by James A. Byrne, complete with a sheaf of wheat and a sickle to symbolize the harvest of death.

The cemetery has struggled since it closed to new burials in 2005. It is no longer irrigated and has lost many of its horticultural specimens, but the Friends of Historic Riverside Cemetery is working to rescue it. ⚜

Grand Lake Cemetery, the only public cemetery open for burial inside an American national park predates the foundation of Rocky Mountain National Park in 1915.

Grand Lake Cemetery

**Rocky Mountain National Park,
Grand Lake, Colorado
http://www.townofgrandlake.com/
cemetery.htm**

The U.S. government acquired the land that would become Colorado as part of the Louisiana Purchase in 1803. Although Native Americans had hunted in the Rocky Mountains for 10,000 years, European and American settlers began to occupy the land in the 19th century.

Originally owned by the Harbison family, this cemetery was used as early as 1875. Several pioneer families were buried on this corner of the Harbison Ranch. Local miners, trappers, ranchers, and homesteaders opened it as Grand Lake Cemetery in 1892.

On January 26, 1915, President Woodrow Wilson created Rocky Mountain National Park, the tenth national park in the system. The Park Service issued a special permit that this land could continue to be used as a cemetery for the use of local families. It was surveyed in 1917 as 42 acres. The Grand Lake Women's Club supervised its maintenance.

Several pioneer family cemeteries were threatened by the creation of Granby Reservoir and Shadow Mountain Lake. Graves from those cemeteries were transferred to the Grand Lake Cemetery in 1943.

Among those buried here is Harry Randell, stabbed in the back after a dance in the Young family's boathouse. Nearby lies James W. Mitchell, who served 18 months for the murder, although the short sentence leaves doubt that he was guilty. His wife Polly left him after the murder, but she is buried with him now.

Mary Gregg is buried in the same grave as Josie, Ralph, Harold, and Alec, four of her seven children. In 1905, Mary was so depressed that she killed them and herself with a shotgun. The surviving children weren't home at the time.

Several of the epitaphs here attest to the dangers of the Rockies. Andy Myers was struck by lightning as he dug a well near the courthouse. Doc Duty was killed in an avalanche at the Toponas Mine in February 1883, but wasn't buried until the snow melted and they recovered his body.

Many of the graves have local boulders labeled with bronze plaques, but the grave of Gustav Anton Spitmiller, whose epitaph reads "Pioneer Plumber," is marked by a bright red wrench. ❧

Mormon Pioneer Memorial Monument

**140 1st Avenue, Salt Lake City, Utah
https://utah.com/mormon/
pioneer-memorial-monument**

Born in Vermont in 1801, Brigham Young was baptized into the Church of Jesus Christ of Latter-day Saints in 1832. After Mormon leader Joseph Smith was killed, Young led the LDS migration from Illinois to Salt Lake City. Mormons consider him "the American Moses."

Young died in 1877 of peritonitis from a ruptured appendix. He was buried in a corner of his own land that had been set aside as a graveyard.

In 1927, Young's descendant Richard W. Young, president of the Brigham Young Cemetery Association, signed over the cemetery's deed to the Church of Latter-day Saints, on the condition that the burials there "shall in no manner or way be disturbed."

Brigham Young rests in the back corner of this pocket-size park. An ornate fence surrounds the plain concrete ledger slab that covers his grave. A brass plaque illustrated with a cow skull explains that, from 1850 to 1856, Young served simultaneously as the territorial governor of Utah and head of the Church of Latter-day Saints.

Beside Young lie 6 of his 55 wives. Some of these wives have ornate marble ledger stones. Others have only a modern paper marker stuck into the sod.

Of these women, only Mary Ann Angell—whom he married after the death of the first Mrs.

In 1877, Brigham Young was buried on a corner of his own property. Now the area is a park owned by the Church of Jesus Christ of Latter-day Saints.

Young—is legally recognized as his wife. After Young had a vision that God would allow Mormons to take multiple wives, Lucy Ann Decker became his first plural wife in 1842. She was 20. He was 41. Her 16-year-old sister, Clara, became his fourth wife.

Also in the cemetery lies Young's eldest son, his first child with Mary Ann Angell. The third of Brigham Young's 57 children, Joseph Angell Young was a teenager when the family settled in Salt Lake City. As a young man, Joseph traveled to England as an LDS missionary. Upon returning, he served three terms as a member of the Utah Territory's House of Representatives, then six terms in the Territory's Senate. ⚜

75

Salt Lake City Cemetery

200 N Street, Salt Lake City, Utah
http://www.slcgov.com/cemetery

The first burial in Salt Lake City Cemetery was of 17-month-old Mary Wallace, buried on her father's land grant in September 1847, two months after the first pioneers followed Brigham Young to the Promised Land. Her brother George was the second burial.

Six months later, Young appointed three men to buy 20 acres for a burying ground. Wallace offered his land and was appointed the cemetery's first sexton. Salt Lake City Cemetery has now swelled to 120 acres.

Pioneer graves dot the cemetery, pointed out by small brass plaques. Some of the pioneers pulled handcarts from as far away as Illinois. One gravestone said that they walked so far that their feet left bloody prints in the snow.

At least 11 of Brigham Young's 55 wives lie here, some in unmarked graves. Several were widows of Joseph F. Smith, the sixth prophet of the church, before they married Young.

Also buried here are 11 presidents of the Church of Jesus Christ of Latter-day Saints, from John Taylor, who followed Brigham Young, to Gordon Hinckley, who died in 2008.

Elsewhere in the graveyard is buried Hiram (or Hirum) Bebee, who claimed to be Harry Longabaugh, the Sundance Kid. In 1945, at the age of 78, Bebee killed a Utah marshal in a bar. After he was sentenced to death, Bebee revealed that the Sundance Kid had not died in Bolivia, as reported. Instead, he snuck back across the border, married, raised a family, and changed his name. Whether Bebee really was the famous train robber or not, his grave lies at the back of the cemetery, near the plot for inmates who died at the Utah State Penitentiary.

One of the most beautiful monuments in the cemetery is the *Christmas Box Angel*, dedicated

John Taylor, president of the Church of Latter-day Saints, was known as the Living Martyr. He was wounded in the attack that killed Joseph Smith.

Ortho Fairbanks's *Christmas Box Angel*, dedicated to all who have lost a child, was unveiled on December 6, 1994.

to all who have lost a child. Unveiled on December 6, 1994, the monument was sculpted by Ortho Fairbanks, who lost a child himself. It was inspired by an earlier angel in the cemetery, which had been destroyed in 1984. That missing angel inspired the book *The Christmas Box Angel* by Richard Paul Evans, who had a stillborn sister. The current angel's face was modeled on one of Evans's daughters. Grieving parents leave trinkets and food at the monument's base. ⚜

76

Custer National Cemetery

**Little Bighorn Battlefield National Monument
Interstate 90 Frontage Road,
Crow Agency, Montana
https://www.nps.gov/libi/planyourvisit/
custer-national-cemetery.htm**

In 1875, gold was discovered in the Black Hills of South Dakota. The U.S. Army demanded access to the gold fields despite treaties signed with the Lakota Sioux. As many as 10,000 Native Americans refused.

Lieutenant Colonel George Armstrong Custer was assigned to move the natives to a reservation. On the morning of June 25, 1876, Custer led five companies of the 7th Cavalry to attack the Lakota, Cheyenne, and Arapaho camped on the Montana prairie.

Chief Sitting Bull, too old to fight, protected women and children in the village, while Crazy Horse led the warriors into battle. Almost 3000 Native Americans slaughtered all 200 of Custer's battalion.

If Custer had waited another day, another column of the 7th Cavalry could have joined him. As it was, it took the reinforcements two days to chase the Lakota and Cheyenne from the field. On June 28, they found Custer's body sprawled at the highest point of the battlefield. 7th Calvary flags fluttered nearby. He had been shot twice: once in the left temple and once in the chest. Around him,

Rows of headstones stand in memory of members of the 7th Cavalry, who died at the Battle of the Little Bighorn.

Oglala Sioux sculptor Colleen Cutschall created the ironwork traces of Native Americans who ride against the sky at the Little Bighorn Battlefield National Monument.

corpses of his men had been stripped, scalped or decapitated, and disemboweled.

The 7th Cavalry survivors dug Custer a grave 18 inches deep and marked it with a piece of paper placed in a spent cartridge hammered onto a stake. With wounded waiting to be escorted 500 miles to the nearest hospital, the other officers' shallow graves were quickly marked with stakes. The enlisted men had scant handfuls of dirt thrown over them. As soon as the living retreated, wolves and coyotes moved in.

Several attempts were made to collect the remnants of the dead and bury them deep enough that they wouldn't be troubled. Families of the officers begged to have their loved ones sent home. Eventually, Custer's bones were sent by train to West Point, where he received a military funeral on October 10, 1877. Most of his other officers were buried at Fort Leavenworth.

In 1881, the 7th Cavalry assembled a granite marker near the place where Custer had been found on Last Stand Hill. They reburied all the bones they could find in trenches around the monument. First Lieutenant Roe planted stakes "where the men actually fell," so that visitors could understand the battle. Those stakes were replaced with marble markers in 1890, at which time more remains were discovered.

President Grover Cleveland set aside a square mile for the National Cemetery of Custer's Battlefield Reservation in 1886. A nearly seven-acre plot surrounding the monument was surveyed for the burial ground proper. President Franklin Roosevelt transferred administration of the battlefield from the War Department to the National Park Service in 1940.

After more than a century of Native American requests for a monument of their own, President George H. W. Bush acknowledged that "The public interest will best be served by establishing a memorial…to honor and recognize the Indians who fought to preserve their land and culture."

Only 60 Native casualties have been documented from the battle, but estimates reach as high as 300. Probably no Native dead had been left behind on the battlefield. The Lakota placed their dead in abandoned teepees. The Cheyenne buried their dead beneath rock overhangs or in caves. On Memorial Day 1999, polished red granite markers were placed where two Native American warriors died. Ten more markers were placed over the next seven years.

A grander Native American memorial was designed by John R. Collins and Alison J. Towers. It combines a spirit gate, a mound, and polished granite panels that tell the Native side of the battle. To that was added a trio of wrought iron tracings of Sioux, Cheyenne, and Arapahoe warriors that stand against the open sky. These figures were created by Oglala Sioux sculptor Colleen Cutschall. ❖

Fort Yellowstone Army Cemetery

Grand Loop Road, Yellowstone National Park, Wyoming

Although Yellowstone was set aside as a national park in 1872, civilian superintendents were not given enough money or manpower to protect it. Hunters poached its wildlife, souvenir hunters chipped away the limestone formations, and campers bathed and did laundry in the hot springs.

Eventually, the U.S. Army was assigned to guard Yellowstone Valley in August 1886. Soldiers lived in frame buildings that barely withstood the harsh winters. Congress finally budgeted for a permanent post, christened Fort Yellowstone, in 1891.

The cemetery was essential in this wild land. In all, there were 58 burials between 1888 and 1925: soldiers or civilian employees of the U.S. Army and their families. Causes of death ranged from runaway horses, drowning, senility, avalanche, exposure (in June), scarlet fever, lightning strikes, falling 800 feet into the Grand Canyon of

the Yellowstone, and injuries inflicted by a grizzly bear. Private John W. H. Davis froze to death while carrying the mail between Lake and Thumb stations. It took a week to find his body. Peter Hanson, a civilian engineer, asphyxiated when an embankment caved in around him. William M. Johnson, a "Colored" civilian employed by Major Pitcher, died of "double catarrh" at the post hospital. Harry Dicks, a pack train cook, died of "aortic insufficiency aggravated by chronic alcoholism."

When the park returned to civilian control in 1917, 20 military graves were moved to the Custer National Cemetery at the Little Bighorn Battlefield.

One of the particularly sad things about this cemetery is the number of infants buried in it. Sometimes the child's grave is the only family member marked. Sometimes the story is tragic: Infant Sarah Clark was buried here in October 1905. Her father, Eugene, a civilian assistant electrical engineer, committed suicide the following year by drinking carbolic acid. Devastated, widow Jeannett moved away from Yellowstone. Decades later, she asked in her will to be interred beside her husband and daughter. After the Park Service honored her request, she was buried here in May 1957. ⚜

Before the formation of the National Park Service, the U.S. Army stationed men at Mammoth Hot Springs to protect the park from vandals and commercial threats. Family members of some of those soldiers became permanent residents.

Virginia City, in the heart of Comstock silver-mining country, had 22 graveyards. Many gravesites are surrounded by stone curbs or ornate iron fences.

Silver Terrace Cemeteries

381 Cemetery Road, Virginia City, Nevada
https://www.nps.gov/nr/travel/nevada/sil.htm

In 1859, two Irish miners discovered one of the richest lodes of gold in history on the slopes of Mount Davidson, a mountain previously considered uninhabitable. The mining camp became a boomtown—and then silver was discovered 900 feet below the surface. Samuel Clemens got his start here as Mark Twain, writing for the *Territorial Enterprise*.

Virginia City became the largest town between Denver and San Francisco. Although it boasted 110 saloons, Virginia City had only seven churches. On a terraced hilltop overlooking town, Virginia City had 22 adjacent graveyards, each devoted to a fraternal organization, religious congregation, tradesmen's union, or ethnic group. Among the groups who had their own burial grounds were the Masons, Odd Fellows, Knights of Pythias, Pacific Coast

Pioneers, and Ancient Order of Redmen. The Exempt Firemen graveyard was intended for men who had served as volunteer firemen. They became exempt from fighting fires when they retired or died.

The appeal of fraternal orders for single men was immense. Men who chased their fortunes to the gold fields often came alone. Joining the Odd Fellows or becoming a Mason meant that someone would see to their remains in the event of their untimely demise. Someone would contact their family. Often fraternal affiliation was the difference between a marked grave and an anonymous one.

Virginia City declined in the 1880s, but the mines didn't close until 1942, when the federal government decided that gold and silver were inessential to the war effort. After World War II, the town remade itself as a tourist destination, advertised for 14 seasons by the TV show *Bonanza*. The National Park Service established the Virginia City National Historic Landmark District—one of the largest landmark districts in the nation—in 1962. The cemeteries lie inside that district. ❧

78

Ketchum Cemetery

1026 North Main Street, Ketchum, Idaho
http://www.ketchumcemetery.org

The Wood River Valley area was originally a Native American wilderness rarely visited by trappers. In the 1880s, Ketchum became one of the richest mining districts in the Northwest. When the mines petered out, sheep ranchers moved in.

The pioneer section of the cemetery dates to the 1880s. In the early days, townspeople marked graves with simple signs on wooden staves planted in small cans of cement. On Memorial Days, neighbors decorated all the graves in the cemetery, related or not.

In the 1930s, Ernest Hemingway was invited to a new ski resort near Ketchum. He fell in love with the area, staying to write part of *For Whom the Bell Tolls* at the Sun Valley Lodge. He and his fourth wife, Mary, bought a house in Ketchum in 1958.

Author of *The Sun Also Rises*, *A Farewell to Arms*, and *The Old Man and the Sea*—for which he won the Nobel Prize in Literature—Hemingway may be better known these days for his tough guy persona. When he committed suicide in July 1961, he followed the path taken by his father, brother, and sister.

Hemingway was buried beneath a simple granite ledger slab inscribed only with his name and dates. He was almost 62. A cross stands at the head of the grave, which lies in the shadow of four pines. Fans seek out his grave to leave half-smoked cigars, empty bottles of bourbon, and flowers.

At his side is buried journalist Mary Walsh Hemingway, the last of Hemingway's wives and his literary executor, who oversaw the posthumous publication of *A Moveable Feast*. Her ledger slab matches his.

Other notable interments in Ketchum Cemetery include Melvin Schwartz, a Noble Prize–winning physicist who studied subatomic particles; skier and filmmaker Dick Barrymore; actress Ann Sothern; and actress Margaux Louise Hemingway, who scored the first million-dollar modeling contract for her work for Faberge. She was Hemingway's granddaughter. ⚜

Winner of a Nobel Prize in Literature, Ernest Hemingway was buried beneath a simple granite slab without an epitaph beyond his name and dates.

Churchyard of Misión San Francisco de Asís

3321 16th Street, San Francisco, California
http://www.missiondolores.org/64

Sixth of the mission parishes founded by Spain in its quest to colonize Alta California, Misión San Francisco de Asís predates the signing of the Declaration of Independence. On June 29, 1776, Father Francisco Palou performed mass at a makeshift altar, consecrating the peninsula to the founder of the Franciscan Order of poor monks. When the village that sprang up took the mission's name, the mission itself became known as Mission Dolores.

The mission's purpose was to convert the local Miwok and Ohlone peoples to Catholicism. Unfortunately, Mission Dolores had one of the highest death tolls of all of Spain's Californian missions. The first burial in the graveyard took place shortly after the mission's foundation. First Californians were buried under wooden markers that have vanished.

Old photographs show a graveyard that was much larger, before the church began to sell off its land. An estimated 5,187 Native Americans lie under streets and buildings around the mission.

The mission itself is the oldest intact building in San Francisco. Beneath its floor were buried several of the city's founding fathers, including Lieutenant José Joaquin Moraga, who led the June 1776 expedition, and William Leisdesdorff, a pioneer who became America's first African-American millionaire before his death in 1848.

80

Buried in the churchyard beside the old mission are Spanish and Mexican families who gave their names to the surrounding city streets.

These days, about 200 tombstones remain in the churchyard, most of them post–Gold Rush. Among them stand monuments to Don Luis Arguello, first governor of Alta California under the Mexican government; Don Francisco de Haro, the first alcalde (mayor) of San Francisco; as well as land grantees who provided their names to neighboring streets. There are even three victims of the Vigilance Committee, killed by vigilantes who took the law into their own hands in the 1850s.

The cemetery has been renovated several times. For a while, it had a large replica of the Grotto of Lourdes, which was featured in Alfred Hitchcock's *Vertigo*. Currently, the cemetery includes a tule reed house to demonstrate how the local natives lived. ⚜

Fort Ross State Historic Park

19005 Coast Highway 1, Jenner, California
http://www.parks.ca.gov/?page_id=449

In March 1812, a large ship sailed into a cove below a bluff settled by the Native American Kashaya. Twenty-five Russians and eighty Aleutians had come to hunt sea otters and grow crops to support Russian settlements in Alaska. While the Russians built a wooden stockade in Alta California, Napoleon's army advanced toward Moscow.

The Spanish would have preferred to colonize Alta California without challenge, but they hadn't explored as far north as Fort Ross. By the time they became aware of the Russian settlement, the well-armed fort had been completed. "Ross" is believed to be short for "Rossiya," as their home country was called.

By 1839, the parent company of the Russian colony reached an agreement with the Hudson Bay Company to supply the Russian settlements in Alaska. After that, Fort Ross was no longer necessary.

The California Historical Landmarks Committee took control of the plundered fort in March 1906. The Great Earthquake of April 18, 1906 knocked down all its remaining buildings.

A historic photo of the graveyard from 1895 shows redwood grave houses over some of the graves. In 1912, several of the graves still had redwood curbs. Over time, the original wooden Russian Orthodox crosses were lost, either to decay, vandalism, or wildfires that periodically swept the area. Some graves were destroyed in 1972 when construction crews built Highway 1 through the graveyard.

Several archaeological digs have explored the graveyard. In 1991, anthropologists from the University of Wisconsin at Milwaukee discovered people buried in redwood coffins with traditional Russian cross medallions on their chests. The acidic soil destroyed all of the soft tissue and some of the bones, but teeth were uncovered among the coffin nails, trade beads, and uniform buttons. Without complete sets of bones, it is difficult to identify the 131 people buried in the graveyard, even to guess genders. Children were recognized by the smaller patterns of coffin nails.

After the archaeologists had finished, the Russian Orthodox Church took an active part in the reburials. In fact, Fort Ross is a source of pride for Russians, who trek 110 miles north of San Francisco to visit. ⚜

At its peak, the Fort Ross settlement housed 350 Russians, Aleuts, and native Kashaya. An unknown number of them rest in the fort's graveyard.

A re-creation of the original chapel stands inside Fort Ross. The chapel was the first Russian Orthodox structure built in North America south of Alaska.

Yosemite Pioneer Cemetery

Yosemite Village, Yosemite National Park, California
http://www.yosemite.ca.us/library/pioneer_cemetery

When gold fever struck him in 1856, John C. Anderson traveled from Illinois to stake a claim in Yosemite Valley. The gold claim didn't pan out as richly as the hotel he and three other prospectors built for Yosemite visitors.

In the old days, people in Yosemite were buried wherever they fell. After he was killed by a horse in 1867, Anderson was buried at the foot of the Four-Mile Trail. Friends thrust his green locust-wood switch into the ground to mark his first grave. All locust trees in the valley supposedly descend from that sapling.

As more people came to Yosemite, a quarter-acre of the valley was chosen for a graveyard because Native Americans had already used it as a burial ground. The Miwoks and Paiutes did not mark their graves, but remains have been uncovered during construction projects in the Valley.

Around 1870, bodies were gathered from around the valley into the pioneer graveyard.

These days, the Yosemite Pioneer Cemetery is tucked behind the grocery story and employee housing. Shaded by trees and surrounded by a low split-rail fence, most of the graves are marked with plain wooden signboards, painted Park Service brown. Some are marked with Yosemite boulders. Anderson received a real gravestone decorated with a willow bending under the weight of its own branches.

On a marble marker "In Memory of Albert May, native of Ohio," two manly hands clasp, signifying friendship. Marble doesn't occur inside the boundaries of Yosemite; the Sierra Nevada Mountains are granite. This stone must have been brought in by mule train to mark May's grave, hinting at the high regard A. G. Black, who erected the stone, must have held for him. May worked as a carpenter and caretaker at Black's New Sentinel Hotel until his death in 1881.

A weathered board marks the grave of Effie Maud Crippen, "age 14 yrs, 7 mos, 22 days." Effie moved to Yosemite with her family in 1877. She explored Yosemite on horseback, sketching it and describing it in her poetry. Wading in Mirror Lake, Effie stepped on a broken bottle and severed an artery in her foot. She bled to death in 1881.

Yosemite is one of the busiest tourist destinations in the country—averaging 3 million visitors annually—but very few find their way to the peaceful little Pioneer Cemetery. ❧

A willow weeps over the grave of John C. Anderson in the Yosemite Pioneer Cemetery.

A copy of William Wetmore Story's *Angel of Grief (Weeping Over the Dismantled Altar of Life)* marks the grave of Teddy Roosevelt's cousin Jennie Roosevelt Pool. It is attributed to Antonio Bernieri, who made a larger copy for Stanford University.

Cypress Lawn Memorial Park

1370 El Camino Real, Colma, California
https://www.cypresslawn.com

In 1890, financier Hamden Noble watched a funeral at San Francisco's Laurel Hill Cemetery. The cemetery had been built on sand dunes, anchored by nonnative trees that struggled to survive the long, dry summers. Remembering the lush garden cemeteries of Cambridge and Philadelphia, Noble bought 47 acres of fertile farmland south of the city. By the dawn of the 20th century, Cypress Lawn sported more trees and shrubs than any park in the United States.

Its timing was perfect. A series of legal maneuvers eventually chased the existing cemeteries out of San Francisco. Families were given the option of paying to move their ancestors. In consequence, Cypress Lawn boasts the highest concentration of historic Californians of any cemetery in the state. Among them are newspaper magnate William Randolph Hearst and his mother Phoebe Apperson Hearst, founder of the kindergarten movement; Lillie Hitchcock Coit, benefactor of Coit Tower on San Francisco's Telegraph Hill; Charles de Young, who founded the *San Francisco Chronicle* and was assassinated by the son of the mayor of San Francisco; and Lefty O'Doul, who traveled to Japan thirty times to help them develop baseball.

San Francisco's Laurel Hill Cemetery had been the last refuge of the pioneers who built San Francisco, who were for the most part single men with no family to move their bodies. Laurel Hill had been a "garden" cemetery until 1906, when the earthquake damaged many of the monuments. Since there was no perpetual care in those days, and these gentlemen had no family to repair their graves, the damage was one of the pretexts used to kick the cemeteries out of San Francisco so the real estate interests could take over the land. When Laurel Hill was dismantled, 35,000 pioneers were identified if possible and reburied in a concrete mausoleum beneath Cypress Lawn's Laurel Hill Pioneer Mound. Among those under the mound are Andrew Hallidie, father of San Francisco's iconic cable cars; anti-slavery Senator David Broderick, victim of the last historic duel in the U.S., and Phineas Gage, who entered psychology textbooks after surviving an iron rod through his skull.

Cypress Lawn has a fine collection of sculpture, including a recording angel placing a plumed pen on the grave of Thomas O. Larkin, signer of the California Constitution. A copy of William Wetmore Story's *Angel of Grief* marks the grave of Theodore Roosevelt's cousin, Jennie Roosevelt Pool.

In Cypress Lawn East stands the exquisite public mausoleum with Tiffany chapel windows and 36,000 square feet of stained glass ceiling. Cypress Lawn displays more stained glass in one place than anywhere else in the United States. ⚜

83

84 Hollywood Forever

**6000 Santa Monica Boulevard,
Hollywood, California
http://www.hollywoodforever.com**

Established in 1899 as Hollywood Memorial Park, the cemetery changed its name in 1998. The iconic palm trees remain the same.

In the early days of the film industry, Hollywood Memorial Park was to die for. Film folk flocked to the cemetery, which backs against the Paramount Studios lot.

Douglas Fairbanks's widow paid $75,000 in 1939 ($1.2 million these days) for a theatrical Greek Revival monument that combined a wall adorned with a bronze relief of the actor, a blindingly white sarcophagus, and a 100-foot reflecting pool.

Not to be outdone, William Randolph Hearst bought a tiny island for the mausoleum for his mistress, actress Marion Davies.

Other stars—Tyrone Power, Cecil B. DeMille, Peter Lorre, Mel Blanc—also came to rest here. Rudolph Valentino, the smoldering "Latin lover," rests in a modest niche in the grand mausoleum at the back of the cemetery. His sudden death in 1926 from a perforated ulcer and ruptured appendix brought throngs of distraught mourners to the graveyard. For decades, mystery women in black left roses at his grave.

The Old Hollywood glamour wore thin and the cemetery fell on hard times, compounded by damage caused by the Northridge earthquake in 1994. Luckily, the cemetery was rescued in 1998 by a young entrepreneur who changed its name, showed movies on the mausoleum walls, booked concerts, hosted a huge annual Día de los Muertos event—and generally lured young people back to the graveyard.

Most recently, punk icons have been making Hollywood Forever their final destination. Both Johnny and Dee Dee Ramone are buried there. ⚜

Artist Wayne Toth sculpted Johnny Ramone playing his Mosrite guitar for the punk rocker's monument at Hollywood Forever.

Angelus Rosedale Cemetery has appeared in numerous movies and TV shows, including *Buffy the Vampire Slayer* and *Six Feet Under.*

Angelus Rosedale Cemetery

1831 West Washington Boulevard, Los Angeles, California
http://angelusrosedalecemetery.com

In 1884, when Los Angeles was a city of under 30,000 people, Rosedale Cemetery was founded on 65 acres of land facing Washington Boulevard.

Designed as a lawn cemetery with beautiful trees and flowering shrubs, Rosedale now has mostly upright headstones, interspersed with some beautiful sculptures and family mausoleums. The cemetery also sports several pyramid tombs, including one for George Shatto, who developed Catalina Island as a resort.

America's first crematory west of the Rocky Mountains—only the second in the country— opened at Rosedale in 1887. By 1913, it had already performed almost 2400 cremations.

Among those buried in Angelus Rosedale is Hattie McDaniel, the first African-American woman to sing on the radio. While her cinematic career spanned over 300 movies, she is best remembered for playing Scarlett's Mammy in *Gone with the Wind*—the role that made her the first African-American recipient of an Academy Award.

Ms. McDaniel's last wish was to be buried at Hollywood Memorial Cemetery. Because of her race, they rejected her. Instead, her modest headstone lies near the gates of Angelus Rosedale, the first integrated cemetery in Los Angeles. (Hollywood Forever installed a cenotaph to her memory in 1999.)

Other permanent residents include Tod Browning, director of Bela Lugosi's *Dracula*; Eliza Donner Houghton, who survived the Donner Party's winter in the Sierras at the age of 3 and went on to marry a congressman; Maria Rasputin, daughter of the mad Russian monk; Harry Kellar, a stage magician whose performances influenced Houdini; and Anna May Wong, the first Chinese-American movie star. She appeared in Douglas Fairbanks's *Thief of Baghdad* and with Marlene Dietrich in *Shanghai Express*.

With its photogenic lines of palm trees, Angelus Rosedale has appeared in *Nightmare on Elm Street 4: the Dream Master* and *Wes Craven's New Nightmare*, as well as many episodes of *Buffy the Vampire Slayer*, *Charmed*, and *Six Feet Under*. ⚜

Manzanar Cemetery

Manzanar National Historic Site
5001 Highway 395, Inyo County, California
https://www.nps.gov/museum/exhibits/manz/
cemetery.html

After the Japanese attacked Pearl Harbor in December 1940, more than 120,000 people of Japanese ancestry—the majority of whom were American-born, American-educated, and had never known any other home—were rounded up from the West Coast of the United States and forced into concentration camps.

Manzanar War Relocation Center was the first to open. Tar-papered barracks stood in the desert 210 miles north of Los Angeles. At its height, Manzanar imprisoned 10,000 people.

Despite strong winds and temperatures over 100 degrees, residents tended an orchard, raised hogs and chickens, and built Japanese-style gardens at the order of their captors, who sought to keep the internees busy.

In December 1942, a mass demonstration at Manzanar spooked the military police into firing into the crowd. One camp resident was killed and 11 more wounded, one of whom subsequently died. The dead were buried in a small cemetery outside the barbed-wire fence.

The 15-foot "Soul Consoling Tower" was built by internees under the direction of Ryozo Kado, who had been the landscaper and stone mason for the Los Angeles Catholic Diocese before his imprisonment. Each family in the camp donated 15 cents for the tower's construction. Its inscription was written by Manzanar's Buddhist priest, Shinjo Nagatomi.

As many as 150 people died at Manzanar. Most were cremated and their ashes given to their families. The first person buried in the cemetery had been a Japanese-born bachelor with no family in the United States. In addition to those killed during the protest, several children, including an unnamed stillborn child, were buried here. In all, 14 people were buried in the cemetery.

Most of the remains were removed by families after the camp closed, but six people remain. Jerry Ogata was 3 months old when he died in 1943 of a congenital heart defect. His headstone was stolen in the 1980s. Camp survivors replaced it in the 1990s.

While most of the camp was demolished, the obelisk-shaped Soul Consoling Tower remains the most prominent feature at the Manzanar site. The area became a California Historical Landmark in 1972 and a National Historic Site in 1992. ⚜

The Soul Consoling Tower stands at the heart of the cemetery at the Manzanar War Relocation Center, a concentration camp where Japanese Americans were imprisoned during World War II. As many as 150 of them died there.

Site of many memorial services, the *Circle of Friends* is dedicated to everyone whose lives have been touched by AIDS.

National AIDS Memorial Grove

Bowling Green Drive and Nancy Pelosi Drive, Golden Gate Park, San Francisco, California
http://www.aidsmemorial.org

In the late 1970s and early 1980s, a new disease swept through San Francisco, New York City, and Los Angeles. Doctors scrambled to get ahead of what was initially derided as the "Gay Plague," a sexually transmitted collection of rare cancers, fungal infections, and organ failures that came to be called acquired immune deficiency syndrome.

Infection, in those days, was lethal. Senator Jesse Helms proposed quarantine for anyone who tested positive for HIV, the human immunodeficiency virus. Since gay couples could not legally marry, lovers were barred from sickrooms and deathbeds across the country.

Because of the social stigma attached to the disease, obituaries often lied about the cause of death. Many victims chose to be cremated because they expected they would have no survivors to mourn them. Unlike the plagues of the past, graveyards do not record the AIDS epidemic.

A group of San Franciscans envisioned a serene place dedicated to all lives touched by AIDS. Donations in memory of prominent local landscape architect Stephen Marcus provided initial funds for what would become the AIDS Memorial Grove.

The groundbreaking took place September 21, 1991, attended by Mayor Art Agnos. The permanency of the Grove remained in question until 1993, when the Grove's board of directors signed a 99-year lease with the City of San Francisco.

Thanks to a bill supported by Representative Nancy Pelosi and Senator Dianne Feinstein, the AIDS Grove attained National Memorial status in October 1996. President Bill Clinton recognized

it as the first AIDS memorial in the nation. The official designation "proclaims to the world that there is a dedicated space in the national public landscape where anyone who has been touched by AIDS can grieve openly without being stigmatized."

In February 1995, the Main Portal was dedicated by benefactor Steve Silver, creator of San Francisco's long-running variety show *Beach Blanket Babylon*. Volunteers have planted thousands of trees and shrubs. They've installed six flagstone gathering areas, an accessible gravel path, eighteen benches, and granite boulders marked with names of those who have been lost.

The Belvedere Overlook, funded by the Elizabeth Taylor AIDS Foundation, was added in 2002. Its balcony displays polished black granite plaques with a timeline of the epidemic. At that time, 40 million people worldwide had been infected with HIV—and 22 million had already died of AIDS. An unknown number of ashes have been buried or scattered inside the AIDS Grove. ⚜

Lone Fir Cemetery

SE 26th Avenue, Portland, Oregon
http://lonefir.org

Portland's lovely Lone Fir Cemetery began as a family graveyard in 1846 with the burial of Emmor Stephens, the father of a man who owned property nearby. In 1854, victims of a steamship accident were buried near Stephens.

The ground was formally dedicated as a cemetery in 1855.

Many Oregon pioneers are buried in graves no longer marked. There may be as many as 10,000 unknowns buried here. Some are Chinese laborers. These men intended that, after their bodies had been buried a suitable length of time, their bones would be exhumed, scraped of flesh, bundled together, and sent home to China to rest with their ancestors.

The Soldiers Monument at Lone Fir Cemetery was erected in memory of veterans of the Civil War, as well as the Mexican, Indian, and Spanish-American Wars. It was unveiled in 1903.

Unfortunately, a large number of them still reside in "temporary" graves.

A tall obelisk marks the grave of Dr. James C. Hawthorne. Shortly after Oregon achieved statehood, Hawthorne opened the Oregon Hospital for the Insane in 1862. He cared gently for his patients, who were allowed musical performances and time outdoors. If patients—who were often abandoned by their families—died at the hospital, Dr. Hawthorne saw that they had a decent burial at Lone Fir, and 132 of them rest here now.

Among them, in an unmarked grave, rests Charity Lamb, who murdered her husband with an ax as he sat down to dinner. She had hoped to escape his abuse, but was convicted of second-degree murder and sentenced to life in the Oregon State Penitentiary, where she was the only female prisoner. Eventually she was released to Dr. Hawthorne's asylum, where she died.

Lone Fir has a good number of beautiful tree stump graves. One might suspect that the men remembered by these stones had been loggers, especially since many of them say "Woodsman of the World," but in fact the stones were purchased from an early burial insurance company. ⚜

The graves of Bruce Lee and his son Brandon stand near the crest of Lake View Cemetery in Seattle.

Lake View Cemetery

1554 15th Avenue E, Seattle, Washington
http://www.lakeviewcemeteryassociation.com

Established as Seattle's Masonic Cemetery in 1872, this hilly cemetery was renamed in 1890. At its crest rest four generations of the Denny family. Arthur Armstrong Denny and his wife, Mary, are credited with founding Seattle. Also in Lake View rests Washington's first governor, as well as Seattle's first mayor, first banker, and first shopkeeper.

Buried here is Princess Angeline, eldest daughter of Chief Sealth, who gave his name to Seattle. Angeline's given name was Kikisoblu, but after her conversion to Christianity, she was given a new name because she was "too handsome a woman to carry a name like that."

In the northeast corner stands the Nisei War Memorial Monument, dedicated in 1949 to Japanese-Americans who volunteered to fight in World War II in order to escape the concentration camps.

89

Lake View's most famous resident is Bruce Lee, who died at the age of 32 from cerebral edema caused by a bad reaction to a headache tablet. Beside him lies his son, Brandon, who perished 20 years later at the age of 28, after he was shot with an improperly loaded gun on the set of *The Crow*. Both graves lie just beneath the crest of the hill, facing the water.

Bruce's large red granite slab identifies him as the founder of Jeet Kune Do (the Way of the Intercepting Fist), but fans adore his movies *Enter the Dragon* and *Fists of Fury*. He upstaged the Green Hornet when he played Kato in the 1960s TV series. San Francisco–born Bruce Lee opened a martial arts studio in Los Angeles, where he taught Steve McQueen and James Coburn. They served as his pallbearers.

Brandon Lee's monument is even more striking. Made of polished black granite, it has a swooping protuberance as if a shrouded figure is stepping clear of the stone. The marker includes a long epitaph, which says in part: "How many more times will you watch the full moon rise? Perhaps twenty. And yet it all seems so limitless." ❧

90 Greenwood Memorial Park

350 Monroe Avenue NE, Renton, Washington
http://www.dignitymemorial.com/
greenwood-memorial-park-funeral-home/
en-us/index.page

When Jimi Hendrix suddenly died in London on September 18, 1970, his father, James "Al" Hendrix, barely had enough money to bring his body home. Among the fans attending the Seattle funeral were Miles Davis, Johnny Winter, and drummer Buddy Miles.

The elder Hendrix purchased a small family plot in Greenwood Memorial Park near the family home in Renton, Washington, south of Seattle and east of Sea-Tac. Jimi was the first Hendrix to be buried there, under a simple granite headstone illustrated with a Stratocaster guitar and the epitaph "Forever in Our Hearts."

In 1995, Al Hendrix finally regained control of Jimi's music with the help of Microsoft billionaire Paul Allen, founder of the Seattle Experience Music Project and owner of the largest collection of Hendrix memorabilia in the world. With these new funds, the senior Hendrix bought a 54-plot space in Greenwood and had plans drawn up for a suitable monument to his son. Unfortunately, Al didn't survive to see it completed.

The monument, designed by architect Mark Barthelemy of Cold Springs, is a granite-capped gazebo. Each of its three supporting pillars features a laser-etched portrait of Hendrix and some of his lyrics in his handwriting.

On November 26, 2002 (the day before his 60th birthday), Jimi Hendrix was exhumed and reburied with his father in a vault beneath the new monument. His original headstone, newly restored, was encased in granite in the center of the memorial. As many as 100,000 fans visit Hendrix's grave each year. ❧

91 Kawaiaha'o Churchyard

957 Punchbowl Street, Honolulu, Oahu, Hawaii
https://www.kawaiahao.org

A product of the Mission Church movement founded in Boston in 1819, Kawaiaha'o Church was built at an oasis around a spring, which still flows. The spring was cared for by a Hawaiian high chiefess named Ha'o, so the church's Hawaiian name means "water of Ha'o." To this day, the church offers services in the Hawaiian language. It is considered Hawaii's "Westminster Abbey," because Hawaiian monarchs, chiefs, and their families attended services, were married, and laid in state there.

Alongside Christianity, missionaries brought a tradition of marked burials inside a fenced churchyard. Early converts could not afford tombstones. It's estimated that there are at least

Architect
Mark Barthelemy
designed this
granite-capped
gazebo in memory
of guitarist
Jimi Hendrix.

One of the oldest Western-style burial grounds in Hawaii, Kawaiaha'o Churchyard serves as the final resting place of King Lunalilo and other native royalty. In the foreground of the photograph is the spring for which the church is named.

200 unmarked gravesites in the churchyard. In addition, the remaining 296 headstones may mark the graves of more than one person.

Kawaiaha'o Churchyard serves as the final resting place of King Lunalilo. His tomb, one of the earliest concrete block buildings in Hawaii, stands near his mother's grave on the northwest side of the churchyard. Lunalilo was invested as king at Kawaiaha'o Church in 1873. He served only 13 months before dying of tuberculosis, a disease brought to the islands by outsiders.

Among the graves in the churchyard lie several missionaries, including Hiram Bingham Jr., who authored a native language dictionary, as well as a translation of the Bible.

Another missionary, James Kekela (known as Kekela O Ka Lani), became the first Hawaiian Christian minister upon his ordination in 1849. In 1853, Kekela went as a pioneer missionary to the Marquesas Islands, where, for 49 years,

he preached against cannibalism and tribal warfare. President Abraham Lincoln recognized Kekela in 1861 for rescuing an American seaman from cannibals.

Also buried in Kawaiaha'o Churchyard is Sanford Ballard Dole, who orchestrated the overthrow of Queen Liliuokalani and ended the Hawaiian monarchy. Dole served as president of the Republic of Hawaii between 1894 and 1898. After its annexation by the United States, he became governor of the Hawaiian Territory. His cousin James founded the Dole Pineapple Company.

Among the unmarked graves lies David Douglas, for whom the Douglas fir is named. He worked as a botanist for the Hudson Bay Company, cataloging plants in the Northwest. He came to Hawaii in 1833 to study its plants and fell to his death in a pit dug for capturing wild animals. A plaque on the church wall is dedicated to his memory. ⚜

Seamen's Cemetery

Waine'e Street, Lahaina, Maui, Hawaii

More than half the humpback whales in the world winter between Maui and nearby Lana'i. They travel down from Alaska to calve and breed in the warm, shallow waters. In the 1800s, they were easy pickings.

In those days, Lahaina was a loud, lawless town where sailors drank and brawled and died. The State Department funded the U.S. Seamen's Hospital to serve sailors, particularly whalers, who swarmed the island between 1820 and 1860. In 1859, the government investigated rumors that it was being charged per diems for patients who'd already been transferred to the Seamen's Cemetery. Charges were never filed.

Not much survives of the Seamen's Cemetery, which was originally much larger. Most of the men buried here were young, victims of their rigorous life at sea and primitive shipboard health care.

Among the dead lies one of Herman Melville's cousins, along with a shipmate of Melville's from the whaler *Acushnet*, a Black sailor named Thomas Johnson who died at the Seamen's Hospital of a "disreputable disease."

Ships came and went from Lahaina, leaving behind sick or wounded men to the mercy of strangers. Charity bought the inexpensive and impermanent markers that once crammed the cemetery. Currently, only one or two tombstones still mark the graves of sailors, but more recent gravestones still reference the Rock of Ages in the midst of the storm-tossed sea. ✤

Originally the graveyard of the U.S. Seamen's Hospital, this small plot of ground stands in memory of the era when Lahaina served as the capital of the Pacific whaling industry.

Saint Philomena Catholic Churchyard

Kalaupapa National Historical Park, Kalawao, Molokai, Hawaii
http://www.philomena.org/damien.asp

The first case of leprosy in Hawaii was found on the island of Kauai in 1835. The Hawaiians already living on the Kalaupapa Peninsula of Molokai were displaced by order of King Kamehameha V in order to isolate the leprosy victims. Without a cure, the contagious disease was a death sentence. Infected victims were rounded up and exiled to Kalaupapa. Surrounded by such rough seas that ships could

The black stone cross marks the original gravesite of Father Damien, who ministered to victims of leprosy imprisoned at Kaluapapa, Molokai. He was canonized in 2009 by Pope Benedict XVI.

land only rarely, sufferers were often thrown overboard and told to swim. A 2000-foot cliff on the southern side of the peninsula kept them penned in.

The first exiles consisted of nine men and three women dropped off on January 6, 1866. They lived in caves or such lean-tos as they could cobble together. Supplies were seldom delivered, so those who could grew taro, sweet potatoes, fruit, and gathered seafood from the tide pools.

The Belgian Joseph de Veuster was ordained in the Cathedral of Our Lady of Peace in Honolulu and became known as Father Damien in 1864. Nine years later, he traveled to Kaluapapa to minister to the victims of leprosy. With Father Damien's help, the exiles built themselves homes, a church, and a hospital. Damien, who spoke Hawaiian, ministered, nursed, and encouraged them. In 1885, after 12 years of aiding the sick, Damien himself was diagnosed with leprosy. He eventually died of it on April 15, 1889. He was 49.

Damien was buried beside the walls of Saint Philomena Catholic Church, beneath the pandanus tree under which he'd slept when he first arrived on the island. The Congregation of the Sacred Hearts, to which Damien had belonged as a young man, erected a black marble cross above his grave. It read, "Died a martyr to his Charity for the Afflicted Lepers." A movement to have Damien beatified—the first step on the path to sainthood—began the year following his death.

After an arrangement had been reached between President Franklin D. Roosevelt and King Ferdinand III of Belgium, Father Damien's remains were exhumed in 1936 and reburied at Louvain, Belgium. Internees of Kaluapapa were left only with the cross marking his grave.

Starting in 1866, more than 8000 people, mostly Hawaiians, died at Kaluapapa. Damien himself buried around 200 victims of leprosy each year. The National Park Service estimates there are 1200 grave markers and several thousand unmarked graves spread over 15 cemeteries inside the park.

In 1977, Pope Paul VI declared Father Damien venerable, the next step up the ladder to sainthood. A relic—Damien's right hand—was returned to his original grave in 1995. He was canonized as a saint on October 11, 2009.

With the discovery of sulfone drugs, leprosy could be put into remission. The isolation order was finally lifted in 1969. Internees at Kaluapapa were free to leave, but many stayed in the place they considered home.

In 1980, President Jimmy Carter established Kaluapapa National Historical Park. The Park Service describes Kaluapapa as a reminder of how a nation in crisis treated people who were exposed to a disease for which they had no immunities.

The national park is limited to 100 visitors per day. Visitors must be at least 16 years old. Photographs of the few remaining residents are forbidden without their written permission. ⚜

The *USS Arizona* Memorial

No. 1 Arizona Memorial Place, Pearl Harbor, Oahu, Hawaii
https://www.nps.gov/valr/index.htm

There had been talk of turning the shallow harbor on Oahu to American military usage during the Spanish-American War, before the United States even annexed Hawaii. Construction of the naval base began in 1908. By 1941, American warships literally encircled the island in the center of Pearl Harbor. Hostilities had not been formally declared, but they were clearly anticipated.

Still, military advisors on both sides of the ocean counseled against war. Japan's Admiral Yamamoto had attended university in the United States and spoke fluent English. He understood that Americans might be balked by a surprise defeat, but once battle was joined, the larger country would win. When he spoke against provoking the United States, his countrymen threatened his life. Cornered, Yamamoto lobbied for a decisive first strike to destroy the fleet at Pearl Harbor. With any luck, the United States would be disarmed until after Japan conquered Asia.

James O. Richardson, admiral in command of the Pacific, called it suicidal to mass the entire fleet in one place. President Franklin Roosevelt replaced him. Military consensus was that the Japanese wouldn't dare more than sabotage. To prevent that, Lieutenant General Walter Short ordered American warplanes parked wing to wing and tail to nose to make them easier to guard. That made them impossible to fly on December 7, 1941.

When a modified torpedo hit the *West Virginia*, the U.S. fleet was completely undefended. Three minutes later, a bomb cut through the *Arizona* and ignited its forward magazine. It sank in nine minutes, all hands aboard, and now sits on the harbor floor.

The *USS Arizona* is considered a cemetery— 1102 of the 1177 men who died when she sank remained buried on her. Some were cremated at their posts. Others were killed by the concussion. In many cases, their bodies were not recoverable.

Since the 1980s, approximately 30 urns of ashes of men who survived the Pearl Harbor attack have been placed in the *Arizona*'s gun turret by Park Service divers. Other men, who served on the *Arizona* prior to December 7, 1941, have had their ashes spread over the waters. The *USS Arizona* memorial at Pearl Harbor is the most popular tourist destination in Hawaii, with up to 4000 visitors a day. ✤

A white chapel straddles the *USS Arizona*, which rests on the bottom of Pearl Harbor, Hawaii. More than 1,100 men remained on her when she sank and their bodies were never recovered.

Saint Nicholas Orthodox Churchyard

**Eklutna Historical Park, Eklutna Village Road,
Chugiak, Alaska**
http://eklutnahistoricalpark.org

The Athabascans settled around the mouth of the Eklutna River 800 years ago. Circa 1650, they formed the village that became Eklutna. It has been inhabited by descendants of the Danaina tribe of the Athabascans ever since.

In 1830, Russian missionaries came to Eklutna. Over the years, the communities melded. They share the graveyard around the old Saint Nicholas Orthodox Church, which was initially built in 1870. It's the oldest building in the greater Anchorage area.

Before the Russians came, Athabascans cremated their dead. As they became Christianized, they accepted burial, with customs of their own. After a funeral, Athabascan graves are covered with a blanket to comfort the soul. Forty days after burial, a spirit house—three or four feet long and two or three feet high—is built over the blanketed grave. Family members paint the grave house colors that represent their family name and decorate it with geometric shapes.

Athabascan tradition requires that everything must be allowed to return to the Earth, so they allow the spirit houses to decay and fall apart.

Some Athabascan graves are marked by both a spirit house and a Russian Orthodox cross. Others are marked only with a cross to indicate non-Native church members. The upper bar on a Russian Orthodox cross represents the label above Christ's head: Jesus, King of the Jews. The longer middle bar signifies Christ's outstretched arms. The diagonal lower bar symbolizes the thief on Christ's right, who repented and went to Heaven, and the one of the left, who didn't. In some stories, the slanted bar illustrates Christ's footrest, knocked askew in his agony.

The cemetery and the church, 25 miles outside of Anchorage, are now part of the Eklutna Historical Park. It is open to the public on weekdays in summer for guided tours. ⚜

Some Athabascan families choose to mark graves with both a traditional spirit house and a Russian Orthodox cross. These are painted in colors that represent the family name.

CANADA

Graves of more than 100 of the *Titanic*'s victims are marked by black granite headstones paid for by White Star Line.

Fairview Lawn Cemetery

3720 Windsor Street, Halifax, Nova Scotia
https://www.findagrave.com/cgi-bin/
fg.cgi?page=gr&GRid=2550

On the evening of April 15, 1912, the "unsinkable" *RMS Titanic* struck an iceberg on its maiden voyage and broke apart. As soon as word of the disaster reached the White Star Line, they dispatched four Canadian ships to recover as many bodies as possible. Two of the ships sailed from Halifax, stocked with ice, coffins, and canvas bags.

Fifteen hundred of the *Titanic's* passengers died in the disaster. Of that number, 1175 of them either vanished into the sea before the rescue ships arrived or were officially buried at sea after they were recovered. Forty-nine of those buried at sea remain unidentified.

A total of 209 corpses were brought back to Halifax. Fifty-nine of them were shipped via

train to their loved ones. The rest were buried in Halifax. Some went to Mount Olivet Catholic Cemetery. Ten identified as Jewish went to Baron de Hirsch Jewish Cemetery, although since most of them were anonymous, they may have been misidentified. The remainder—121 of them—came to Fairview Lawn Cemetery.

Simple black granite blocks, paid for by the White Star Line, stand side by side, each marked with the same final date. The gravestones are arranged in lines curved to represent the hull of a ship. The right-side lines are broken, to indicate where the iceberg tore the *Titanic* open. Because the ship wasn't seen again until Robert Ballard rediscovered it in 1985, it's a coincidence that the headstones face the same direction as the wreck.

In place of names, 44 people who remain unidentified have only a number to represent the order in which they were retrieved from the water.

Tourists come by the busload to pay their respects in the summertime. ⚜

96

Cimetière Notre-Dame-des-Neiges

**4601 Chemin de la côte des neiges,
Montréal, Quebec**
http://www.cimetierenddn.org/fr/cimetiere

Early in 1854, the parish corporation board of Notre-Dame-des-Neiges bought a large piece of farmland adjoining the Anglo cemetery on Mount Royal. In its first decade, more than 3500 trees were planted in the cemetery, mostly elms and maples. The processional route from the gate to the chapel was lined with trees to form an allée. The trees seem to stand at attention as funeral corteges pass.

At 280 acres, Our Lady of the Snows is the largest cemetery in Canada, with almost 1 million permanent residents. Family mausoleums line up like houses in a city of the dead, reminiscent of Père Lachaise.

The cemetery is strenuously Catholic, down to a full-size copy of Michelangelo's *Pieta* and the Grotto of Lourdes, although this last has been converted to family crypts. The massive gray

Monument aux Patriotes of 1837–38 obelisk was erected by the Institut Canadien. Its goal was to define French-Canadian identity by naming political exiles and those executed in Montreal, as well as all those who died in the struggle for representative government against the British colonial authorities.

In 1921, the Imperial War Graves Commission bought plots in Notre-Dame-des-Neiges and the adjoining Mount Royal Cemetery for burial of the Canadians who died in World War I. The Commission insisted that a gate connect the two plots. The Cross of Sacrifice, designed by Sir Reginald Blomfield, stands over both. On the Notre-Dame side, it is inscribed in French, without mentioning the British King for whom the English-speaking men on the Mount Royal side gave their lives.

In addition to a copy of William Wetmore Story's *Angel of Grief*, Notre-Dame has a copy of a monument in Cimitero Monumentale in Milan. In *The Last Kiss*, a kneeling woman bends to kiss the brow of a prone woman wrapped in a sheet. On the other hand, a very modern monument of twisting granite slabs leaning together at their apex marks the grave of Robert Bourassa, a premier of Quebec, who fought for the legality of the French language. ⚜

The epitaph reads, "United in life, reunited in death."

Drummond Hill Cemetery

6110 Lundy's Lane, Niagara Falls, Ontario
https://www.niagarafalls.ca/city-hall/
municipal-works/cemetery/locations-and-
histories/drummond-hill.aspx

In the final year of the 18th century, a pioneer graveyard opened atop the hill beside the First Presbyterian Church on Lundy's Lane. Buried in the churchyard were British settlers who farmed the fertile land near Niagara Falls.

John Burch was one of the earliest Loyalist pioneers in the area. In 1786, he was one of the first to harness the Niagara River by erecting saw and grist mills. His headstone, the oldest surviving in the churchyard, dates back to 1797. Initially buried on his own farm, Burch was reburied here in 1799.

To this day, the Niagara River forms a natural boundary between the United States and Canada. This proved too close for comfort during the War of 1812, when American troops invaded in an attempt to annex Ontario.

When American officers commandeered Laura Secord's home, she overheard them plotting an attack on the British outpost at DeCew's Falls. Laura walked nearly 20 miles alone through woods and swamps to warn the British. A monument erected by the Ontario Historical Society marks her grave.

The bloodiest battle of the war, which Canadians consider their Gettysburg, took place on July 25, 1814, in the churchyard of the First Presbyterian Church. American forces repeatedly attacked Lieutenant General Gordon Drummond's men, who held the hilltop after six hours of fighting. Both sides suffered casualties estimated at 800 men each. In the end, the Americans claimed victory but withdrew to nearby Fort Erie, which they abandoned in November that year. The American invasion of Canada was over, but if the battle had gone differently, Ontario would now be an American state.

Drummond's men were left with the task of burying the 1600 dead men in trenches in the old cemetery. The Battle of Drummond Hill monument, which marks some of these graves, includes an obelisk, a pair of cannons, and a British flag.

Also buried in the four-acre graveyard is Karel Soucek, a daredevil who successfully went over Niagara Falls in a barrel in 1984. His monument is decorated with his portrait amid a stylized cascade of water. It quotes him as saying, "It is better for a person to take a chance at life…than to live in that gray twilight and know not victory nor defeat." ❧

This monument marks the high-water mark of the American invasion of Canada during the War of 1812. The battle was fought in this pioneer churchyard.

99 Necropolis Cemetery

200 Winchester Street, Toronto, Ontario
http://www.mountpleasantgroup.com/en-CA/
Locations/Cemeteries/toronto-necropolis.aspx

Necropolis, the ancient Greek word meaning "City of the Dead," was chosen to name this cemetery in Toronto as a way to indicate it welcomed anyone, regardless of religious affiliation.

The Necropolis's initial residents were transferred from an old Potter's Field, where an estimated 6000 pioneers had been buried on six acres of land between 1826 and 1850. The use of "potter's field" to refer to a graveyard for paupers traces back to a field near Jerusalem where potters dug clay. When Judas returned the 30 pieces of silver he had been paid for betraying Christ, the Jewish high priests used the money to buy the potters' field. That original ground was used to bury strangers. In the original biblical potter's field, strangers meant non-Jews. As potter's fields became Christianized, "stranger" came to mean anyone traveling through who didn't belong to a local church.

Beneath a broken pillar in the Necropolis Cemetery lie Samuel Lount and Peter Matthews, hanged for taking part in the 1837 Rebellion against the Tory government. The two men had been buried as criminals in the Potter's Field, but when their friends moved them to the Necropolis Cemetery, they were honored as patriots who died for political freedom. Elsewhere in the cemetery lies William Lyon Mackenzie, the first mayor of Toronto, who led the 1837 Rebellion and lived for another 36 years. His Celtic Cross monument makes no mention of his part in the uprising.

Also buried here is Captain Anderson Ruffin Abbott, the first Black surgeon in Canada, who graduated from the University of Toronto at 23. He served in the Union Army during the American Civil War, along with seven African-American doctors. Mary Todd Lincoln gave Abbott the shawl her husband had worn at his first inauguration.

Toronto native Henry Langley designed the mortuary chapel, superintendent's lodge, and entrance gates in the American "Carpenter Gothic" style, using Toronto "buff" brick. He is also buried in the Necropolis. ⚜

The ornate entry to Toronto's Necropolis Cemetery has smaller arched entrances for pedestrians. These are called lychgates, from the Old English word for body. This is where the coffin waited, out of the weather, for the arrival of the clergyman.

Beneath Carlo Bossi's bust are lilies, which indicate casting off earthly cares for heaven. Beneath his wife Petronilla's bust are passionflowers, symbolizing Christ's passion and a belief in redemption.

Ross Bay Cemetery

1495 Fairfield Road, Victoria, British Columbia
http://www.oldcem.bc.ca/cem_rb.htm

In 1872, cemetery trustees purchased 12 acres from Isabella Mainville Ross, widow of Charles Ross, the chief trader for the Hudson Bay Company for whom the bay and cemetery are named. Thirteen years later, Isabella was buried in the cemetery within sight of her former house.

The cemetery is the oldest surviving formal landscape in British Columbia. Victorian carriageways still wind around gravestones made of marble, sandstone, and granite. The oldest plots in the cemetery have curbstones or cast-iron fences.

The cemetery had been intended to be nondenominational, but the Roman Catholic Church and the Church of England demanded segregated portions for their congregations. The Presbyterians, Wesleyans, and Reformed Episcopalians followed suit, leaving only 10 percent of the little 27-acre cemetery available to everyone else.

Since Victoria is a coastal city, strangers sometimes washed up here, friendless and nameless, and ended up in the Potter's Field section of this cemetery. The cemetery's southwest corner, which once extended all the way to the beach, was reserved for "Heathens": all non-Christians, including First Nations people who had not converted to Christianity, the

Chinese, and Japanese Buddhists. The Sikh community cremated their dead on open pyres in the cemetery, but scattered the ashes on the water rather than interring them.

Approximately 600 African-Americans emigrated from California for the Fraser River Gold Rush in 1858–59. Some of them were buried in Ross Bay Cemetery with others of their church affiliation, rather than being isolated by race. Among those commemorated here are Nancy and Peter Lester, who came to Victoria in search of equal rights. Peter led an antislavery movement in Philadelphia and San Francisco in the 1840s and 1850s, before emigrating to Canada. His burial site is unknown.

Artist and author Emily Carr is buried here. Although she didn't paint until after her parents' deaths, she was one of the first Canadian painters with a modernist, post-Impressionist style. She chronicled life in British Columbia and paid homage to the First Nations' cultures. After a stroke limited her ability to travel, she became an author, winning the Governor-General's Award for her first book *Klee Wyck*, "The Laughing One." Fans leave paintbrushes at her grave.

Of the 28,000 people buried here, only a handful are said to haunt the graveyard, including Isabella Ross, original owner of the land, who gazes out at the ocean. David Fee, murdered on Christmas Eve 1890 on the steps of Saint Andrews Cathedral, sometimes appears out of the mist. Also an elderly Victorian couple occasionally strolls the cemetery's west end. ⚜

100

Heart of the Día de los Muertos celebrations in Mexico, Pantéon Antiguo flickers with candlelight as families welcome back their ancestors. Marigolds guide spirits back with their scent and vivid orange color.

CENTRAL AND SOUTH AMERICA AND THE CARIBBEAN

Panteón Antiguo

Santa Cruz Xoxocotlán, Oaxaca, Mexico
http://www.oaxaca-mio.com/fiestas/
muertos_xoxo.htm

Five kilometers southwest of the state capital of Oaxaca, Santa Cruz Xoxocotlán is the heart of the Día de los Muertos celebrations in Mexico.

On October 30, families prepare household altars for those who have died. In addition to photos and mementos, offerings are made of an egg bread called pan de muerto, alongside chocolate, nuts, fruit, jicama, and pumpkin. Once everything is arranged, it cannot be touched again until after the holiday without angering the ghosts.

The church bells ring at 3 p.m. on the 31st, summoning the Little Angels, the spirits of children who have died.

Around 5 or 6 in the evening on November 1, families go to the graveyard with candles and flowers to decorate the graves. They also bring picnics and mescal or beer to help them withstand the chill. They will sit by the graves until 5 or 6 the following morning. Copal incense burns to purify the souls of the "faithful departed."

The colonial Chapel of San Sebastian, in the heart of the Panteón Antiguo, stands on the site of the first Catholic church in town, built from 1535 to 1555. The current chapel was consecrated to the martyr on May 8, 1657, but is in such terrible condition that it is no longer open. People continue to stand outside it during religious processions. The cemetery has been around as long as the chapel itself.

Thousands of tourists come to Santa Cruz Xoxocotlán for the Day of the Dead celebrations. Visitors are welcome and encouraged to support the celebrations, but must ask before photographing families. ⚜

Panteón Civil de Dolores

Avenida Constituyentes S/N, Miguel Hidalgo,
Bosque de Chapultepec Parque Nacional,
Mexico City, Mexico
http://www.ciudadmexico.com.mx/
atractivos/panteon_dolores.htm

In 1870, Dolores Murrieta de Galloso bought 593 acres near the Chapultepec ravines to build the largest cemetery in Mexico. When she died four years later, the project hadn't been completed. Her family continued the construction and named the graveyard in her honor when it opened in 1875.

President Sebastián Lerdo de Tejada decreed that the cemetery would set aside burial space for heroes the nation wished to honor. Near the cemetery's main entrance stands the *Rotonda de las Personas Ilustres*: gravesites of Mexicans famous for art, literature, cinema, or politics. The rotunda is one of the most visited sites in Mexico City.

Buried here are muralist Diego Rivera, painters David Alfaro Siqueiros and José Clemente Orozco, composers Agustín Lara and Juventino

Rosas (the first Mexican composer to receive worldwide attention), union leader Vicente Lombardo Toledano, politician and poet Vicente Riva Palacio, and poet Rosario Castellanos, the first woman from Chiapas to become a published author. She served as the Mexican ambassador to Israel, where she died.

The grave of actress Dolores Del Rio is marked with a striking explosion of stainless steel cones. She came to Hollywood in the 1920s and did very well. In the 1940s, she returned to Mexico, where her first Spanish-language movie made her the biggest movie star in Mexico.

Outside the Rotunda are buried other interesting figures. The grave of Italian-born photographer and activist Tina Modotti was damaged by vandals, but a newer monument to her memory stands in the Italian section of the graveyard now. Carlos Chavez was a composer who wedded Mexican music with native Indian melodies and wrote ballets, symphonies, and

an opera. Soprano Angela Peralta, the Mexican Nightingale, was the premier opera singer of her age. She was touring with her own Mexican opera company in 1883 when she and 75 members of her company succumbed to a yellow fever epidemic.

Both Dolores Murrieta de Galloso, original owner of the cemetery, and Sebastián Lerdo de Tejada, the president who envisioned the *Rotonda*, are buried in the cemetery. ✤

The Rotunda of Illustrious People in the Dolores Civil Cemetery is one of the most visited sites in Mexico City.

103 Corozal Cemetery

Carretera Omar Torrijos, Corozal, Panama
https://www.wmf.org/project/
corozal-cemetery

The country of Panama straddles the narrowest point between the Atlantic and the Pacific Oceans. During the California Gold Rush in 1849, tens of thousands of 49ers—and those who wanted to profit from them—crossed Panama, steaming as far as they could up its rivers before making the rest of the trek by foot or on mules.

In the six years following 1849, the "Silvermen" came to Panama to build the Panama Railroad across the isthmus. Although Spaniards, Eastern Europeans, Chinese, and other Asians participated in the so-called Silver Roll workforce, they were vastly outnumbered by West Indians from Jamaica, Barbados, Martinique, Saint Lucia, and other islands. Some stayed on to build the first Panama canal for the French. More than 20,000 Silvermen succumbed to tropical diseases and the heat before the French gave up.

Another wave of Silvermen worked on the American canal, begun on August 15, 1914. They did the backbreaking work of carving the canal out of the mountains of the continental divide, often with dynamite, and built the locks that raise and lower ships from ocean to lake to river to ocean as they cross the continent.

At the Pacific end of the canal, the American Battlements Cemetery (now the Corozal American Cemetery and Memorial) opened in 1914 for U.S. citizens—the "Gold Roll" employees—who died during the construction of the canal.

Alongside it, the segregated 46-acre Corozal Cemetery opened for Silver Roll employees. Until 1979, the cemetery was under American jurisdiction. When the Canal Zone reverted to Panamanian control, oversight of the cemetery passed to Panama City. Erosion, vandalism, and the creeping return of the jungle threaten the cemetery. In 2010, it was placed on the World Monuments Fund list of the 100 Most Endangered Heritage Sites.

Carved out of the jungle, the Corozal Cemetery is lovely and sad. It records a history that will be lost without immediate action. ✤

West Indians came to Panama in the early 1900s to build the Panama Canal. Many of them lie in the lovely Corozal Cemetery.

Cementerio de la Recoleta

Junín 1760, 1113 CABA,
Buenos Aires, Argentina
https://turismo.buenosaires.gob.ar/es/
atractivo/cementerio-de-la-recoleta

The ten acres where La Recoleta now stands was formerly a vegetable garden farmed by the Recoletos monks. The land was seized in 1822 by Governor Martin Rodriguez and his minister Bernadino Rivadavia, who went on to become the first president of Argentina. Rodriguez followed the lead of Napoleon in Europe and banned burial inside churches in Argentina.

Mausoleums pack Recoleta Cemetery, which makes all the lists of the most beautiful cemeteries in the world.

Originally called the Northern Cemetery, the cemetery was laid out by Prosper Catelin, a French engineer. In 1946, it was declared a National Monument. In 1949, the name changed to La Recoleta Cemetery.

For many years, this was the only cemetery in Buenos Aires. As the wealthy class of Argentina expanded, they chose to fill Recoleta with marble sculpture inspired by the statuary in Père Lachaise and Staglieno Cemetery. Of the 5500 mausoleums in La Recoleta, several have been declared national treasures.

Portrait sculpture fills the cemetery. Among the politicians, generals, and bankers stands David Alleno, a caretaker in the cemetery who hired an Italian sculptor to portray him—life-size—with his broom and watering can. Boxer Luis Angel Firpo is depicted in his robe as if waiting for the fight to begin. Several bronze soldiers stand guard throughout the cemetery.

Buried here is Pierre Benoit, a painter believed to be the Dauphin of France, who would have become Louis XVII if he had not been poisoned in Argentina. Benoit helped design the cemetery and is the architect responsible for the frontispiece of the Buenos Aires Cathedral.

After a series of conservative governments post–World War II, Colonel Juan Perón was popularly elected as president of Argentina in 1946. His wildly popular wife, Evita Duarte, died of gynecological cancer at the age of 33. Millions filed past her corpse as it lay in state. After Perón was deposed, Evita's corpse was exiled as well. The generals sent her to be buried in Milan's Monumental Cemetery, where she remained for 20 years. Once her body was allowed finally to come home, it was kidnapped once more. Now it lies in the Duarte family mausoleum, encased in cement. ⚜

105 Cementerio Museo de San Pedro

Carrera 51 #68-68, Manrique, Medellín, Colombia
http://www.cementeriosanpedro.org.co

A couple of blocks north of Hospital Metro Station in Medellín stands Cementerio Museo de San Pedro. The 54-acre cemetery was consecrated on May 21, 1845. The cemetery is full of monuments and mausoleums imported from Italy, alongside gems made by local artists Marco Tobón Mejía and Bernardo Vieco, both of whom are buried here.

The original chapel was replaced by the current one in 1929, built by Belgian architect Agustín Goovaerts. Pedro Justo Berrio, who was president of the Sovereign State of Antioquia before his death in 1875, is buried just outside the chapel in a tomb with a stern marble mourner and an altar with a book held open with a sword.

Minister for Education and External Relations Dr. Luis López de Mesa's towering family mausoleum has an enormous three-pronged anchor on it. The anchor symbolizes Christian faith.

At the base of the obelisk on José María Amador's grave, a fully dressed woman has flung herself facedown to grieve. These sorts of statues are called pleureuses—weepers—who mourn perpetually over the dead. José was the 24-year-old son of Carlos Coriolano Amador, an entrepreneur who funded both the telephone system and the mining industry in Colombia.

Jorge Isaacs, author of *Maria* (one of the most-read novels from Colombia), was originally buried in Cemetery San Pedro under a monument with another grieving woman, this time in high relief. Originally this pleureuse was nude, but the cemetery forced the sculptor to cover her up. Now she's wrapped in a skin-tight marble sheet that leaves little to the imagination. In the end, Isaacs's remains were moved to Cali.

Also buried here is Union Brigadier General Edward Augustus Wild, who lost an arm in the Battle of South Mountain but went on to lead a company of African-American soldiers called Wild's African Brigade. Wild managed a silver mine in Nevada before coming to South America, where he died in 1891.

In the 20th century, Medellín was the heart of international traffic in cocaine. Mausoleums

Flowers brighten this mausoleum arcade at Medellín's Cementerio Museo de San Pedro.

built in the 1980s and 90s are remarkable for mimicking the architecture of the time, complete with aluminum doors.

After one of Pablo Escobar's hitmen was buried here, his family mausoleum blared loud music around the clock. The public utilities company shut off the power repeatedly, only for the music to mysteriously start up again. Eventually, the cemetery informed the dead man's mother that she would lose her rights to the mausoleum if the music didn't stop.

The Antioquia Museum Network declared the cemetery a Site Museum in October 1998. Since 2000, the museum has offered a wide range of tours about the history, artwork, and symbolism found here, such as "Florists of the Beyond" about the sculpted flowers. On full moon nights, the museum offers programs of theater and dance. ⚜

San Pedro Cemetery

Ninacaca, Cerro de Pasco, Peru
http://expedienteoculto.blogspot.com/2009/03/ninacaca-la-ciudad-de-los-muertos.html

In all the world, Peru's San Pedro Cemetery of Ninacaca is unique. Instead of tombstones or crosses, the cemetery is full of architectural models. Moorish-style buildings stand next to Peruvian cathedrals, the Vatican, the Taj Mahal, and Moscow's Saint Basil's Cathedral.

Although the mortuary models seem to echo the spirit houses built by North American native cultures, the tradition in Cerro de Pasco began after a terrorist attack in March 1989 left six people—including the mayor—dead. Townsfolk re-created the Municipal Palace to mark the mayor's grave.

106

Soon after that, a popular educator died. His grave was marked with a replica of the local school. The fashion for architectural models caught on.

The specially built memorials cost between $250 and $1000. Survivors choose a building and its bright colors to reflect the deceased: their heritage, their religious beliefs, places they wished they'd visited in their lifetimes.

Although the tradition sprung from tragedy, the San Pedro Cemetery is now cheerful in its originality. ✤

Cerro de Pasco, located at the top of the Andean mountains, is one of the highest cities in the world.

107 Cementerio General de Santiago

**Avenida Profesor Alberto Zañartu 951,
Santiago, Chile
http://www.cementeriogeneral.cl**

In 1821, the Cementerio Generale de Santiago was established about a mile and a half north of Santiago's city center in the Recoleta neighborhood. It's one of the largest cemeteries in Latin America, with 2 million buried in 210 acres of elegant mausoleums, towering palm trees, sweet-smelling flowers, and exotic birds flying around.

The cemetery has a political side, too. All but two of Chile's former presidents are buried here. A large monument marks the grave of former president Salvador Allende, who received a proper burial here in 1990, 17 years after his suicide on the first day of the coup d'état led by Augusto Pinochet in 1973.

Orlando Letelier, a Socialist associate of Allende's, was arrested during the coup and tortured in a concentration camp on Dawson Island. Released into exile, Letelier took an academic post in the United States. In 1976, he was assassinated by a car bomb in Washington, DC. After Pinochet fell from power in 1990, Letelier's body was repatriated.

Near the cemetery's Recoleta entrance stands a memorial to victims of the Pinochet dictatorship, erected in 1994. The left side of the wall lists 1000 names of those who "disappeared," along with the date they were last

Santiago's Cementerio General, one of the largest graveyards in South America, combines beautiful architecture with monuments that remember victims of the Pinochet dictatorship.

seen. On the right side are 3000 names of those known to have been executed, along with their ages and dates of death. Some were children. At the foot of the wall, families leave photos of their loved ones.

Another memorial is called Patio 29, where more than 100 victims of the dictatorship were buried in graves marked with simple iron crosses labeled NN (no name). As forensic investigators

identify the bodies, more of the crosses bear the correct names.

Along the far wall of the cemetery is the niche of Victor Jara, a songwriter and political activist. At the beginning of Pinochet's takeover, Jara was detained, had his fingers broken so he couldn't play guitar again, then was shot forty or fifty times before his body was dumped on the street. Now his grave is a shrine. ⚜

Cimetière de Morne-à-l'Eau

**Rue de Moule, Morne-à-l'Eau,
Guadeloupe Island
http://www.ville-mornealeau.com/
decouvrir-la-ville/patrimoine/16-cimetiere**

The Guadeloupe Islands in the southern part of the Caribbean are part of the French West Indies. They lie between Puerto Rico and Venezuela. Hilly Grand-Terre, the bigger island, is known for its sugarcane fields and long beaches.

Fifteen kilometers north from Point-à-Pitre across Grand-Terre lies the town of Morne-à-l'Eau. The town was the birthplace of soccer player Jocelyn Angloma. On Guadeloupe, it is known for the crab feast it throws on Easter.

Before the town of Morne-à-l'Eau was founded in 1827, wealthy families used private burial grounds on their sugarcane plantations. Masters and slaves did not mix, even after death. Today, everyone shares the graveyard, from the families of béké (descendents of the French settlers) planters to modest farmers, musicians, and even

the founder of the Communist Party of Guadeloupe. The oldest tomb in the public cemetery dates back to 1847 and belongs to a béké family.

Morne-à-l'Eau's beautiful cemetery houses 1800 tombs, which climb the sides of a natural amphitheater. Marble and granite are banned, so the tombs are made of cement decorated with faience tiles. The majority are decorated in black-and-white checkerboard patterns. No one is entirely sure why, although one theory points out that white is a symbol of mourning in Africa, while black is the color of mourning in Europe. Occasionally, tombs are simple white; others are blue or discreetly pink. Some are quite elaborate. The most imposing belongs to the Moutoussamy family: a two-story pavilion with a terrace and French window. Others echo the sloping roofs of the Creole houses in town. Not surprisingly, the oldest tombs are soberest.

Two weeks before All Saints' Day (November 1), young people from the village offer their services to help clean graves. They paint, pull weeds, and do repairs. On the evening of the 1st, families gather at their ancestors' tombs. Vendors sell Guadeloupan fry bread, peanuts, and chipped-ice snowballs. Hundreds of candles bathe the tombs in golden light. ⚜

Intricate black and white tilework decorates the mausoleums of Cimetière de Morne-à-l'Eau.

Reggae superstar Bob Marley is buried in a brightly colored mausoleum in the village where he grew up.

Bob Marley Mausoleum

Nine Mile, Saint Ann Parish, Jamaica
http://www.jamaicascene.com/attractions/
ocho_rios/bob_marley_mausoleum_tour.php

Rastafarian reggae star Bob Marley hurt his toe playing pickup soccer while on tour in France in 1977. The wound turned out to be cancerous, but surgery was against Marley's religion. The cancer spread to his lungs, stomach, and brain. By the time Marley pursued radiation treatments, it was too late. He died in Miami in May 1981.

Marley's albums had earned $190 million: approximately 10 percent of Jamaica's gross domestic product. As he lay in state in the National Heroes Arena in Kingston, more than 150,000 people—the largest gathering in the nation's history—filed past his casket.

After a funeral attended by Jamaica's past and current prime ministers, Marley was laid to rest at Nine Mile, 75 miles outside of Kingston. He was buried at his family's compound in the mountainside village, where he grew up and wrote some of his hits. Now he lies in an eight-foot-tall marble mausoleum, with his Bible and red Stratocaster guitar at his side. When his dreadlocks had fallen out from the radiation, his wife, Rita, saved them to be buried with him. Marley's half brother lies in the upper part of the tomb and their mother is buried nearby.

Marley's family still owns the compound and offers tours. ⚜

109

Cementerio Santa María Magdalena de Pazzis

Old San Juan, Puerto Rico
http://sanjuanpuertorico.com/santa-maria-
magdalena-de-pazzis-cemetery/#15/
18.4702/-66.1204

Considered by many to be one of the most beautiful cemeteries in the world, Santa María Magdalena de Pazzis Cemetery stands on a hill between the city walls of Old San Juan and the blue Atlantic. On its west side stands Castillo San Felipe del Morro. On weekends, the breeze carries the laughter of children as they fly kites at the fort.

When the cemetery opened early in 1863, it was administered by Carmelite nuns. It is named

110

A lovely domed mortuary church dominates the colonial-era cemetery of Old San Juan.

for Santa María Magdalena de Pazzi, a 16th-century Carmelite who suffered religious ecstasies. She is the patron saint against sickness.

Symbolizing the journey to the afterlife, the beauty of the cemetery's oceanfront site is meant to challenge the Spanish fear of death. Inside the cemetery's yellow-and-white gate, the tightly packed marble statuary and whitewashed graves gleam brightly. The heart of the graveyard is an unusual round mortuary chapel, built in Renaissance Revival style, with a bright rose-colored dome. Colorful flowers, vivid blue sky, and elegant sculpture make this a photographer's dream.

Among the historic figures buried here are Academy Award–winning actor José Ferrer, abolitionist and politician José Julián Acosta, poet and advocate for independence José de Diego, composer and songwriter Rafael Hernandez, doctor and politician José Celso Barbosa, journalist and historian Salvador Brau, and leader of the Puerto Rican Nationalist Party, Pedro Albizu Campos.

The cemetery lies near La Perla, one of the oldest slums in Puerto Rico, but the cemetery area is well policed and safe to visit during the day. ⚜

111 Necrópolis de Cristóbal Colón

Zapata and 12th Street, Vedado, Havana, Cuba
http://www.lahabana.com/guide/
necropolis-de-cristobal-colon

Just south of Revolution Square lies the beautiful Cemetery of Christopher Columbus, the Spaniard who "discovered" Cuba in October 1492. The 140-acre cemetery was designed by Madrid-educated architect Calixto de Loira. The cemetery's first burial was de Loira himself, who died before the cemetery was completed.

The larger streets of de Loira's grid are lined with 500 major mausoleums, chapels, and family vaults belonging to the wealthy and well connected. They vary in style from Classical Revival to Neo-Gothic to Art Deco: often, smaller-scale copies of their owners' homes. In the center of the cemetery rises the Capilla Central, the central chapel. Its design was inspired by the Duomo in Florence, Italy, but its octagonal shape is unique in Havana.

In 1959, 80 percent of Cubans were Roman Catholic, although few attended church. After the Revolution, Cuba was declared an atheist nation. That stance softened in the 1990s. Now church—and the cemetery—are places with freedom of expression in Cuba.

The most visited grave in the cemetery belongs to Amelia Goyri, a 24-year-old who died in childbirth. She was buried with her still-born infant at her feet in 1901. Years later, when her body was exhumed, the dead child was in her arms. She's called *La Milagrosa*, the Miraculous One. Cubans come to her grave to pray for safe pregnancies, then return with flowers to thank her. The ritual is that visitors touch her tomb three times, make their request, then walk away from the grave without turning their backs to it.

Also buried in Colon Cemetery are composer Hubert de Blanck, who wrote the opera *Patria* about Cuba's independence from Spain; Ibrahim Ferrer, singer for the original Buena Vista Social Club; and Orthodox Party leader Eduardo Chibas, who committed suicide live on the radio in 1951—and on whose grave Fidel Castro gave his first speech.

The cemetery suffered in the decades after Castro came to power, when families in exile could no longer care for their ancestors' monuments. Despite the need for conservation, the Colon Cemetery is among the most visited sites in Cuba, with as many as a million and a half visitors each year. ⚜

Named for Christopher Columbus, this cemetery surrounds a mortuary church modeled after the Duomo in Florence, Italy.

EUROPE

Sutton Hoo

**Tranmer House, Woodbridge,
Suffolk, England
https://www.nationaltrust.org.uk/sutton-hoo**

Eighteen Anglo-Saxon barrows have survived since the 7th century AD on a bluff above the River Deben near Woodbridge, Suffolk. The name *Hoo* derives from the Old English word *haugh*, which means "high place."

This area of England was inhabited by Iron Age farmers, then Romans, before it was invaded by Anglo-Saxons around 500 AD. King Raedwald ruled from 599 to around 624, when he died. It's believed the largest mound at Sutton Hoo was his grave.

When the king died, an entire ship, capable of crossing the sea, was dragged up from the River Deben. A burial vault inside it was stocked with treasures: silver dishes from Byzantium, a horned stag on a ring that probably fit over a scepter, and a purse lid with gold decorations.

Beneath the purse lid lay 37 gold coins, which can be dated to around 625.

Victims of the acid soil, neither the body nor the ship survived the centuries. The treasures were discovered in 1939, when Mrs. Edith Pretty, the landowner, sponsored an excavation. The dig concluded hastily when World War II was declared in Europe.

A second, smaller ship burial lay at the upper end of the burial ground. This time, the ship was placed atop the burial chamber. While this grave had been robbed, archaeologists found clues that the warrior had been buried with a sword, a shield, drinking horns, and a cauldron.

After a second excavation in 1985, this mound was rebuilt to its original height. The larger mound has been left excavated, with posts to mark the boundaries of the ship. A viewing platform allows visitors to look down into the grave.

Other burials at Sutton Hoo included a nobleman's grave, alongside the grave of his horse. Buried with him were a bucket, a bronze

Eighteen Anglo-Saxon barrows stand on a bluff overlooking the River Deben in Suffolk, England.

cauldron, and his horse's harness. Other graves held a woman of rank, a child with a silver spear, and cremated remains.

The Sutton Hoo burial ground was acquired by the National Trust in 1998. They discovered a smaller Saxon cemetery while building a Visitor Center.

The Visitor Center, opened in 2002, explains the burial ground and the archaeological explorations. The mound's treasures are on display in the British Museum, including an iron helmet pieced together from fragments taken from the largest mound. It has a mask to hide the wearer's features, decorated with bronze eyebrows, inlaid with silver wire and garnets, that end in gilt boar's heads. The re-creation is truly spectacular. ❖

This beautiful helmet is a re-creation of one found in the largest of Sutton Hoo's barrows. A gilded dragon covers the nose and meets a second dragon, which runs over the crest of the cap. At the bridge of the nose, the two dragons meet two boars to form a bird with outstretched wings.

Westminster Abbey

City of Westminster, 20 Deans Yard, London, England
http://www.westminster-abbey.org

Westminster Abbey has served as the site of every British coronation since 1066. The tradition predates the current Gothic building, begun by Henry III in 1245. The Abbey is also stuffed nearly to bursting with mortuary sculpture.

Seventeen British monarchs were buried in the Abbey, ranging from Henry III, whose heart lies at Fontevrault Abbey in France among the tombs of his ancestors, to Henry VIII's fourth wife, Anne of Cleves, and Mary, Queen of Scots. Protestant Elizabeth I shares a tomb with her Catholic sister, Mary I, beneath an epitaph that says, "Consorts both in throne and grave, here rest we two sisters…in the hope of one Resurrection." Elizabeth's coffin was stacked atop Mary's. Elizabeth's effigy is the only one visible.

Geoffrey Chaucer, Rudyard Kipling, Charles Darwin, and Sir Isaac Newton were also honored with burial in the Abbey. Charles Dickens was

Anne Seymour, Dutchess of Somerset, was the aunt of King Edward VI, son of Henry VIII. This portrait sculpture shows her on her deathbed. It was possibly carved from her death mask.

Westminster Abbey holds the most significant collection of monumental sculpture—either as tombs or memorials—in the United Kingdom.

interred here against his will. Composer Henry Purcell was buried in the Abbey near the organ he played. George Frederic Handel requested burial in the Abbey in his will, since he had composed the coronation hymn. African explorer David Livingstone was offered burial in the Abbey after his death in Africa, so his attendants unearthed his body, embalmed it, and sent it back to England without its heart, which they reburied in his original grave. During the 20th century, coffins were no longer buried in Westminster. In

1905, actor Sir Henry Irving was the first to have his ashes interred.

At the west end of the nave lies the tomb of the Unknown Warrior. After World War I, unidentified British servicemen were exhumed from graveyards in the Aisne, the Somme, Arras, and Ypres. Brigadier General L. J. Wyatt, commander of British troops in France and Flanders, chose one to represent all of the unidentifiable dead. The chosen unknown was buried beneath the Abbey floor on Armistice Day, November 11, 1920. ⚜

114 Saint Giles' Churchyard

Church Lane, Stoke Poges, Buckinghamshire, England
http://www.stokepogeschurch.org/welcome/ history/st-giles

Eighteenth-century poet Thomas Gray composed the "Elegy Written in a Country Churchyard" while visiting this small churchyard in the heart of England.

The manor, which stands 200 yards away, was a Saxon thane's home until the Norman

Conquest in 1066. By the 1080s, the Normans were building the first church here. The chancel (the part near the altar), walls, and pillars in the main body of that Norman church survive.

The word *Stoke* meant a "stockaded place." In 1086, the lord of the manor became known as William of Stoke. In the 13th century, Amicia of Stoke, heiress of the manor, married Robert Pogeys, and their land became known as Stoke Poges.

Inside the chancel stands the tomb of Sir John de Molyns, Marshal of the King's Falcons and Supervisor of the King's Castles. Although he served both Edward II and Edward III, Sir John was a robber baron believed to have murdered his wife's uncle and cousin to inherit their land. He died in March 1360.

Around 1558, Lord Hastings of Loughborough added a chapel for inmates of a nearby almshouse. The chapel serves as a burial place for the Hastings family. On the chapel's south wall is a mural with skulls and cherubs' heads. Sir Thomas and Sir Walter Clarges were buried here with their families, but the graves have been lost.

The oldest monument is a flat tombstone dug out of the churchyard, now moved into the Hastings chapel. In Norman French, the stone says, "All those who pass by here, Pray for the soul of this one. William of Wytermerse he had for a name."

Out in the churchyard, Thomas Gray lies beneath a brick sarcophagus next to his mother and her unmarried sister. His name doesn't appear on the grave, but a tablet on the church's wall records his burial. Immediately opposite the southwest door of Saint Giles' Church stands the yew tree under which Gray composed his poem.

The boast of heraldry, the pomp of pow'r,

And all that beauty, all that wealth e'er gave,

Awaits alike the inevitable hour:

The paths of glory lead but to the grave.

The inspiration for Thomas Gray's "Elegy Written in a Country Churchyard" is the final resting place of the poet himself. Its small Norman church is echoed by cemetery chapels around the world.

Highgate Cemetery

Swain's Lane, Highgate, London, England
http://highgatecemetery.org

When the London Cemetery Company founded Highgate Cemetery, they envisioned the "garden cemetery" as a place of beauty where Londoners could escape the smoke and dirt of their city. The graveyard offered controlled nature—serene, parklike, safe—beside the wilderness of Hampstead Heath.

In the 19th century, people flocked to Highgate Cemetery. They brought picnics and strolled the lanes, marveling over the wealth of statuary and beautiful greenery. Inspired by the birdsong, they courted here. With 30 funerals a day, people flowed constantly in and out.

Then the 20th century dawned. England endured World War I. One of every three soldiers perished. At the war's end, the influenza pandemic swept the country, killing thousands. World War II wiped out most of the next generation of men. By the 1950s, few survived to tend the graves. No money came from new burials in family plots to pay the army of gardeners. Highgate Cemetery was abandoned to nature.

By the end of the 1960s, Highgate Cemetery was choked with weeds, shadowed by a dense forest of ornamental trees, and colonized by wildlife from Hampstead Heath that included foxes, hedgehogs, and rabbits. The overgrown cemetery was featured in *Taste the Blood of Dracula*, one of Hammer Studio's costume thrillers starring Christopher Lee. Perhaps that inspired the outbreak of vampire hunting that mutilated Highgate Cemetery in the 1970s.

The Friends of Highgate Cemetery formed in 1975. Volunteers cleared brambles, felled invasive trees, and reopened access to gravesites. Eventually, the Friends bought the entire cemetery. They now offer tours to fund their work.

Among the famous dead buried at Highgate lie Karl Marx, as well as authors Christina Rossetti, George Eliot, Radclyffe Hall, and Douglas Adams, author of *The Hitchhiker's Guide to the Galaxy*. Other gravesites worthy of social calls include impresario Malcolm McLaren; actor Sir Ralph Richardson; social reformer George Jacob Holyoake, the last man arrested for atheism in Great Britain; William Friese-Green, inventor of "kinematography"; as well as various balloonists, menagerists, and scientists. ❧

The Friends of Highgate Cemetery treat the Eastern Cemetery as managed woodland, celebrating nature among the old monuments.

Inspired by the translation of the Rosetta Stone, Highgate's magnificent Egyptian Avenue fanned a fascination with Egyptian architecture in cemeteries worldwide.

Brookwood Cemetery

**Cemetery Pales, Brookwood, Woking,
Surrey, England**
http://www.brookwoodcemetery.com

Ten years after Highgate opened, it was clear that the ring of London cemeteries called the Magnificent Seven would not provide enough burial space for the booming Victorian metropolis. In 1849, Sir Richard Broun and Richard Spyre proposed a graveyard "devoted to the Continental usage of giving to each corpse a separate grave."

In 1852, Parliament empowered the London Necropolis and National Mausoleum Company to purchase 2000 acres in Woking. The last great London cemetery would be 30 miles from London on the desolate heaths of Surrey.

It took two more years for the cemetery to be renovated into "a garden of sleep" as inspired by Mount Auburn. Brookwood was planted with pines, birches, Californian sequoias, and South American monkey puzzle trees.

The cemetery was made possible by the railroads. The London Necropolis Railway took people from London's Waterloo Station into the enormous cemetery, which had two stations: North for Dissenters and South for Anglicans. The South Station catered funeral parties, served afternoon tea, and also operated as a pub.

Hedges and lych gates delineated each parish church's burial ground. Brookwood was the first cemetery in Britain to offer burial to Muslims, Sikhs, and Zoroastrians. It encloses the largest military cemetery in the United Kingdom, with sections for British, American, Canadian, Czech, and Turkish soldiers.

Among the quarter of a million people buried here are Impressionist portrait painter John Singer Sargent; anatomist Dr. Robert Knox, who purchased corpses from infamous bodysnatchers Burke and Hare; and Dennis Wheatley, prolific author on the occult. Edward the Martyr was the first millennium English king murdered in favor of his half-brother Ethelred the Unready. Although Edward was never canonized by the Catholic Church, he has been reckoned a saint since 1001. In 1984, his bones were installed in Saint Edward the Martyr Orthodox Church in Brookwood.

The funeral train was destroyed during World War II and Brookwood is no longer the largest cemetery in the world, but it is still a remarkable place. It offers guided tours and regular lectures. ⚜

Amid a field of crosses, an angel points the way to Heaven in Brookwood Cemetery, once the largest graveyard in the world.

Golders Green Memorial Gardens

Hoop Lane, London, England
http://www.thelondoncremation.co.uk/
golders-green-crematorium

C remation was legalized in Britain in 1884. For its first 17 years, Londoners had to travel to Brookwood Cemetery to be cremated. When Queen Victoria died in 1901, her surgeon, Sir Henry Thompson—president of the Cremation Society—opened Golders Green the following year.

Golders Green is the name of the once largely Jewish neighborhood. Although the crematorium stands across from a Jewish cemetery, its scattering gardens accept all denominations. An estimated 2000 people are cremated at Golders Green each year, more than 320,000 people so far.

The redbrick crematorium was built in an Italianate style with a large tower that hides its chimney. Its three columbaria contain the ashes of thousands of Londoners. On almost every wall hang commemorative tablets. The earliest ones hang on the cloister walls. The 12-acre scattering garden contains several large tombs, ponds and a scenic bridge, and a large crocus lawn.

Among the people cremated at Golders Green whose ashes were either scattered here or placed in the columbaria: Kingsley Amis; children's author Enid Blyton; rock star Marc Bolan; Sigmund Freud; *Rocky Horror*'s narrator Charles Gray; Who drummer Keith Moon; playwright Joe Orton, whose ashes were combined with those of his murderous lover, Kenneth Halliwell; ballerina Anna Pavlova; actor Peter Sellers; and Bram Stoker, the author of *Dracula*.

Many more have been cremated there, but their ashes were either scattered or enshrined elsewhere. Among these were England's Prime Minister Neville Chamberlain, poets Rudyard Kipling and T. S. Eliot, and the writers Henry James and H. G. Wells, whose ashes were scattered off the coast of Dorset.

Because of vandalism, the columbaria are kept locked, although they can be visited with a guide. Golders Green also has a tearoom. ⚜

Perhaps the best-known crematorium in the world, Golders Green has cremated more than 300,000 people. Some of them are remembered with plaques.

Reilig Odhrán

Isle of Iona, Inner Hebrides, Scotland
http://www.isle-of-iona.net/attractions/
historical/st-orans-chapel

T he Hebridean island of Iona, off the western coast of Scotland, is only three and a half miles long. It is considered the Westminster Abbey of Scotland, where 48 Scottish kings lie buried. An inventory done in 1549 recorded that eight Norwegian, four Irish, and two ancient French kings are buried in the churchyard as well. If true, there are more kings in Reilig Odhrán than in Westminster Abbey. Unfortunately, their grave markers are no longer legible.

Still, the churchyard was the traditional burial place of the Argyllshire kings from the earliest times to Gabhran Mac Domangart, who died in battle around 560. Also buried there lie Duncan and Macbeth, made famous by Shakespeare. After a relatively peaceful reign during which Macbeth made a pilgrimage to Rome, his body was carried over the water in 1057.

The Reilig (Gaelic for graveyard) lies beside Saint Oran's Chapel. According to legend, Saint Oran (Odhran in Gaelic) was buried alive beneath the chapel as a sacrifice to keep its walls standing.

Near the chapel's doorway lies a stone called Clach Brath. Legend holds that when the stone is worn through, the world will end. For centuries, pilgrims to the burial ground turned

The Reilig Odhrán on the Hebridean island of Iona is the final resting place of kings from Scotland, Ireland, and Norway.

pebbles in the cavity of the stone to speed the day of reckoning.

Another legend foretells a great flood that will drown all the other islands. Iona will rise on the waters, floating like a crown. The dead buried in Reilig Odhran will arise dry, which is how they will be recognized on Judgment Day.

Iona is accorded this honor because Saint Columba founded his abbey here in May 563. Columba, great-grandson of King Conall of Ireland, had a fiery temper. After he won a bloody battle against King Diarmit, he was excommunicated. In penance, he went into exile on Iona. He worked as a scribe, authored several hymns that survive, and brought Christianity to the Picts in Scotland.

Some of the old stones in the graveyard are adorned with lotus leaves, spiral vines, swords, a stag chased by dogs, and even a Norse galley with furled sails.

After all the centuries, the churchyard continues to be used. During World War II, a German airman was shot down over Iona. He was buried in the churchyard beside a British pilot. John Smith, leader of the British Labour Party, was buried there in 1994. ⚜

Greyfriars Kirkyard

Greyfriars Place, Edinburgh, Scotland
http://www.greyfriarskirk.com/visiting-kirk

In 1447, Franciscan monks (the so-called Gray Friars) built their friary at the north end of the Grassmarket on a slope with a lovely view of the castle. The Franciscans were a medical order who served the poor. The Reformation chased them out of Scotland in 1558.

Their yard was claimed by Queen Mary for a public burial place in 1562. Just in time, too. The burial ground was used "extensively" during the plague of 1568.

The first peer buried here was James Douglas, Earl of Morton, executed in 1581 after being accused of the murder of Queen Mary's husband. Douglas was followed by historian George Buchanan the following year. Both graves went unmarked, common practice at the time. Painters George Jamesone and Sir John Medina and poet Allan Ramsay also lie in unmarked graves.

At the foot of the east walk stands the Covenanters' Monument, which remembers Scottish Presbyterians who died for their faith, rather than convert to the Anglican Church founded by Henry VIII in England.

Greyfriars Kirkyard is considered one of the most haunted graveyards in the world. Visitors to the kirkyard claim to have been scratched, bruised, and bitten near one of the largest mausoleums in Scotland. The mausoleum's owner, Sir George Mackenzie of Rosehaugh, was Lord Advocate during the "Killing Times." He relished the opportunity to execute so many Covenanters for choosing the wrong Christian faith. In all, Sir George sent 18,000 to their deaths. Many of his victims are buried around him.

The most famous denizen of Greyfriars Kirkyard is a Skye terrier named Bobby. When John Gray died of tuberculosis and was buried here, his dog Bobby spent the rest of his life guarding the old man's grave. The dog died in 1872 and is buried nearby in unconsecrated ground. ⚜

The most famous resident of Greyfriars Kirkyard is Bobby, a terrier who refused to leave his master's grave. This statue stands outside the Kirkyard walls at the top of Candlemaker Row.

Glasgow Necropolis

**Castle Street, Cathedral Square,
Glasgow, Scotland
http://www.glasgownecropolis.org**

By the early 1800s, Glasgow was one of the leading industrial cities of Europe. Cholera and typhus swept through it regularly; as many as 5000 people died each year. The soot-blackened city churchyards were packed full.

The Church of England's requirement that people were to be buried in their churchyards was a point of friction for the growing Protestant middle class. They admired the landed gentry's ability to bury their dead on their country estates. With the example of nondenominational Père Lachaise in mind, Protestants found a righteous cause in establishing a landscaped burial ground separate from the Church of England.

Before the cemetery was drawn up for a partly quarried hill known as Fir Park, a monument to Calvinist reformer John Knox was unveiled here in 1825. Atop a 58-foot Doric column stood a 12-foot sandstone statue of Knox, towering 230 feet above sea level.

A single-span sandstone bridge called the Bridge of Sighs leads to the ornamental facade of the Necropolis. Beyond the cemetery gates, they'd intended to build catacombs as a way to foil grave robbers. The Anatomy Act in 1832 ended the reasons people stole corpses for anatomy classes, so the public mausoleum was never completed.

Local landscape gardener George Mylne directed the layout of the cemetery. Its terraces of lawn were divided by gently curved paths. The site was lined with elm, plane, poplar, sycamore, and oak trees, but not the fir trees for which the park had been named, since they struggled in Glasgow's polluted air. Many of the larger memorials were created by famous sculptors of the day, including Charles Rennie Mackintosh, J. T. Rochead, and Alexander "Greek" Thomson.

Among the 50,000 buried here is Irish-born William Thomson, Lord Kelvin, who proposed the absolute scale of temperature and added the word *thermodynamics* to the dictionary. He also helped lay the first transatlantic telegraph cable. Also here is John Henry Alexander, who created the trick where an actor catches a bullet in his teeth. His memorial is shaped like a Victorian theater, with its curtain about to fall. Finally, Corlinda Lee, Queen of the Gypsies, is buried here with her son. She read Queen Victoria's fortune in 1878.

The stony crags near the Glasgow Cathedral were transformed into an exquisite cemetery during the Victorian era.

Poulnabrone Dolmen, a 6,000-year-old megalithic tomb, is remote but accessible, since it stands along the R480. Its gravel parking lot is a great place to stargaze.

Poulnabrone Dolmen

The Burren, County Clare, Ireland
http://www.burrengeopark.ie/
discover-and-experience/
geosites-discovery-points/poulnabrone

Poulnabrone is one of Ireland's most photographed archaeological sites. "The hole of the sorrows" stands in the stark Burren, a massive region of fossil-filled limestone formed 350 million years ago when a tropical sea covered Ireland. The portal tomb was erected by Ireland's very first farming communities. Radiocarbon evidence reports that the burials were made at regular intervals between 3800 and 3200 BC.

Strangely, similar structures stand in India, the Koreas, Africa, Spain, and across the British Isles. Approximately 174 portal tombs still exist in Ireland. Most of them stand in the north, with outliers like Poulnabrone in counties Clare and Waterford. A portal tomb, also called a dolmen, consists of two large stones that delineate the tomb's entrance. Together with a back stone,

they support an enormous slanting roof stone. The north-facing entrance at Poulnabrone stands almost six and a half feet high.

Poulnabrone is one of the few portal tombs in Ireland to be investigated by archaeologists. In 1985–86, Ann Lynch led an excavation that recovered remains of sixteen adults and six children buried inside the tomb. Those whose genders could be determined were split evenly between female and male.

The bones had been defleshed before burial, hinting that they were stored or buried elsewhere before being interred here. The way some of the bones were scorched indicated they had been held over a flame, maybe in a purification ritual.

Only one of the people buried here was older than 40. Even the young people suffered from arthritis in their necks and shoulder bones: evidence of carrying heavy loads. Their teeth revealed infections and periods of malnutrition. Some of the bones showed evidence of violence. One hipbone had a flint projectile point embedded in it. A skull exhibited a fracture like a stone projectile might have made.

Archaeologists also found stone tools, bone and quartz jewelry, and pottery. ✤

Stone Age farmers built Newgrange, an acre-in-diameter passage tomb, in 3200 BC. The winter solstice sunrise illuminates it inside.

122

Newgrange Stone Age Passage Tomb

Brú na Bóinne Visitor Centre, Donore, County Meath, Ireland
http://newgrange.com

In County Meath, north of Dublin, stands a manmade mound that covers an acre of land. Built by Stone Age farmers around 3200 BC, this passage tomb predates Stonehenge, the Great Pyramids of Giza, and the Mycenaean culture of ancient Greece.

Kidney-shaped Newgrange stands 39 feet high and 249 feet in diameter. The white quartz facing its eastward side glows gold in the sunrise. Of the 97 large curbstones serving as a retaining wall around the tomb, only some are adorned with megalithic art. Most striking is the entrance stone, engraved with spirals that look like oversize fingerprints.

A stone-lined passage stretches 60 feet into the tomb, to a chamber with three smaller chambers sprouting off it. Excavations done in the 1960s and 70s uncovered both burned and unburned human bones in the passage, although most of the skeletons were missing. Archaeologists also found pendants, beads, and fragments of bone pins.

Like Stonehenge, Newgrange is aligned with the Winter Solstice sunrise. On the days around December 21, the rising sun beams through an orifice called the roof-box straight into the tomb's heart. Beginning around 9 a.m., the sunbeam broadens into the chamber until the entire room is illuminated. This lasts about 17 minutes. The demand to be inside the chamber during the solstice is so immense that there is a free annual lottery.

During the rest of the year, visitors can see the tomb on guided tours that leave from the Brú na Bóinne Visitor Centre on the north side of the River Boyne. In addition, the Visitor Centre has a full-scale replica of the chamber at New Grange, as well as a model of a smaller tomb called Knowth.

In fact, as many as 35 smaller mounds rise along the River Boyne. After Newgrange, Knowth is the next largest, followed by Dowth. UNESCO designated all of them the Brú na Bóinne World Heritage Site in 1993. ⚜

Glasnevin Cemetery

Finglas Road, Dublin, Ireland
http://www.glasnevinmuseum.ie

Daniel O'Connell founded the Dublin Cemeteries Committee in 1828 to develop a garden cemetery like Paris's Père Lachaise. Four years later, Glasnevin Cemetery was established outside Dublin to bury "people of all religions or none." Prior to that, there were no Catholic graveyards in Dublin, only Anglican churchyards.

O'Connell was a Catholic politician who became known as the "Great Liberator." When he was elected to Parliament in 1828, he forced that body to accept Catholics. He agitated for secession from Great Britain—for which he was arrested in 1843. He died in 1847 on a pilgrimage to Rome. The epitaph in his crypt says, "My heart to Rome, my body to Ireland, my soul to Heaven."

Funded by public subscription, O'Connell's

monument is the centerpiece of Glasnevin. The round granite tower, standing 168 feet tall, was designed by George Petrie and completed in 1869. At its top is a viewing room large enough for six people, offering a view that spans from the sea to the Wicklow Mountains in the south and the Mourne Mountains in the north.

At the bottom of the tower is the crypt where O'Connell is buried in a sarcophagus. Members of his family lie in a side chamber.

In 1971, during The Troubles, Loyalists bombed O'Connell's monument. Its three-foot Wicklow granite walls withstood the blast, but the spiral wooden staircase to the viewing room was destroyed. Reconstruction of the stairs was completed in 2014.

Many Irish patriots lie in Glasnevin, including Michael Collins, leader of Sinn Fein during the Anglo-Irish War, who negotiated the 1921 peace treaty before he was ambushed and killed; Eamon de Valera, who opposed the peace treaty and may have ordered Collins's death, but was elected president of the Irish Republic more than once before his death in

Dublin's Glasnevin Cemetery is dominated by a 168-foot-tall tower in memory of Daniel O'Connell; it was bombed by Loyalists in the 1970s. In front of it stands the warrior angel Michael.

1975; and Constance, Countess Markievicz, who was sentenced to death for her part in the Easter Rebellion in 1916, although she was later released. When she died of appendicitis 1927, eight trucks brought funeral flowers to her grave. Charles Stewart Parnell, the uncrowned king of Ireland, believed in Home Rule in the 1880s. He is buried beneath a boulder surrounded by a grove of trees.

Patriot Patrick Pearse delivered the eulogy at the grave of journalist and publisher Jeremiah O'Donovan Rossa, which is echoed in his epitaph: "They have left us our Fenian dead, and while Ireland holds these graves, Ireland unfree shall never be at peace." Rossa died in exile in New York.

Another fierce believer in Irish independence was Maud Gonne MacBride, a legendary English beauty whom Yeats courted unsuccessfully for 30 years. He immortalized her in poetry. A large granite slab marks her grave.

Also buried in Glasnevin is Christy Brown, author of *My Left Foot*, who was born with severe cerebral palsy. ⚜

Aître Saint Maclou

186 Rue Martainville, Rouen, France

Rouen, in northwestern France, was one of the biggest, wealthiest cities of medieval Europe. It served as capital for the Anglo-Norman dynasties, which ruled both England and large parts of France from the 11th to the 15th centuries.

When the Black Plague struck in 1348, it wiped out three-quarters of Rouen's inhabitants. To accommodate the plague victims, a new graveyard opened near the Church of Saint Maclou. All bodies, regardless of social standings, sank into a mass grave.

For centuries, the Catholic Church had preached bodily resurrection. When the trumpet sounded on the final day, all the dead around the world would rise out of their graves to be judged. Bodiless spirits would not rise.

Therefore, bones had to be buried in hallowed ground.

Once Rouen recovered from the Black Death, shops and homes surrounded the little cemetery. Many of these half-timbered medieval buildings survive.

The Plague returned in the 16th century. This time, two-thirds of Rouen succumbed. In order that the Atrium of Saint Maclou could be used again to bury the victims, all the bones remaining in the ground were exhumed and placed into a cloister surrounding the graveyard. The cloisters, begun in 1526, were decorated with skulls, spades, mattocks, and coffins.

When the burial ground was closed by royal decree in 1781, the bones were taken elsewhere. The area became a historical monument in 1862. Today the lovely, macabre atrium remains as the only surviving medieval ossuary courtyard in a European city center. Tour groups in every possible language often disrupt the atrium's peace, but despite that, it is a breathtaking, thought-provoking little space. ⚜

Ossuary, from the Latin for "bones," means a container or vault for the remains of the dead. The only medieval ossuary cloister left in the world remembers victims of the Black Plague.

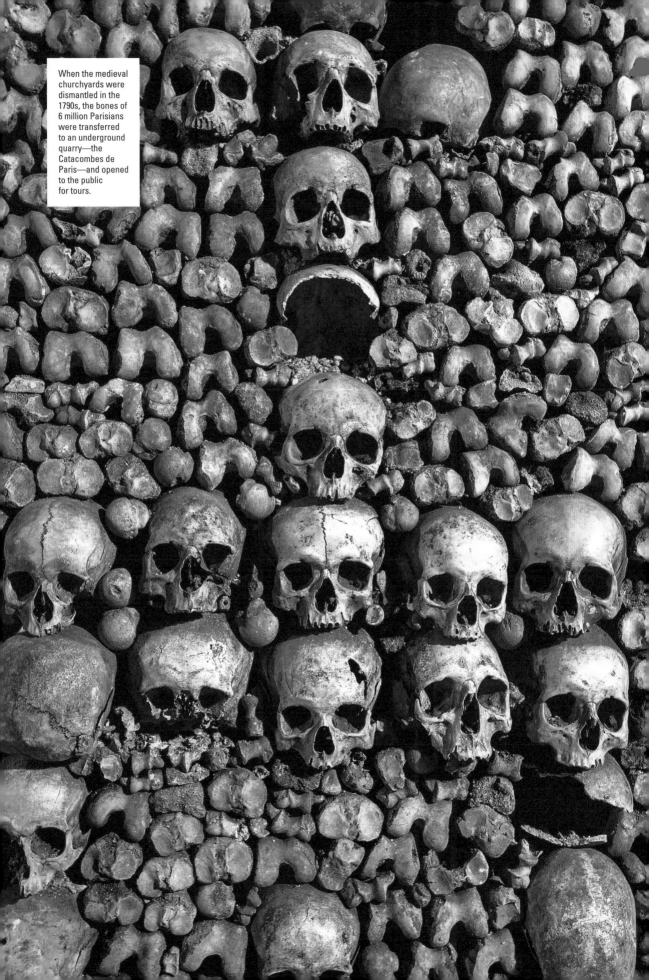

When the medieval churchyards were dismantled in the 1790s, the bones of 6 million Parisians were transferred to an underground quarry—the Catacombes de Paris—and opened to the public for tours.

Catacombes de Paris

1 Avenue du Colonel Henri Rol-Tanguy, Paris, France
http://www.catacombes.paris.fr/en/homepage-catacombs-official-website

The catacombs of Paris originally had nothing to do with death. They began as a network of quarries beneath the city, providing gypsum to build the metropolis. After they'd been mined, the tunnels stood empty and unused.

Simultaneous with the reconstruction of Paris in the 1780s, a movement gained momentum to clean out the old churchyards. The most notorious of them, the Cimetière des Innocents, had been in use since the Middle Ages. Accounts of the period speak of a pestilential hellhole, jammed with liquefying cadavers. Fearing epidemics, the city fathers overrode the protests of the clergy.

Beginning at dusk, workmen emptied the Parisian charnel pits by bonfire light. It was impossible even to consider individualizing the remains. After the bones were loaded onto carts, priests chanting the funeral service followed them to the underground quarry.

In 1786, after the ossuary was filled, the Archbishop of Paris consecrated the bones of approximately 6 million people. Lost among the anonymous dead were Lavoisier, father of modern chemistry; Madame de Pompadour, Louis XV's girlfriend; Saint-Germain, alchemist, spy, and reputed immortal; Montesquieu, the philosopher of the Enlightenment; Mirabeau, who advocated constitutional monarchy and whose corpse was ejected from the Panthéon; Danton, who participated in storming the Bastille to subsequently be guillotined during the Reign of Terror; Robespierre, who engineered the Reign of Terror, then became its prey; and numberless other victims of the Revolution.

In 1874, the Municipal Ossuary opened to viewers, including Bismarck and Napoleon III.

Twenty meters below the streets, a sign warns, "*Arrêtez. C'est ici l'empire de la mort.*" Stop. Here is the kingdom of death. The warning frightened away the Nazis, who never discovered the French Resistance hiding in the catacombs with a radio capable of reaching London.

Beyond the warning, brown knobs of fibulas and femurs rise eight feet high. Skulls form contrasting lines among the leg bones. Empty eye sockets gaze out patiently. French inscriptions, set among the bones, remind visitors of the inevitability of death—as if there could be any question here. Several groups offer tours of the catacombs, or you can rent an audio tour when you buy an entry ticket. ❧

The Panthéon

19 Place du Panthéon, Paris, France
http://www.monuments-nationaux.fr

In 451, Attila the Hun threatened the Roman settlement called Lutecia, where Paris now stands. A shepherdess named Genevieve rallied the people to pray for deliverance. When the Huns broke off the siege, Genevieve was proclaimed a savior. After she died in 502, a small oratory was built over her grave. Clovis, King of the Franks, built a church there after his wife (who became Saint Clotilde) converted him to Christianity. Clovis and Clotilde were both buried inside the church alongside the shepherdess.

In 1754, Louis XV praised Genevieve for helping him to recover from illness and funded a renovation of her church. By the time it had been completed in 1790, the French Revolution had dispensed with both religion and the king. The Marquis de Villette proposed turning the church into a secular temple to honor the great men of France. With much fuss, the philosopher Voltaire's ashes were transferred to the crypt of the newly named Panthéon on July 21, 1791.

Architect Quatremère de Quincy took over the Panthéon that same year. He bricked up the lower windows and replaced all the religious statuary with images of Liberty and France. Even the relics of Saint Genevieve were evicted.

Jean-Jacques Rousseau was pantheonized in October 1794 and his monument placed in the crypt directly across from Voltaire's. During Napoleon's reign, 41 people were pantheonized.

With the restitution of the monarchy in 1816, Louis XVIII signed the Panthéon back over to the Catholic Church. The building was consecrated for the first time in January 1822. Genevieve's relics were somehow reconstituted and returned to the church.

When Victor Hugo died in 1885, he lay in state beneath the Arc de Triomphe before being inhumed in the Panthéon. He was joined by Émile Zola in 1908. They share a vault with Alexandre Dumas, who was not added until 2002. Other internees in the Panthéon range from statesmen to military heroes to scientists. Louis Braille, inventor of the most common alphabet for the blind, was added in 1952. The ashes of

France's national monument to its "great men" holds the graves of Voltaire, Victor Hugo, Louis Braille, and Marie Curie.

Pierre and Marie Curie were transferred to the Panthéon in 1995. She was the first woman to be buried there on her own merits. Pantheonizations continue to this day. Currently, there is a push to add more diversity to those honored. ❧

Cimetière du Père Lachaise

16, rue du Repos, Paris, France
http://www.pere-lachaise.com

In June 1804, Napoleon declared an end to burial within churches, temples, synagogues, and their surrounding properties inside the cities of France. With one proclamation, he undid 1500 years of ecclesiastical history. He also went a long way toward improving the health of city dwellers, who lived crowded around overstuffed burial grounds that had been in use since the Middle Ages.

By December of that year, just as Napoleon declared himself Emperor, the Cemetery of Père Lachaise opened beyond the eastern boundary of Paris. Although it was nondenominational, the cemetery was named for François d'Aix de La Chaise, the Catholic confessor to Louis XIV, who had owned the land in the 17th century. Created as a secular burial ground, Père Lachaise welcomed anyone as long as they could afford a gravesite, which was revolutionary. Père Lachaise allowed families to purchase burial space in perpetuity, rather than requiring the bones to be exhumed after a certain number of years and stored in an ossuary. Even more inspiring, the cemetery of Père Lachaise was designed to look like a park, complete with benches and trees. It welcomed the living as well as the dead.

Despite that, people didn't embrace the new graveyard. For one thing, it lay too far outside the heart of Paris. Also, it initially seemed strange to bourgeois families to spend money to build monuments to themselves.

Père Lachaise, the first ornamental cemetery in the West, is the most visited cemetery in the world.

In response, cemetery organizers hit on the perfect gimmick. In 1817, they relocated the remains of storied medieval lovers Heloise and Abelard and united them for the first time under life-size statues lying in repose beneath a Gothic Revival canopy. A skeleton that had been displayed as Molière's at Alexandre Lenoir's museum of French monuments was transferred to Père Lachaise and given a grand sarcophagus. Like the bodies of Christian saints before them, these relics drew patrons who wanted to be buried nearby.

An anonymous benefactor reclaimed the body of Oscar Wilde from his pauper's grave and transferred it to Père Lachaise. Wilde's new grave was marked by a generously endowed winged sphinx sculpted by Sir Jacob Epstein. For decades, visitors left lipstick kisses on the marble monument. Only recently has a Plexiglas barrier been erected to protect the monument from being loved to death.

As early as 1830, Père Lachaise became a bona fide tourist attraction. It was considered an appropriate place for a family cultural excursion: edifying and a source of national pride. The cemeteries of Paris even had their own guidebook: *Vèritable Conducteur aux Cimetières aux Père Lachaise, Montmartre, Montparnasse, et Vaugirard*, published in 1836. Two centuries later, Père Lachaise is the most visited cemetery in the world, with an estimated 3.5 million visitors each year.

Numerous celebrities came to rest at Père Lachaise: writers (Honoré de Balzac, Colette, Alfred de Musset, and Marcel Proust), painters (Jean-Baptiste-Camille Corot, Honoré Daumier, Jacques-Louis David, Eugène Delacroix, Max Ernst, Amedeo Modigliani, Camille Pissarro, and Georges Seurat), photographers (Nadar), composers (Bizet and Poulenc), and entertainers (Sarah Bernhardt, Georges Méliès, Edith Piaf, and Isadora Duncan), and even Americans (Gertrude Stein and Alice B. Toklas).

The most popular (and most controversial) resident of Père Lachaise is American singer Jim Morrison of The Doors. After he died in a Paris bathtub—the official cause was listed as heart failure, although no autopsy was performed—Morrison was buried in an unmarked grave in Père Lachaise. Various monuments have marked his grave over the years, all of which have been stolen. Currently, the grave is marked by a granite cube with an epitaph in Greek that translates to "True to his own spirit."

The cemetery has struggled with how to accommodate the estimated 1.5 million visitors who come each year to commune with Jim. In sheer numbers, Morrison's grave is one of the major tourist attractions of Paris.

Père Lachaise also has a number of monuments to those who are not buried there. A series of ten memorials remember the French citizens deported to the Nazi concentration camps in World War II. The first monument, unveiled in June 1949 in memory of those who died at Auschwitz, was designed by French deportee Françoise Salmon. ❧

Normandy American Cemetery

Colleville-sur-Mer, France
https://www.abmc.gov/cemeteries-memorials/ europe/normandy-american-cemetery#. WJOqWbYrL2Q

On D-Day, June 6, 1944, the steep bluffs of France's beaches in Normandy were heavily fortified by German forces. Before the Allies took Omaha Beach, 2499 Americans fell. The end of World War II had begun.

Americans slain at Omaha Beach were buried in a cemetery hastily established by the U.S. First Army. Next-of-kin could either request repatriation or else allow their loved ones to be buried permanently in France. About 60 percent of the bodies were sent home. The rest were interred at the Normandy American Cemetery on land donated by France in thanks for America's sacrifice. The Normandy American Cemetery is the largest U.S. World War II graveyard overseas.

A half-mile-long access road leads to the cemetery, which covers 172.5 acres on the headlands above the D-Day beaches. Its $30 million Visitor Center was dedicated by the American Battle Monuments Commission on

Donald Harcourt De Lue's *Spirit of American Youth Rising from the Waves* remembers the soldiers who gave their lives on the beaches of Normandy in World War II.

the anniversary of D-Day in 2007. As the main entrance to the cemetery, the Visitor Center welcomes approximately a million people each year to pay their respects at the most visited American military cemetery outside the United States.

The vast green lawn is divided by paths that form a Latin Cross. Buried here are 9383 men and 4 women who died throughout the war in France. At the time of burial, 307 men were unidentified. Thirty-three pairs of brothers lie side by side.

Past the graves, Donald Harcourt De Lue's 22-foot bronze *Spirit of American Youth Rising from the Waves* stands on a granite pedestal. The naked young man, seeming to soar skyward, is surrounded by a semicircular limestone colonnade that says, "This embattled shore, portal of freedom, is forever hallowed." At each end of the colonnade is a loggia with a blue-tiled ceiling. These display maps of the Battle of Normandy.

Beyond the statue, two olive trees frame the entrance to the Garden of the Missing. The dedication reads: "Here are recorded the names of Americans who gave their lives in the service of their country and who sleep in unknown graves. This is their memorial. The whole Earth their sepulcher. Comrades in Arms whose Resting Place is Known Only to God." Of the 1557 names listed, some are marked with rosettes to indicate that they have since been recovered and identified.

A viewing platform overlooks the battlefield, now nothing more than a peaceful sandy beach that stretches farther than the eye can see. ⚜

The first American cemetery on European soil in World War II is filled with the graves of D-Day forces and other Americans who died in World War II.

129 Cementiri de Poblenou

Avenida Icaria, s/n, Barcelona, Spain
http://www.cbsa.cat

Poblenou Cemetery dates to 1775, when it was the first modern cemetery in Europe to be built outside its city's walls. The original cemetery was destroyed by Napoleon's troops in 1813. After the invasion, the graveyard was expanded and rebuilt by architect Antonio Ginesi. The Bishop of Barcelona reconsecrated it in April 1819.

Poblenou consists of three sections. The first is a labyrinth of seven-story-high mausoleum niches, which is the modern manner of burial in Spain. Beyond that lies a section filled with Gothic Revival mausoleums and chapels built for Barcelona's wealthiest families in the 19th century. The third section mixes niches, monuments, and common graves where the poor are buried.

The monuments include works by some of the most important sculptors and architects working in Barcelona in the 19th and 20th centuries. Plaques identify the significant works.

The best-known grave monument in Poblenou marks the final resting place of textile manufacturer Josep Llaudet Soler. *El Beso de la Muerte* (*The Kiss of Death*) was designed by Joan Fontbernat and carved by Jaume Barba in 1930. The larger-than-life marble statue shows a

The first modern cemetery in Europe to be built outside its city's walls holds one of the world's most affecting grave monuments: *The Kiss of Death.*

young man slumping to his knees, being supported by a winged skeleton. Death bends over to touch her teeth to the youth's brow.

Another lovely sculpture shows a winged angel raising the swooning soul of a maiden toward heaven. The sculpture, carved by Fabiesi, dates to 1880 and adorns the grave of Pere Bassegoda.

Also buried in Poblenou is "Santet," or Little Saint Francesc Canals I Ambrós, who died in a fire at a neighbor's home in 1899. The 22-year-old was selfless in life and is believed to have supernatural powers after death. People leave photos and flowers in the niches surrounding his grave. ⚜

Cementerio de Fisterra

Rúa Alcalde Fernández, 14, Fisterra, A Coruña, Spain
http://www.xn--csarportela-bbb.com/ cementerio-municipal-de-fisterra/

The Romans called this area of Spain *finis terrae*, the end of the earth. The Spanish call it Costa da Morte, the coast of death, because of all the ships that have wrecked here. Cape Finisterre is a rock-bound peninsula on the west coast of Spain, the westernmost point on the European mainland.

In 2000, Spanish architect César Portela chose this sloping site for a very modern cemetery. Sixteen granite cubes, each containing twelve burial niches, were placed at random overlooking the sea. Connected by a winding path, they imitate flotsam washed up by the tide.

In order to match the surrounding native rock, the burial cubes are constructed of locally

quarried slabs of gray Modariz granite, held together by gravity and a thin layer of mortar. The cubes stand 11 feet high and 16 feet long. Their dense stone is impermeable, so that vegetation should be unable to find a foothold.

Near the burial cubes stand the cemetery's chapel, the morgue, and a forensic laboratory. These are also faced with local granite.

Finisterre Cemetery, which has been called one of the most architecturally astonishing new cemeteries in Europe, echoes both the Stone Age dolmens of nearby Galicia and modern minimalist theories of land art. ⚜

130

This 21st-century graveyard applies modernist theories of "land art" to a minimalist burial ground on the edge of the earth.

Trafalgar Cemetery

Gibraltar GX11 1AA, Gibraltar
http://www.visitgibraltar.gi/trafalgar-cemetery

Gibraltar lies at the end of the Iberian Peninsula at the mouth of the Mediterranean. While it shares its northern border with Spain, Gibraltar was captured by the British in 1704 and remains under British protection.

This pretty little graveyard, originally called the Southport Ditch Cemetery, is mostly filled with people who died in the recurrent yellow fever epidemics of the early 19th century. Consecrated in 1798, it was named for the Southport Ditch, part of the town's natural defenses, which dates back to Gibraltar's Spanish era in the 17th century.

Among the approximately 108 people buried here are two sailors wounded during the Battle of Trafalgar in October 1805. Lieutenant William Forster of the *HMS Mars* and Lieutenant Thomas Norman of the *HMS Columbus* succumbed to their injuries after the battle was over. All the men who died during the course of the battle with Napoleon's fleet were buried at sea.

Victims of other Napoleonic sea battles are buried here, however. Among them are Thomas Worth and John Buckland of the Royal Marine Artillery. They were killed by the same shot in the Bay of Cadiz in 1810.

Also here lies John Brugier, who served as purser on the *HMS San Juan Nepomuceno*. That Spanish ship was captured at the Battle of Trafalgar, then towed into the harbor to be used as a supply warehouse.

After 1814, the little cemetery was considered full. Its final burial took place in the tomb in the northeast corner in 1838.

In 1992, the Royal Navy donated an anchor as a memorial to those buried at sea during the Battle of Trafalgar. ⚜

Tourists visit this pretty little cemetery to see the graves of British sailors wounded in the Battle of Trafalgar against Napoleon.

Cemitério Alto de São João

Parada Alto de São João, Lisbon, Portugal
http://www.cm-lisboa.pt/equipamentos/
equipamento/info/cemiterio-alto-de-sao-joao

The monument to Fernando de Olivera stands in Cemitério Alto de São João. In 1904, De Olivera was one of the first Portuguese bullfighters to be unhorsed in the ring. He died of his injuries.

Cholera struck Lisbon in 1833, inspiring Queen Maria II to declare this hill—the Heights of Saint John—a cemetery. Originally intended to serve residents of the eastern side of the city, the First Republic chose Alto de São João as the burial place of its heroes. A cenotaph remembers the victims of the revolution that toppled the monarchy and created the First Republic on October 5, 1910. Buried here is Antonio José de Almeida, who served both as prime minister and as sixth president of Portugal.

The huge cemetery has nearly a hundred streets. They are lined with marble mausoleums, temples, and shrines like Roman aediculae. Architecture ranges from Art Nouveau to Art Deco to Neo-Manueline or Portuguese Gothic Revival. Some tombs have doorposts, window boxes, and tile roofs like the *casas portuguesas* of northern Portugal.

A mausoleum of rough stones is topped by a bronze soldier in a rounded helmet and long coat. Interred here are casualties from World War I.

The domed Gothic Revival mausoleum built by the Viscounts of Valmor hints at why the annual architectural prize in Lisbon is called the Premio Valmor. Between the female statues, the arched doorways, and the flaming urn finials, hardly a surface is left undecorated.

Portuguese bullfighters don't kill the bull, but sometimes the bull kills the fighters. Several bullfighters are buried here under complicated monuments, including Fernando de Oliveira, Daniel Do Nascimento, and Tomas Da Rocha.

The country's first crematory, embellished with flaming skulls, opened here in 1925. It closed 11 years later. The city government blamed politics, although its morbid adornments can't be discounted. The crematorium did not reopen until 1985, after pressure by the local Hindu community. Its remarkably hellish decoration remains intact. Author José Saramago was cremated here in 2010. ⚜

Necropoli della Banditaccia

Via della Necropoli, 43/45, Cerveteri RM, Italy
http://www.comune.cerveteri.rm.it/
turismo-e-cultura/le-necropoli

The Etruscans, who predated the Romans in Italy, stopped cremating their dead in the 9th century BC and started burying their bodies whole.

The hills outside of Cerveteri are made of soft stone called tufa, which is easy to dig and sturdy enough to have withstood millennia. At first, the Etruscans dug simple ditch graves. Then they cut gullies, which became trenchlike streets.

They burrowed into the walls of these sunken streets to dig out caves. More than simple holes in the stone, doorways into these mortuary caves are dressed and decorated, with precisely squared corners. Inside the caves, the Etruscans carved small square rooms, each with a stone bed or burial niches.

As time went on, the underground mausoleums separated from one another. Circular tombs, with their conical caps of sod, look like beehives. Some stand 40 feet high, the dressed stone of their heavy retaining walls braided with carvings. Steep stone steps lead down inside to large antechambers that separate into smaller rooms.

It's not accidental that the exteriors of Etruscan tombs resemble houses. Not only do they have beds—and bedside chairs—some have

Dating to the 7th century BC, the Etruscan Necropolis is composed of thousands of tombs carved out of the soft rock.

reliefs of everyday objects such as sandals, a knife, or a jug, so the dead could use those things in the afterlife. Some graves even have reliefs of pets: a dog, a cat, a goose. Wealthy Etruscans were laid to rest surrounded by familiar things.

Later still, the Etruscans began to build perfectly round tumuli over their tombs. *Tumulus* and *tomb* share the same Greek root, which means "swelling." Tumuli, artificial mounds built over burials, appear around the world from Sutton Hoo to Sweden to Marietta, Ohio.

With their streets and their neighborhoods, their fashionable districts and their run-down areas, the Etruscan burial ground is a true necropolis, literally a city of the dead. ⚜

134 Tomb of Cecilia Metella

Via Appia Antica 161, Rome, Italy
http://archeoroma.beniculturali.it/en/
archaeological-site/mausoleum-caecilia-
metella

Censor Appius Claudius Caecus envisioned the Appian Way, begun in 312 BC, as an easy way to move Rome's army southward during the Second Samnite War. The road is wide enough for five soldiers to march abreast. It stretched almost 350 miles from the Roman forum to the Adriatic Sea.

Even before the road was built, Rome prohibited burial inside city walls. Because of this, roads out of the city were lined with grave monuments. Few of these survive, but the enormous mausoleum of Cecilia Metella, now a museum, gives an indication of what once stood along the Appian Way.

Cecilia was daughter of Quintus Metellus Creticus, conqueror of Crete. She was the daughter-in-law of Crassus, the richest man in Rome, who formed the First Triumvirate with Pompey and Julius Caesar in 60 BC. Not much is known about Cecilia herself, who may have died young. Her tomb was built between 30 and 20 BC

Lord Byron, J. M. W. Turner, and Charles Dickens were all inspired by the round noblewoman's tomb that towers above the ancient Appian Way.

by Crassus's eldest son. The tomb is 60 feet in diameter and stands 71 feet high.

The tomb inspired Lord Byron to daydream about Cecilia in *Childe Harold's Pilgrimage*. J. M. W. Turner's painting *Tomb of Cecilia Metella* hangs in London's Tate Britain Museum. Charles Dickens visited in 1845, writing in *Pictures from Italy*. "Here was Rome indeed at last; and such a Rome as no one can imagine in its full and awful grandeur! We wandered out upon the Appian Way and then went on, through miles of ruined tombs and broken walls."

Out beyond Cecilia Metella's mausoleum, fragments of other tombs still line the old road. Among them are the tombs of Emperor Gallienus, murdered in 268 AD; Seneca, the Stoic philosopher; Romulus, 14-year-old son of Emperor Maxentius; and others. Ten miles of the old Via Appia—its road base of large volcanic stones cemented together with softer gravel—are still visible today. It's possible to walk the same stones as Julius Caesar and Saint Peter. ☙

Emperor Constantine built a church above the early Christian catacombs to hold Saint Sebastian's bones. It is one of the seven traditional pilgrimage churches in Rome.

Catacombe di San Sebastiano

Via Appia Antica 136, Rome, Italy
http://www.catacombe.org/uk_index.html

When this area along the Appian Way was used as a Roman burial ground, it was called *cata cumbas*, the low place near the quarries. Since it already served as a necropolis, it made sense for Christians to bury their dead here as well. From this place, the word *catacomb* spread to refer to any hall of Christian tombs.

Early Christians buried their dead because Christ had been placed whole in his tomb. They anticipated a bodily resurrection, the way Christ had come back. Rather than follow the Roman custom of cremation and entombment of the ashes, persecuted Christians dug their graveyards down into the earth, level after level. The catacomb beneath the Basilica of Saint Sebastian Outside the Walls stretches four levels down into the ground and includes almost seven miles of tunnels.

Shallow niches were carved into the walls of the catacombs just deeply enough to tuck a body inside. The dead would be wound in a sheet and placed here without a coffin, then a slab of

The word *catacomb* originated in this graveyard, where early Christians buried their dead in mazes carved underground.

marble—if they were wealthy—or terra-cotta would seal them inside. These slabs were decorated with birds, fish, or a lamb: symbols of Christianity to people who couldn't read.

Early Christians, many of whom spoke Greek rather than Latin, referred to their burial places as *coemeteria*, equivalent to dormito-ries. The root of *dormitory*, of course, means "to sleep." Christians believed that their dead were merely resting until Christ came again. This is why we refer to a graveyard as a cemetery.

Sebastian, for whom the catacomb is named, was a Roman soldier who realized he could no

longer persecute Christians. Other soldiers tied him to a tree and shot him with their arrows. When he recovered from his wounds, Sebastian began to preach. The Romans captured him a second time and killed him, but Christians buried his body beneath an altar in their catacombs on the Appian Way. When Constantine converted to Christianity in 312 AD, he had a church built above the catacombs and Saint Sebastian's bones moved into the basilica.

In fact, no bodies remain in the catacombs. Most were removed in the 4th and 5th centuries, when the catacombs were pillaged by barbarians who couldn't breach the walls of Rome. ⚜

136 Ancient Pompeii

Scavi di Pompei, Via Villa dei Misteri 2, Pompeii, Italy
http://www.pompeiisites.org

Pompeii was a Roman market town, home to 20,000 people. In 62 AD, a small earthquake caused damage to the city that was still being repaired 17 years later, but Mount Vesuvius appeared to settle back to sleep. What Pompeians didn't know was that

the quake hadn't eased the volcano's internal pressure. Instead, gasses built until they blew off the mountain's crown on August 24, 79 AD. Rocks flew from the volcano, raining down to crush Pompeii. Constant tremors threw down roofs and walls on people who'd just sat down to lunch. Most survivors grabbed what they could and fled.

Others, who remembered the previous earth-quake, gathered provisions and hunkered down in their wine cellars to wait out the eruption. Some, like the priests of the Temple of Isis, spent too long gathering up their treasures. *Everyone* who remained behind died in the city that day.

More than 1500 bodies have been found beneath volcanic ash and debris up to 20 feet deep. The soft parts of the buried bodies dissolved over the centuries, leaving skeletons inside people-shaped cavities. An archaeologist discovered a way to fill the holes with plaster, to make casts in the form of people long gone. Some plaster casts remain at the death scenes, like the Garden of the Fugitives inside Pompeii. Others are in the National Museum of Naples.

In 1748, almost 1700 years after Pompeii was wiped from the map, the discovery of the first tombs outside its walls on the old road to Noceria gave the world a glimpse of Roman mortuary customs. After archaeologists excavated urns in the tombs (where they held ashes from cremations), stone carvers were inspired to engrave urns on headstones that can still be found throughout Europe and the United States. Grave ornamentation changed throughout the Western world.

As many as 3 million people pay their respects at the ruins of Pompeii each year. Dead Pompeii seems enormous. Some villas have red tile roofs—modern restoration work—but most remain mere walls. Behind the city ruins looms the murderer, Vesuvius, a little more than five miles away. ⚜

Mount Vesuvius stands over the ruins of the ancient Roman town of Pompeii. The remains of more than 1500 people have been found where they were buried by volcanic ash. This photo looks across the ruins of ancient Pompeii to the modern city of the same name.

Il Cimitero Acattolico di Roma

Via Caio Cestio 6, Rome, Italy
http://cemeteryrome.it

Prior to 1738, the Vatican forbade burial of unbelievers and foreigners inside Rome. Bodies of Protestants either had to be transported to Leghorn, 160 miles away, or buried with the prostitutes below the Pincian Hill. That changed only after a British ship captured one of Napoleon's vessels and returned treasures it had looted to the Vatican. In gratitude, the pope set aside a field beside the old Roman-era pyramid for the burial of non-Catholic foreigners.

The pyramid tomb of Caius Cestius was built in 12 BC. It's the last Roman-era pyramid to survive, although many of them sprouted up in the last years of the Roman Republic, after Caesar

A Murano glass mosaic enlivens this monument, which combines an unstrung lyre and a simple Protestant cross. The lyre often indicates the grave of a poet.

John Keats didn't want his name to appear on his gravestone, since he was certain he would be forgotten after his early death from tuberculosis.

conquered Egypt. Saint Paul walked past it on the way to his beheading in 65 AD.

Until 1870, a Vatican commission reviewed every monument proposed for the Protestant Cemetery. Since they believed there could be no salvation outside the Mother Church, they forbade the epitaph "Rest in Peace."

Twenty-five-year-old poet John Keats came to Rome in September 1820, already suffering from the tuberculosis that would kill him. He felt he was dying without leaving a mark on the world, so he chose the epitaph "Here lies One Whose Name was writ in Water." A lute with missing strings adorns his tombstone.

In July 1822, poet Percy Shelley disappeared while sailing. Two weeks later, when his body washed up near Viareggio, it was identified by the book of Keats's poetry in its pocket.

Italian law required that anything washed ashore had to be buried immediately, as a precaution against the plague. A month later, Edward Trelawny, Lord Byron, and Leigh Hunt exhumed Shelley's body, doused it with wine, and set it afire. They brought his ashes to be buried in the Protestant Cemetery. His Latin epitaph translates to "Heart of Hearts."

Close by Shelley's grave kneels an angel that has been copied around the world. This is the original *Angel of Grief Weeping over the Altar of Life*. Sculptor William Wetmore Story made his last work to mark the grave of his wife Emelyn in 1895. He died later that same year and is buried beside her. Their son, Joseph—named for his grandfather, who gave the dedication at Mount Auburn Cemetery—was reburied with them. ⚜

From Russian Orthodox crosses to mosaics to statuary, grave monuments jam the Protestant Cemetery of Rome. The old Roman wall stands in the background.

Cimitero di San Michele in Isola

30121 Venice, Italy
http://www.italyheaven.co.uk/veneto/venice/sanmichele.html

Monuments line the cemetery walls on the island of San Michele in Venice.

When Napoleon took control of Venice, he banned burial in the city's churches and churchyards. Since then, Venetians have buried their dead on an island near Murano: San Michele in Isola, the island of the dead.

Originally there were two islands: San Michele in Isola and San Cristoforo della Pace. Venetian churchyards were emptied onto Cristoforo, but when that didn't provide enough space, engineers joined the two islands by filling the canal between them. To this day, San Michele in Isola remains the civil cemetery of Venice.

The cemetery island takes its name from the Church of Saint Michael, built on the island in the 10th century. Dedicated to the archangel Michael, who will hold the scales on Judgment Day, it was restored in 1562 and several times since.

Grave monuments lining the wall of the cloister begin to hint at the impressive skills of Italian sculptors showcased in the cemetery. A breathtaking relief depicts a seated nude holding a book across his hips. Death, wimpled like a nun, grasps his shoulder.

In a garden dedicated to servicemen, a brilliant Murano glass mosaic sparkles on a monument to the ambulance drivers of World War II. On a field of gold, four white-coated men lean above a bleeding soldier.

Inside the Reparto Greco, the section for the Orthodox faith, composer Igor Stravinsky and his wife Vera lie in graves along the back wall. Not far from Stravinsky stands the monument to Sergei Diaghilev, impresario of the Ballet Russe, who brought Russian dancers to the West and changed the history of ballet. Often visitors leave their ballet slippers in tribute.

Tucked away in a tattered garden called the Reparto Evangelico lay Protestant foreigners who died while visiting Venice. The gravestones read "*Hier ruht*" and "Here lies" instead of "*Requiescat en pace*." A rusted iron cross, tilted against the weathered brick wall, bears the simple legend "*Auf wiedersehen.*" Buried here are Russian poet Joseph Brodsky and American poet Ezra Pound. ⚜

The walls of the Cimetero di San Michele are made of beautiful brickwork.

Cimitero Monumentale di Staglieno

Piazzale Resasco, Genoa, Italy
http://www.staglieno.comune.genova.it/en/node/199

In 1886, 35 years after the Monumental Cemetery of Staglieno opened, Parisian newspaper *Le Figaro* crowned it the most beautiful cemetery in the world. To this day, Staglieno is considered the largest open-air museum in Europe, full of one-of-a-kind marble artwork, and repeatedly makes lists of the world's most beautiful graveyards.

Spread over 250 acres, Staglieno has more than 117,000 gravesites, 290 of which are chapels in the arcade around the cemetery. The statuary, which dates to the mid-19th and early 20th centuries, spans Neoclassical, Symbolist, Art Nouveau, and Art Deco in style and ranges from spiritual to erotic to macabre in subject matter. Many sculptures were commissioned pre-need, so the living could enjoy them before being buried beneath them.

The most famous statue in Staglieno is Giulio Monteverde's angel at the Oneto family tomb. The androgynous angel holds one hand to his bare chest, gazing down with a fierce fixed expression. At his side he holds a long trumpet, indicating that he is the angel of resurrection. He will blow the trumpet at the end of the world to call the dead from their graves. Monteverde's angel has been copied in cemeteries around the world. Brooklyn's Green-Wood has at least two copies. Another stands on Monteverde's grave in Rome.

One of the most remarkable sculptures is Giuseppe Navone's monument to Salvatore Queirolo. It combines a rounded sarcophagus decorated with busts of Salvatore and his wife. A life-size skeletal Death, with scythe in hand, sprawls atop the sarcophagus, one hand raised against the angel looming above him. Her hand is raised in benediction or banishment. From the skull's teeth to the olive branch in the angel's hand, this is a masterwork.

Even Caterina Campodonico, who sold peanuts, commissioned a statue of herself in a fringed shawl and lacy apron to mark her grave. The detail on her portrait is amazing, down to the creases folded into her apron. That her monument celebrates a working-class woman makes it unique. ⚜

This grieving angel was carved by Onorato Toso around 1910 for the Ribaudo family. It's only one of the exquisite works of art in Staglieno Cemetery.

Mycenae Archaeological Site

Mykines 212 00, Peloponnese, Greece
http://odysseus.culture.gr/h/3/
eh351.jsp?obj_id=2573

The archaeological site of Mycenae lies 90 miles from Athens. It was once a fabulous kingdom. Modern excavations found evidence of occupation starting around 1950 BC. It suffered periods of disruption around 1200 BC and again a hundred years later, at which time the town was abandoned. There's no entirely accepted explanation for the disruptions, but the prevailing theory is that there must have been war among rival kingdoms.

In *The Iliad*, Homer described the Greek city of Mycenae as well built and rich in gold. In 1874, graves discovered by German archaeologist Heinrich Schliemann bore that description out.

The entrance to the Citadel of Mycenae passes through the Lion Gates. The relief for which they are named—a pillar supported by a pair of lions—was the symbol of Mycenaean royalty. To the right inside the cyclopean walls lies Grave Circle A, a royal cemetery excavated by Schliemann. The 90-foot circle encompasses the stone-lined grave shafts of six Mycenaean chiefs. Five of them wore tightly fitting masks of hammered gold.

One mask depicted a man with a mustache and beard. Schliemann decided that must be the face of Agamemnon, the king of Mycenae who led the Greeks during the Trojan War. In reality, the burial dated to the 16th century BC, 300 years before the Trojan War. However, it is possible to visit Grave Circle A and to stand where the masked prince once lay. The mask itself is displayed in the National Archaeological Museum in Athens.

Outside the Citadel stand the extensive ruins of merchants' houses. Grave Circle B contained 24 graves, which included a vase shaped like a duck and another made of rock crystal, as well as bronze swords and gold beakers. The original treasures are on display at the National Archaeological Museum.

A quarter-mile down the road stands a tholos tomb Schliemann called the Treasury of Atreus. It dates to the later part of Mycenae's history. This is the best preserved of the so-called beehive tombs because it was built into a hill, which left it somewhat protected. Past a 50-foot path lined with towering stone walls stands the 18-foot-high doorway. The round chamber inside stretches 44 feet high. Its walls form a rounded cone, reminiscent of a wicker beehive. When the tomb was new, bronze rosettes decorated its walls. It predates the Etruscan necropolis by 400 years. ❧

Cyclopean walls lead into the so-called Treasury of Atreus in the ruins of Mycenae.

Kerameikos Cemetery

Ermou 148, Athens, Greece
http://odysseus.culture.gr/h/3/ gh351.jsp?obj_id=2392

Northwest of the Acropolis stands the main cemetery used by Athenians in the classical era. Kerameikos is named for the ceramic workshops that once lined Kerameikos Road. The road led to the Diplyon, the double gate that was the main entrance into ancient Athens.

The graveyard was excavated in the later part of the 19th century. Its main entrance is a small gate on Hermes (Ermou) Street. Inside stand mushroom-shaped grave markers, short stone columns ringed at the top with ridges. These are actually the youngest grave markers, in use after fancier markers were banned.

Stelae—upright marble slabs or pillars—became popular grave markers in Athens in the 5th century. Stelae were cheaper than full statuary, but more expensive than ceramic monuments, so they were a way for families to display their wealth in the graveyard. Athenian stelae were often decorated with portrait reliefs. While sometimes figures on them are grieving, the gravestone images always look back at life, rather than capturing death scenes.

The Street of Tombs, begun in 394 BC, is lined with 20 monuments to wealthy Athenians. The most famous gravestone now stands in the National Archaeological Museum, although a replica remains in the graveyard. It marked the grave of Hegeso, who died late in the 5th century BC. She sits in a chair, holding a gem (now missing) in her right hand. Her sorrowful maid stands before her, offering a jewelry box. Originally Hegeso's stele was painted.

The stele to Eukoline, who died circa 380 BC, has an epitaph: "This woman had a name connected with Ease. Now she lies in the earth and shares the fate common to all." Greek epitaphs rarely match the scenes displayed on the stelae. Athenians bought markers already carved and added names and details later as needed.

The stele dedicated to Mika captures her wishing her husband farewell. It looks as if they are shaking hands, a motif re-created on many Victorian grave markers. ❧

141

Sculptor Yannoulis Chalepas's masterwork, the *Sleeping Maiden*, is the most beloved statue in the Proto Nekrotafio Athinon.

142

Proto Nekrotafio Athinon

Anapafseos and Ilioupoleos Streets, Athens, Greece
http://www.athensinfoguide.com/wtscemetery.htm

After Greece became autonomous from the Ottoman Empire in 1828, Athen's First Cemetery was established by royal decree. It was intended as a final resting place for statesmen, artists, and writers.

The cemetery stands at the end of Anapafseos (Eternal Rest) Street. Its monuments range from tombstones to stelae to statues and mausoleums. Some monuments were directly inspired by stelae in the city's ancient Kerameikos Cemetery, but neoclassical sculpture is common as well. In fact, the First Cemetery is Greece's largest outdoor sculpture collection.

The best known of its monuments is the *Sleeping Maiden* made by sculptor Yannoulis Chalepas in 1878. It marks the grave of Sofia Afentakis, about whom not much is known. The sleeping girl reflects the classical belief that death is an eternal, dreamless sleep. It was the last work Chalepas made before his schizophrenia manifested. One story is that he went mad when he realized his lovely sculpture was wrong: He'd carved the girl's legs as slightly bent, but if she straightened them, the mattress on which she lay would have been too short.

Also buried here lies satirical poet Yiorgos Souris, whose marvelous monument shows him hunched over his writing.

The most notorious non-Greek buried in the First Cemetery is Heinrich Schliemann, the German anthropologist who searched for Troy and found Mycenae. Schliemann is buried in a towering mausoleum designed like an ancient Greek temple by Ernst Ziller, the German architect responsible for the National Archaeology Museum. The base of Schliemann's tomb is decorated with a frieze that shows men excavating with shovels, supervised by Schliemann in a pith helmet.

Greece's minister of culture Melina Mercouri has a tall pillar with the relief of an angel holding a downturned torch that echoes the Kerameikos Cemetery. Before her death, Mercouri worked to have the so-called Elgin marbles returned to Athens, where they once graced the Parthenon.

Many of the monuments in the First Cemetery suffer from Athens's notorious smog. The World Monuments Fund, a New York–based watchdog working to preserve important architectural and cultural heritage sites, placed the Proto Nekrotafio Athinon on their World Monuments Watch list in 2012. ⚜

Wiener Zentralfriedhof

**Simmeringer Hauptstraße 234,
Vienna, Austria
http://www.friedhoefewien.at/eportal2/ep/
channelView.do/pageTypeId/75472/
channelId/-54304**

Vienna's Zentralfriedhof is a monument to the greats of classical music: Brahms, Strauss, Schubert, and Beethoven are all buried here.

Planned the year that the Vienna Universal Exhibition brought crowds to Vienna, the Central Cemetery was calculated from the start as a way to celebrate the cultural heritage of the music capital of the Hapsburg Empire.

Architects were imported from Germany to design the cemetery. They suggested straight tree-lined avenues that cut the cemetery into easily accessible blocks. The first burial took place on All Saints' Day, 1874.

In 1888, the bodies of Ludwig van Beethoven, who died in 1827, and Franz Schubert, who died the following year, were transplanted to the Zentralfriedhof and given new monuments. Both had originally been buried in the Währinger Ortsfriedhof, which closed in 1870 and eventually reopened as Franz Schubert Park. Their original grave markers have been preserved along the walls in that park.

Inside the Central Cemetery, a cenotaph for Wolfgang Amadeus Mozart stands between the monuments of the other two classical giants. Mozart had been buried anonymously in a mass grave at Sankt Marxer Friedhof in Vienna, as was the law in the 1790s. The Mozarteum in Salzburg displays a skull claimed to be Mozart's. So far, DNA evidence has been inconclusive.

Because they died after Zentralfriedhof opened, Johannes Brahms (died 1897) and Johann Strauss (died 1899) were buried here from the start, as was operetta composer Franz von Suppé (died 1895) and Hugo Wolf (died 1903), who composed more than 300 German lieder, even setting the poems of Goethe to music.

Academy Award–nominated composer Robert Stolz, who died in 1975, lies near Strauss, who advised him in his youth. Stolz's best-known song is "Two Hearts in Three-Quarter Time."

The 618-acre cemetery has an estimated 3 million interments in 330,000 graves. Not all of the permanent residents were musicians. ❖

This Gothic mausoleum stands near a row of headstones in the Jewish section of Zentralfriedhof.

Storytellers Jacob and Wilhelm Grimm lie beside Wilhelm's sons in the Alter Sankt-Matthäus-Kirchhof in Berlin.

144 Alter Sankt-Matthäus-Kirchhof

Großgörschenstraße 12-14, Berlin, Germany
http://www.zwoelf-apostel-berlin.de/
page/2327/alter-st-matth%C3%A4us-kirchhof

This cemetery began as the burial place for the Saint Matthew's congregation in 1856. Its most famous residents are Jacob and Wilhelm Grimm, whose collected folktales were published as *Children's and Household Tales* in 1812. The book included the stories of Hansel and Gretel, Cinderella, Rumpelstiltskin, and Snow White. The Grimms' second most important work, a German dictionary, was still unfinished at the times of their deaths: Wilhelm in 1859 and Jacob in 1863. The brothers lie beneath simple stones beside two of Wilhelm's sons.

Old Saint Matthew's Churchyard was one of the largest of the 260 graveyards in Berlin until the 1930s, when Hitler's chief architect tried to level the cemetery to build his Germania project. In the name of elevating Berlin as the capital of the Reich, the northern third of the cemetery was dismantled. Protesters halted the destruction.

During the 1970s, more than 50 tombs were labeled *ehrengrab*: honored graves. The honorees included doctor and politician Rudolf Virchow, who named leukemia and thrombosis, among other conditions; composer Max Bruch; women's rights activist Minna Cauer; and physicist Gustav Kirchhoff, discoverer of blackbody radiation. Prussian Empire architects Alfred Messel and Heino Schmieden and sculptor Friedrich Drake are responsible for some of the impressive architecture and sculptures in the graveyard. They rest in *ehrengrab*.

Claus Schenk Graf von Stauffenberg, the resistance hero who attempted to assassinate Hitler with a bomb plot, is honored with a cenotaph here. After his execution, von Stauffenberg's body was cremated and his ashes thrown into a sewage treatment plant.

The cemetery has several special burial sections. The *Garten der Sternenkinder*—Garden of the Star Children—was set aside for stillborn children or those who died before their first birthday. It's a place where parents can grieve and find community.

Memorial Posithiv took over sponsorship of an old tomb and turned it into a memorial and burial place for those who have died of AIDS. Their goal is to erase the stigma attached to the disease's victims. Atop the tomb swoons a marble angel by sculptor Rudolf Pohle.

The mortuary chapel, which dates to 1906, has been repurposed as a museum. A permanent exhibition explores the economic and intellectual faces of Berlin over the past two centuries.

In 2006, Cafe Finovo opened in the former caretaker's house. It invites visitors to linger in the leafy cemetery with good coffee and cakes. ⚜

Waldfriedhof München

Fürstenrieder Strasse 288, Munich, Germany
http://www.muenchen.de/sehenswuer-digkeiten/orte/120255.html#/

At the end of the 19th century, Munich's city planner, Hans Grassel, proposed the groundbreaking concept of integrating a cemetery into a forest. Starting in 1905, tombs, cemetery lanes, and buildings were all incorporated into the old timber forest that belonged to Furstenried Palace, southwest of Munich's city center. The Forest Cemetery's curved footpaths were intended to mimic nature trails, while the low, plain buildings were designed to be shorter than the trees. The focus was on maintenance of the character of the forest.

The original mourning hall, built in 1907, stands 100 meters inside the forest. From the outside, it looks like a traditional forest chapel. It's decorated with murals symbolizing the salvation of man. In contrast, the new brick-and-concrete mourning hall has a very simple, modern style. It overlooks the natural habitat area around the lake.

More than 64,000 graves sprawl across the Waldfriedhof's 400 acres. Michael Ende, author of *The Never-ending Story*, is buried here under a bronze book marked with a yin-yang symbol. Werner Karl Heisenberg, who won the 1932 Nobel Prize in Physics for quantum mechanics, is buried with his parents under a simple stone with iron lettering. Controversial film director Leni Riefenstahl's white gravestone stands near the vast Italian World War II burial ground in the southern part of the cemetery.

Lena Christ, author of *Die Rumplhanni* and *Memoir of a Superfluous Woman,* is buried here as well. Hers is one of the saddest stories in the graveyard. At the end of World War I, Lena left her husband to live with a young singer. Before long, her lover left her. Struggling to make ends meet, Lena forged signatures on some paintings. She was promptly caught. Just before her trial was set to begin, her former husband met her in the Forest Cemetery with a dose of cyanide. At the time of her suicide, Lena was 38. Her grave is marked with a wooden crucifix beneath a sharply pointed roof.

The first Muslim burial ground in Germany opened inside Waldfriedhof in 1955. The New Jewish Cemetery opened there in 1908. ⚜

All of the buildings in Munich's Waldfriedhof were designed to blend into the forest.

Het Oude Kerkhof

**Weg langs het Kerkhof 1A,
AN Roermond, the Netherlands
http://www.oudekerkhofroermond.nl**

H*et Oude Kerkhof* means "the old grave-yard," the most common name for cemeteries in the Netherlands.

In the 18th century, Roermond, in the southern Netherlands, was ruled by the Hapsburg Emperor Joseph II. He banned burial inside churches and churchyards. In response, Roermond opened this graveyard beyond its city walls, near a small, previously established Jewish cemetery. The kerkhof dates to May 1785, which makes it one of the oldest municipal cemeteries in the Netherlands. Because of that, the separation between its Catholic, Protestant, and the two Jewish sections is starkly visible, delineated by hedges and brick walls.

The cemetery is world-famous for one particular monument. In 1842, 22-year-old Catholic noblewoman J. C. P. H. van Aefferden fell in love with a 33-year-old colonel in the Dutch cavalry.

True love reaches beyond the grave in Roermond's Het Oude Kerkhof.

Not only was J. W. C. van Gorkum not noble born, but he was also Protestant. In spite of the outrage their marriage provoked, they remained together almost 40 years. When he died in 1888, he couldn't be buried in her family's tomb because of his faith. Mrs. van Gorkum buried her husband in the Protestant section, along the brick wall, and ordered a double marker: Two nearly identical tall white monuments, each with sculpted arms outstretched. Hers reaches a feminine hand over the top of the brick wall to clasp his masculine hand. Eight years later, when she passed on as well, she was laid to rest along the wall in the Catholic section, beneath a monument eternally joined to his. ❖

Westerveld Cemetery and Crematorium

**Duin and Kruidbergerweg 2-6,
HG Driehuis, the Netherlands
http://www.bc-westerveld.nl**

On January 1, 1866, burial inside churches and graveyards within city limits was banned by the Dutch government. Wealthy residents of Amsterdam, many of them bankers, banded together to find a tranquil location for a family cemetery, where they could buy graves in perpetuity. They purchased the Westerveld estate in 1888.

Landscape architect Louis Paul Zocher, designer of Amsterdam's Vondelpark, was hired to transform the vast dunes into a more intimate landscape. The cemetery opened officially on May 1, 1890.

Westerveld's crematorium, the first in the Netherlands, opened in 1913.

Although the Society for the Introduction of Cremation in the Netherlands organized in the Hague in 1874, it took decades for the idea of cremation to gain acceptance. Westerveld's crematorium was the first in the nation. Designed by architect Marius Poel, it opened in 1913. Physician Christiaan Joannes Vaillant—a member of the cremation society—was the first person to be cremated in the Netherlands in 1914. His gold-colored urn with a bronze tablet stands in the country's first columbarium.

The first Dutchman to be cremated at all has a much grander monument at Westerveld, even though his cremation was done in Germany. Social critic and author Multatuli, who protested

the treatment of natives in Dutch Indonesia, has a tall marlstone monument that holds aloft a flaming torch.

Women's rights advocate Aletta Henriette Jacobs was the first female physician in the Netherlands. In the second columbarium, she shares a monument with her husband: a bronze relief of a couple kneeling on a globe and holding up a flaming torch.

Aviation pioneer Anthony Fokker, who produced 40 kinds of planes for the German High Command in World War I—including the plane flown by Baron von Richthofen—died in New York after selling his aircraft plans to General Motors. Fokker's ashes are buried in a family plot beneath a bird with outstretched wings.

Pianist Youri Egorov defected from Russia in 1976, fleeing anti-gay violence. After releasing 14 albums, he died of AIDS at the age of 33. He's buried beside his life partner, Jan Brouwer, under matching granite drums.

Each year Westerveld hosts a Concerto in Memoriam, attended by thousands, who come to plant flowers in memory of their loved ones. ⚜

Flanders Field American Cemetery

Wortegemseweg 117, Waregem, Belgium
https://www.abmc.gov/cemeteries-memorials/
europe/flanders-field-american-cemetery#.
WJs-hBIrL2R

In the summer of 1918, 40,000 American soldiers entered World War I in Belgium. They faced heavy losses in the Spitaals Woods, not far from where the Flanders Field Cemetery now stands at Waregem.

The cemetery, the smallest of the eight American World War I cemeteries in Europe, is also the only one in Belgium. After the armistice was signed on November 11, 1918, Belgium granted America these six acres permanently, free of charge, as a burial ground.

A small white stone chapel stands in the center of the cemetery, surrounded by four symmetrical areas of headstones, where 368 Americans are buried. The rest were repatriated at the request of their next-of-kin.

Every Memorial Day since 1922, Belgian schoolchildren come to the cemetery to sing "The Star-Spangled Banner." The ceremony—celebrated only in Belgium—brings hundreds to the cemetery each year. During the ceremony, fighter planes fly over the cemetery in the Missing Man formation.

On Memorial Day 1927, nine days after he flew alone over the Atlantic, Charles Lindbergh flew over the cemetery in *The Spirit of St. Louis*. He dropped a bouquet of flowers wrapped in his silk scarf.

The cemetery was named for a poem written by Canadian poet John McCrae in 1915: *In Flanders Field the poppies blow, Between the crosses, row on row.* ⚜

Memorialized in possibly the most famous poem about war, Flanders Field was a battlefield in Belgium repeatedly won and lost in World War I. It is also the name of the only American WWI graveyard in Belgium.

Borrehaugene Viking Graveyard

Birkelyveien 5, Borre, Norway
http://midgardsenteret.no/en/om-midgard/
the-borre-park

In 1852, road workers took fill dirt from one of the small hills on a bluff overlooking the Oslofjord. Inside the mound, they found the remnants of a boat burial.

Antiquarian Nicolay Nicolaysen supervised the excavation of the Iron Age mound, which came to be called Skipshaugen, literally Ship Mound. The grave held the cremated remains of a couple and their dog, along with the bones of three horses. One horse stood, saddled and bridled, inside the ship. Another stood just in front of the ship, along with a sled. Jewelry and bridle pieces found in the grave were decorated with animals whose elongated limbs twined around each other in complicated interlacings. This has come to be called Borre style, which dates to the late 9th and early 10th centuries AD.

Borrehaugene (*haugene* is Norwegian for "mounds") is believed to be the royal burial ground of one of the wealthiest districts in southern Norway. It holds the largest number of Viking Age burial mounds in Scandinavia: 50 in all. The best preserved mounds cluster above the Oslofjord. The largest mound stretches over 148 feet in diameter and stands 20 feet tall.

Originally, this area had been farmland. The soil in the mounds had been used to cultivate grain before it was piled over the graves. Near the mounds, beneath the sod, are the outlines of two great halls and a long house. The use of the site spans from the 7th century until the country was Christianized around 1000 AD.

A reconstruction of the long house opened in the park in 2013. Nearby the Midgard Historisk Senter, the visitor center, explains the lifestyles of the people who lived and died here.

The park is also a popular place for picnics. Wildflowers flood the woods in the spring. The trees are full of birds, including the rare stock dove. ❧

Fifty Viking-era burial mounds overlooking the Oslofjord in Norway enclosed the remains of royalty buried alongside their horses and dogs.

Vår Frelsers Gravlund

Akersbakken 32, Oslo, Norway
https://www.oslo.kommune.no/helse-og-omsorg/begravelser-og-gravferd/gravlunder-og-kirkegarder/var-frelsers-gravlund

Originally consecrated in June 1808, the Cemetery of Our Savior was created in response to the famine and cholera epidemic Oslo suffered during the Napoleonic Wars. Toward the end of the 19th century, the heart of the cemetery was designated a Garden of Honor. Romanticist painter Hans Gude was the first to be buried there, in 1903.

Also buried at Vår Frelsers Gravlund is Henrik Ibsen, who died in 1906. He's best known in Scandinavia for his play *Peer Gynt*, although the rest of the world knows him better for *A Doll's House*. Ibsen's obelisk is marked with a hammer in reference to his poem "The Miner."

Edvard Munch died of pnuemonia at the age of 80. He left many of his paintings to the city of Oslo, which built a museum in his honor.

Painter Edvard Munch, whom we remember for *The Scream*, died of pneumonia in 1944. His monument is topped with a bust by sculptor Arne Durban. It was stolen from the grave in 2004, months after two of his paintings were stolen in a brazen daylight heist. When the bust was returned a month later, the thief simply put it back on the grave marker. The paintings were recovered the following year.

American opera singer Anne Brown, the first African-American admitted to Juilliard and the woman who created the role of Bess in Gershwin's *Porgy and Bess*, married Norwegian Olympic skier Thorleif Schjelderup and took Norwegian citizenship to escape the prejudice against Black opera singers back home. After a long recital career, she was buried at Vår Frelsers in 2009.

The triangular-shaped cemetery is considered an important historical monument—1600 of its 4500 graves contain "significant national or local personalities." They range from politicians to artists, authors, and, strangely enough, economists. ⚜

151 Friedhof Fluntern

Zürichbergstrasse 189, Zurich, Switzerland
https://www.stadt-zuerich.ch/ted/de/index/
gsz/natur-_und_erlebnisraeume/friedhoefe/
friedhof_fluntern.html

On Zurichberg, one of the hills overlooking the city of Zurich, lies Fluntern Cemetery. The parklike cemetery is enclosed by a birch forest, but the graves still lie in precise lines and the grass is meticulously clipped. The immaculate graveyard offers beautiful views of the surrounding area.

Fluntern's most famous resident is author James Joyce, author of *Ulysses* and *Finnegan's Wake*, two of the most controversial modern books yet written. Joyce died of a perforated ulcer in Zurich in January 1941, far from the rainy streets of Dublin. At his request, he was buried in a simple wooden coffin, without a religious service. Since the cemetery adjoins the zoo, his wife Nora liked the thought of him listening to the lions roaring.

Ten years later, Nora followed James to Fluntern, but the space around Joyce's original gravesite had filled by then. Their bodies were eventually exhumed and reburied together. Their gravesite is marked by a sculpture of a bespectacled old man seated with one leg crossed over the other, holding an open book in his hand. It was made by American sculptor Milton Hebald. The monument was unveiled on June 16, 1966. Some call it Bloomsday, the day that the events in *Ulysses* are relived.

Each of the graves in Fluntern is numbered—as are the birdhouses. The Joyces' plot number is 1449.

Other people remembered at Fluntern include Elias Canetti, winner of the 1981 Nobel Prize in Literature, and Nobel Prize–winning chemists Paul Karrer and Leopold Ruzicka. ⚜

In January 1941, James Joyce was hospitalized with a perforated ulcer. He died early on January 13 and was buried without religious ceremony two days later in Friedhof Fluntern.

Lindholm Høje contains almost 700 Germanic Iron Age and Viking burial sites, outlined in stones.

Lindholm Høje Viking Burial Site

Vendilavej 11, Nørresundby, Denmark
http://www.nordmus.dk

On the southern slope of Voerbjerg Hill, looking across the Lim Fjord toward the city of Aalborg, lies a meadow broken up by field stones. The stones and boulders make suspicious patterns. In fact, Lindholm Høje is an enormous graveyard. Almost 700 Germanic Iron Age and Viking graves cover the meadow, going farther back in time the farther up the hill one climbs. The graves date between 400 and 1000 AD.

Men's graves have a triangular outline of rocks or a pattern that resembles a boat: vaguely curved with pointed ends. Women's graves have rounder shapes. During the Iron Age, graves were covered with mounded earth. The Viking-era dead were cremated inside boats pulled inside the stone perimeters. The Vikings believed that cremation freed the spirit and sent it to join the gods. While grave goods—meant to be enjoyed in the afterlife—often didn't survive the flames, some Arab coins and other metal accessories have been recovered that reveal the Vikings' far-flung trading connections.

Throughout the time that Lindholm Høje was used as a graveyard, a village stood nearby. It moved several times over the centuries to escape the sand that drifted around it.

Around the year 1000, sand completely covered the site, burying both the graveyard and a freshly plowed field nearby. Lindholm Høje remained hidden until 1952, when excavation revealed more than 700 graves and 150 Viking boats burned on the site.

The Lindholm Høje Museum was built by the Aalborg Portland Cement Factory in 1989. It contains artifacts excavated from the burial ground and village. It also has an extensive exhibition about the Iron Age, the Vikings, the village, and the dead. ❧

Fabulist Hans Christian Andersen was recognized as a national treasure by Denmark before his death in 1875 of liver cancer.

Assistens Kirkegård

Kapelvej 4, Copenhagen N, Denmark
http://www.assistens.dk

Assistens Cemetery, whose name simply means the "extra cemetery," opened in 1760 as a mass grave for the poor. Each of Copenhagen's five parishes, along with an orphanage and a hospital, had an allotment. Their borders are still visible in section A.

Because the cemetery lay so far out of town, Assistens remained a cemetery solely for the poor until 1785, when Chancellor Johan Samuel Augustin chose to be buried there. His example made the cemetery fashionable. Now it is a pantheon of Denmark's cultural celebrities.

The most famous denizen is Hans Christian Andersen, author of "The Little Mermaid" and "The Snow Queen," who died in 1875. Also buried here are philosopher Søren Kierkegaard; Niels Bohr, Denmark's most famous physicist; Carl Otto, the father of phrenology; Peter von Scholten, governor-general of the Danish West Indies who liberated the slaves there; Finn Juhl, the country's most renowned architect/industrial designer; and physicist H. C. Ørsted, who discovered both aluminum and electromagnetism. They were recently joined by Natasja Saad, a Danish rapper whose stage name was Little T. She was the first female jockey to win a horse race in Sudan.

Surrounded by a long yellow wall, the cemetery is full of trees, ivy, and rhododendron bushes as big as houses. At one point, there was a movement to close the cemetery and turn it into a park, but public outcry was so great that it has been designated a heritage location to be preserved and protected. The Assistens Cultural Center combines a museum, a park, and the lush, green graveyard, but usage of the area is pretty fluid. Danes sunbathe or stroll in the cemetery, as well as picnicking, jogging, bike riding, studying, even courting.

The old chapel has been adapted into a museum that brings people buried in the cemetery to life. Guided tours, held in English and Danish, point out the highlights in the graveyard. ❧

Kungshögarna, the Royal Mounds

Disavägen, 754 40 Gamla Uppsala, Sweden
http://www.raa.se/gamlauppsala

Before Christianity came to Sweden, the Viking kings ruled from Gamla Uppsala, north of Stockholm. This ceremonial site boasted royal palaces, a royal burial ground, and a great temple to Odin, Thor, and Freyr. In the 1070s, Adam of Bremen described the temple as richly decorated with gold.

The temple was probably destroyed in 1087, when Christian King Ingold the First defeated the pagans. The church built above the temple's ruin served as the cathedral of Sweden until 1273. After a fire and renovations, the present church is mostly a reconstruction of the original, but it contains the tomb of Anders Celsius, who developed the temperature scale. Celsius died of tuberculosis in 1744 and was buried beneath the church's floor.

The Royal Grave Mounds date from the same era as the Sutton Hoo mounds, the 5th and 6th centuries AD. These were also made by Vikings, although they did not contain ship burials.

Sweden's King Karl XV commissioned the first excavation of these mounds in 1830. Bror Emil Hildebrand headed the exploration. In the Eastern Mound, archaeologists found a clay pot of burned bones later determined to have belonged to a woman and a boy of 10 to 14. The mound also contained "some burial gifts": carved bronze panels that may have decorated a helmet, whetstones for sharpening knives, bone game pieces, and bones from a bear, hinting that the deceased had been laid out on a bearskin.

In 1874, Hildebrand opened the Western Mound. Discovered inside were the burned cobbles where the grave's owner had been cremated, along with the remains of two dogs and a goshawk, probably for hunting in the afterlife. The other relics included Roman ivory gaming pieces, three 4th-century cameos from the Near East, and golden foil that may have adorned clothing. There were also remnants of a Frankish sword decorated with garnets and gold.

The Middle Mound has not been investigated.

Around the mounds lies a vast grave field that once held as many as 3000 smaller mounds. Farmers destroyed most of them over the years. Only 250 mounds remain.

Although the people buried in the Royal Mounds remain unidentified, the barrows themselves continue to be Sweden's oldest national symbols. ⚜

These symbols of Sweden date back to the 5th and 6th centuries, the same era as the Viking graves at Sutton Hoo.

<table>
<tr><td>155</td></tr>
</table>

Skogskyrko gården

12233 Enskede, Stockholm, Sweden
http://www.skogskyrkogarden.se

Skogskyrkogården, the Woodland Cemetery, was a collaboration between Sweden's most famous architects, Gunnar Asplund and Sigurd Lewerentz. They wanted to create a new kind of burial ground, neither a landscaped garden cemetery nor a necropolis in the Islamic tradition. They intended that individual graves would be absorbed into the forest and meadows.

They chose a former quarry for their site, then planted it with pine forest. Burial sites were assigned irrespective of status. Grave markers were restricted to small headstones or wooden crosses, tucked between the trees at regular, if not precisely measured, intervals. Reflecting the reserved Lutheran culture that influences so much of Swedish design, there are no sculptural monuments.

Candlelight flickers
from graves in
Stockholm's
Woodland
Cemetery on All
Saints' Day.

Beyond the main gate of the cemetery, the land rises into the long slope of a hill. A tall granite cross stands halfway up the incline. This path, labeled the "Way of the Cross" in Lewerentz's original drawings in 1915, has become the iconic image of the cemetery. The cross's vertical column can be read as a declaration of humanity's presence on earth.

The original crematorium, designed in 1940 by Asplund, has been likened to a functionalist version of the Parthenon. It was the final work he did for the cemetery, where he was buried later that year.

As intended, the minimalist cemetery was a modernist revelation, as influential for the 20th century as Père Lachaise was for the 19th. Architectural historian Marc Treib called the Woodland Cemetery "the most perfect and profound modern landscape on the planet."

Nine years after her death, the ashes of film star Greta Garbo were interred here in June 1999. Her niece Gray Reisfield said, "She had a deep love of Nature—typical of any Swede—and now she has come home to the beautiful Skogskyrkogården." Garbo's simple headstone is adorned with her signature in gold letters, without an epitaph or date of death.

The Woodland Cemetery became a UNESCO World Heritage site in 1994. ❧

156 Hólavallagarður Cemetery

Suðurgata, 101 Reykjavík, Iceland
http://www.kirkjugardar.is/sida_en.php?id=3

Icelanders used to believe that the first person buried in a graveyard would not decay, but would watch over those who came later and lead them to the afterlife. In November 1838, Guðrún Oddsdóttir, a magistrate's wife, was the first to be buried in Hólavallagarður.

The name of this quiet cemetery means "garden on a hill." Once, Iceland was heavily forested, but humans have lived on the island since the 9th century. Most of the trees are gone, which makes heavily forested Hólavallagarður doubly refreshing. The cemetery trees are mostly birch and rowan, although spruce, poplar, larch, and willows thrive here as well. Dozens of redwings hop between the lichen-covered headstones.

Because Iceland was a relatively poor country until recently—it's been independent from Denmark only since 1944—the graves aren't as ostentatious as contemporaries in Britain or America. However, thanks to Iceland's isolation, the cemetery has been untouched by war. The iron fences that surround its family plots weren't

Built into a forest overlooking the capital city of Iceland, this cemetery has been called the largest museum in Reykjavík.

melted down for wartime recycling, as they were in other countries.

Buried here are Jón Sigurðsson, who led the 19th-century Icelandic Independence Movement; Hannes Hafstein, a poet and politician whose beautiful grave has a rondel sculpted by Einar Jónsson; and Bríet Bjarnhéðinsdóttir, a politician who was one of Iceland's early advocates for women's rights.

In 2007, Congresswoman Asta Ragnheiður Johannesdóttir recognized the cultural importance of the cemetery. She moved to put it under the control of the Minister of the Environment so that it could be preserved to teach about Iceland's environmental and cultural heritage.

Art historian Björn Theodor Björnsson wrote *Marks of Remembrance* for the cemetery's sesquicentennial in 1988. He called Hólavallagarður the "largest and oldest museum in Reykjavík…a living exhibition [that] opens itself to anyone who can read the hand of the sculptor and discern from symbols and types of font the thoughts and deeds of the dead." ❧

EASTERN EUROPE

The Old Jewish Cemetery of Prague is twelve layers deep, with gravestones dating back to the Middle Ages.

157

Starý Židovský Hřbitov

23/3 Široká Street, Prague, Czech Republic
http://www.jewishmuseum.cz/en/explore/sites/old-jewish-cemetery

Traditionally, Jews practiced inhumation—burial in earth—in observation of Genesis 3:19: "Earth you are and to Earth you shall return." We hear it most commonly as "ashes to ashes, dust to dust."

Founded early in the 15th century, the Beth-Chaim (Hebrew for "House of Life") served as the only Jewish graveyard in Prague for three centuries. Its oldest surviving monument dates to 1439.

During the years when Jews were confined to the ghetto, the little 2.5-acre Jewish cemetery was penned in by buildings on every side and could only increase in height. Whenever the graveyard filled, a layer of dirt would be brought in and the headstones moved atop it. The ground, now twelve layers deep, is covered by 12,000 surviving tombstones. As many as 100,000 people are buried here.

The most visited tomb belongs to Rabbi Yehudah Loew ben Bezalel (1512–1609). Rather than a tablet marker like the others, the rabbi has a tomb of pink stone, guarded by lions. Rabbi Loew is said to be one of only four men, post-Adam, to see the Garden of Eden. While there, he was granted the secret name of God, which can create life. With it, he created a golem to protect the ghetto.

When visiting a Jewish grave, it's traditional to leave a pebble. The ritual traces back to the Hebrews wandering in the desert after Moses led them out of Egypt. Anyone who fell during that 40-year trek was buried at the wayside. Travelers who passed those lonely graves added a rock as a way of keeping the burial mound fortified.

While the Nazis demolished many Jewish graveyards, this one was spared to become part of a museum to be built to the extinct race. The beauty of this little graveyard must have touched some Nazi soul.

Now overseen by the Federation of Jewish Communities of the Czech Republic, the Old Jewish Cemetery welcomes 10,000 visitors each year. Most bring pebbles in their pockets for Rabbi Loew. ❧

Vyšehradsky Hřbitov

**K Rotunde 10, Vysehrad,
Prague, Czech Republic
http://www.prague.eu/en/object/places/
148/vysehrad-cemetery-and-slavin-
vysehradsky-hrbitov-a-slavin**

Vysehrad means "high castle." The rocky
promontory that bears the name was
the site of the original wooden castle in
Prague, built around the 10th century. This was
where Princess Libuše prophesied that Prague
would become a rich and powerful center of trade.

Founded in 1869 on the site of a small
parish cemetery that no longer exists, Vysehrad
Cemetery was conceived as a shrine to the
heroes of the Czech Nationalist Revival. It contains more than 600 graves, including poet Jan
Neruda and playwright Karel Capek, who coined
the term *robot*.

Vysehrad Cemetery has been called a
gallery of modern Czech sculpture, ranging in
style from Art Nouveau to Cubism. The life-size
bronze bust scowling from composer Antonin
Dvořák's grave was made by Ladislav Saloun,

An angel lays a palm
frond atop the Slavin
Pantheon in Vysehrad
Cemetery. The Roman
use of palm fronds
to symbolize victory
transformed into the
Christian symbol of
triumph over death.

sculptor of the Jan Hus monument in the Old Town Square.

The centerpiece of the cemetery is the towering Slavin Pantheon, after which the cemetery is sometimes mistakenly called. *Slavin* translates loosely to "Hall of Fame." Designed by Antonin Wiehl and completed in 1894, the mausoleum—topped with an angel laying a palm frond—is the final resting place of over fifty Czech artists and sculptors, including Art Nouveau painter Alfons Mucha.

An arcade, also designed by Wiehl, rings the cemetery. Under its covered passageway, curving Gothic arches delineate each burial plot. Baroque ironwork encloses some of the graves. Some display elaborate mosaics: a rain of gold stars on a cobalt glass background or a caparisoned knight like something out of Rackham's *King Arthur*. Others, less romantic, confront the reality of death. One marble sarcophagus is embellished with a gruesome skull crowned with a pair of twining snakes.

The annual Prague Spring International Music Festival starts at the grave of composer Bedřich Smetana on May 12, his birthday, then proceeds into town to the Municipal House. ⚜

Cimitirul Vesel

Săpânța 437305, Romania
http://romaniatourism.com/press-the-merry-cemetery.html

Behind the Church of the Assumption in this small town in northern Romania lies one of the country's most popular tourist sites: the Merry Cemetery.

In 1936, Ioan Stan Patras started carving crosses to mark graves in the old church cemetery. Over the next 40 years, he carved several hundred. Each was individually tailored to the deceased: Mothers cook for their families, shepherds tend their flocks, priests envy carousers. Patras painted the crosses in bright colors, with blue—the color of heaven and freedom—predominating.

More recent crosses have witty poems as epitaphs. The grave of Dumitru Holdis, who was too fond of *tzuica*, the local plum brandy, reads: "Tzuica is a genuine pest. It brings us torture and unrest. Since it brought them to me, you see—I kicked the bucket at 43."

Before his death in 1977, Patras carved his own memorial, complete with a self-portrait. The cross now stands near the entrance to the church. Its epitaph relates that he supported his family since he was 14. The footboard of his grave is emblazoned with *Creatorul Cimitirului Vesel*: Creator of the Merry Cemetery.

Patras's apprentice, Dumitru Pop, carries on the work. He lives in the master's house, now a small museum.

More than 700 handmade monuments brighten the cemetery. Pop creates 20 or 30 new ones each year, as needed. ⚜

The Merry Cemetery was the brainchild of a woodcarver who illustrated the lives—and deaths—of people in his village. The brightly painted grave markers draw tourists from around the world.

Moscow's Novodevichy Cemetery is a sculpture-illustrated Who's Who of Russian culture, from Anton Chekov to Boris Yeltsin.

Novodevichy Proyezd

2 pro. Luzhnetsky, Moscow, Russia
http://www.novodevichye.com

On the Moscow River beside the Novodevichy (New Maiden) Convent lies Novodevichy Cemetery, a Who's Who of Russian culture. Full of statues and inspired, immense works of art, it's well worth a summer afternoon's wander.

The cemetery grew in popularity in the 1930s, after Nikolai Gogol, author of *Dead Souls*, was reburied here. The cemetery where he had previously been buried was demolished by order of Stalin.

When Nikita Khrushchev was buried here—instead of with the other Soviet heroes on Red Square—the cemetery was closed to the public in 1971. Khrushchev lies near the back of the cemetery, at the end of a tree-lined footpath. His monument—composed in alternating black and white to represent the dual sides of his nature—was designed by Ernst Neizvestny, a controversial sculptor whose work Khrushchev had dismissed as "filth."

Thanks to glasnost, the cemetery reopened to the public in 1987. More recent political figures are buried here now. Boris Yeltsin, Russia's first president, lies beneath an enormous tricolor Russia flag carved in stone by Georgy Frangulyan. Raisa Gorbachev, wife of the final leader of the Soviet Union, is buried beneath a bronze statue of a lovely mournful girl with flowers in her hair. Even Vyacheslav Molotov, who gave his name to the flammable cocktail, rests here.

The grave of author Anton Chekhov is marked with a seagull in reference to his play. Also buried here are composers Sergei Prokofiev, Alexander Scriabin, and Dmitri Shostakovich; ballerina Galina Ulanova; film director Sergei Eisenstein; Konstantin Stanislavsky, the father of method acting; Mikhail Bulgakov, author of *The Master and Margarita*; Aleksey Tolstoy, whose novel *Aelita* is considered the foundation of Soviet science fiction; and Vladimir Mayakovsky, whose satirical play *The Bathhouse* critiqued the Soviet State.

Also buried here are a number of cosmonauts, including the second man in space and the first to command the Soviet cosmonaut corps. ❧

Lush, green Rasos Cemetery climbs up and down hills and winds between trees. Its monuments veer between traditional orthodox crosses to extremely modern portrait sculpture.

Rasų Kapinės

Rasu g. 32, Naujininkai, Vilnius, Lithuania
http://www.vilnius-tourism.lt/en/what-to-see/places-to-visit/places-of-interest/rasos-cemetery

Lushly green Rasos Cemetery stands on Ribiskes Hill. It is named for the district of Vilnius, where it's located, which was heavily rebuilt during the Soviet area. The Soviets planned to destroy the whole cemetery in the 1980s to build a major highway across the land. Luckily, a downturn in the economy stalled the project. After Lithuania won its independence in 1990, Lithuanian and Polish authorities collaborated to restore the cemetery.

Beyond its lovely red brick entry gate, the cemetery is divided by Sukileliai Street into an old and a new part. It's been closed to new burials, except in family plots, since 1990, so it's primarily a museum of famous people from the 19th and 20th centuries.

Lithuanians, Poles, and Belarusians are buried here: cultural heroes, composers, book smugglers, organizers of secret performances of banned plays, priests who were political activists, actresses, librarians, filmmakers, architects, poets, botanists, and concentration camp survivors. Buried here are Marek Konrad Sokolowski, a Polish, Ukrainian, and Russian guitarist who invented the harp guitar and won "the first guitarist of Europe" award in Vienna in 1858. Thirty-five-year-old painter, photographer, and composer Mikalojus Konstantinas Ciurlionis died in 1911 after a profound depression. During his ten-year career, he wrote almost 400 compositions, including a cantata for chorus and orchestra, and illustrated many of his musical pieces using synesthesia. Also remembered here is Rimantas Daugintis, a Lithuanian sculptor who died of self-immolation in 1990, protesting the Soviet regime.

The inscriptions in Rasos Cemetery are mostly in Polish, but the grave of Petras Vileisis, a philanthropist and engineer who held art exhibitions in his palace, has a Lithuanian epitaph. Dr. Jonas Basanavicius, a scientist and patriot who signed the Act of Independence of Lithuania, has an epitaph written in a style of Lithuanian that predates its written standardization.

Jozef Pilsudski, Poland's first president, was born in 1867 in what is now Lithuania. He helped reestablish Polish independence and its annexation of Vilnius in 1920. His heart lies in Rasos Cemetery under a black granite slab, beside his mother. The rest of him is buried in Wawel Cathedral in Krakow. ⚜

Rasos Cemetery is the most visited place in this neighborhood, which suffered under the hands of the Soviets and has very few surviving buildings that predate 1940.

Cmentarz Powązkoski

Powązkowska 14, Warsaw, Poland
http://warsawtour.pl/en/tourist-attractions/
pow-zki-cemetery-cmentarz-pow-zkowski-
3487.html

Named for the village outside the walls of Warsaw where it was created in 1790, Powazki Cemetery was designed by Dominik Merlini, architect to King Stanislaw August Poniatowski. The king and his family are buried in the catacombs, an aboveground gallery surrounding the graveyard with burial niches.

The cemetery's church, Saint Karol Boromeusz, was funded by King Stanislaw and his brother Michal, the Primate of Poland. The church was destroyed during the Warsaw Uprising in 1944. Falling shells started a fire that burned so hot that it melted the church's bells. The current church is a reconstruction, completed in the 1960s.

More than a million people may be buried in Powazki Cemetery, but it is impossible to say. The cemetery's records were also destroyed in World War II. Known to be buried here is painter Władysław Podkowiński, whose nightmarish *Frenzy of Exultations* was the first work of Polish Symbolism. Also here is poet and journalist Miron Bialoszewski, who was deported to a German work camp. His *Memoir of the Warsaw Uprising* was published in 1970. Hanka Ordonowna was an actress and cabaret singer who married an earl, but was still deported to the gulag in Uzbekistan. After the war, she rescued Polish orphans and set up an orphanage in Mumbai, funded by Indian princes.

Eugeniusz Bodo was not as lucky. Although he was one of the most popular comedians between the wars, Bodo was arrested by the Soviets and perished in the gulag. The plaque with his name in the catacombs is a cenotaph, since he was buried in a mass grave in "a Russian camp."

The Polish film industry is also represented in Powazki. Krzysztof Kieślowski, the director of *Amator*, lies in a grave beneath a sculpture of two hands forming a square like a framing a camera shot. The sculpture was stolen in 2013 and ended up in a scrapyard, but has been replaced. Jazz musician Krzysztof Komeda was a film composer who wrote the scores for many of Roman Polanski's films, including the haunting lullaby in *Rosemary's Baby*.

Every year since 1975, celebrities gather in Powazki on All Saints' Day to raise money to restore the cemetery. ☀

Perhaps more than a million people are buried in Powazki Cemetery, but the records were destroyed in World War II.

Glorious in the autumn, Warsaw's Powazki Cemetery is an encyclopedia of Polish history.

Kerepesi Cemetery

Fiumei ut 16, Budapest, Hungary
http://nori.gov.hu/nemzeti-sirkert

Kerepesi Cemetery in Budapest was designed as a national pantheon. Buried here are artists, writers, scientists, and politicians, including Ferenc Deak, who negotiated limited autonomy for Hungary from the Austro-Hungarian Empire; Lajos Batthyany, who served as prime minister in Hungary's government during the Empire, but sided with rebels who wanted autonomy and was executed by a firing squad as a traitor; architect Miklós Ybl, who designed Saint Stephen's Basilica and the Opera House; and architect Odon Lechner, whose use of polychrome tile makes Budapest so distinctive. Janos Kadar, Hungary's socialist leader for three decades, was buried here in 1989.

In addition to its historical importance, the cemetery is full of varied and exciting sculpture. The first democratically elected prime minister, Jozsef Antall, was buried here in 1993 beneath a sculpture by Miklos Melocco that combines four full-size horses and riders escaping from a shroud. Lajos Kossuth, the first leader of democratic Hungary—who lived and died in exile in Italy after his planned revolution failed—is buried in an enormous tomb guarded by a snarling lion. Endre Ady, the father of modern Hungarian lyric poetry, has a particularly hunky man seated on his grave. A woman in a long dress holding a wreath overhead stands on painter Mihaly Munkacsy's grave.

One of the most emotionally affecting statues in Kerepesi is a nude man, down on one knee, with his face curled over his knee as if weighed down by sorrow. Lichen crawls over the surface of the stone as if he's been in that position awhile.

November 1, All Saints' Day, is a public holiday in Hungary and the best day to visit the cemetery. Families clean and tidy graves, before decorating them with yellow chrysanthemums. They light red candles and leave them burning on the graves. In the evening, thousands of tiny flames flicker throughout the cemetery. ⚜

Most often, the figures who mourn in graveyards are female. This unusual male statue grieves in Budapest's Kerepesi Cemetery.

Mirogoj Cemetery

Aleja Hermanna Bollea 27, Zagreb, Croatia
http://www.gradskagroblja.hr

East of Italy, across the Adriatic Sea and sandwiched between Slovenia and Bosnia, Croatia was once a Roman province. The Croats settled there in the 7th century, accepted Charlemagne as their king and Christianity as their religion in the 8th century, and defeated the Byzantines and Franks in the 10th century to form their own kingdom. By the 12th century, they had become part of Hungary and remained so for centuries, through the Ottoman Empire, the Hapsburg Empire, and World War I. In 1929, Croatia became part of Yugoslavia, which fell to the Nazis in 1941. The country became Communist after the war. Free elections weren't held until 1990.

Ljudevit Gaj, a 19th-century linguist, owned a mansion at the foot of Medvednica Mountain. After his death, Zagreb's city fathers bought his estate to build a cemetery.

In 1879, construction began on the towering wall that surrounds the cemetery, topped at intervals by 20 cupolas that make it look like a citadel. Austrian architect Hermann Bollé designed the interior of the wall as a neo-Renaissance arcade, now full of memorial statuary. Bollé's design was completed in 1929, half a century after he began, but he was buried in Mirogoj in 1924.

The entrance to Miragoj Cemetery passes by the Church of Christ the King, designed by architect Ivan Meštrović.

The cemetery's motto is "What Père Lachaise is to Paris, Mirogoj is to Zagreb." The cemetery serves as a gallery of artwork by Croatian painters, sculptors, and craftsmen. It repeatedly makes the lists of the most beautiful cemeteries in Europe.

Buried here are Miroslav Krleza, a novelist and playwright who was kicked out of the Communist Party in 1939, but was rehabilitated by Marshal Tito and went on to assemble the *Encyclopedia Yugoslavia*; Franjo Tudjman, an orphan who became the youngest general of the Yugoslavia People's Army under Tito, before becoming the first democratically elected president of Croatia; Nobel Prize–winning chemist Vladimir Prelog; and abstract expressionist painter Edo Murtic, whose murals decorate the cemetery.

Miragoj also has two Olympic medal–winning basketball players: Drazen Petrovic, who played for the Portland Trail Blazers and New Jersey Nets, and Krešimir Ćosić, who went on to coach Yugoslavia's team to an Olympic silver before becoming a diplomat in Washington, DC.

Like Hungary's Kerepesi Cemetery, the best time to visit Mirogoj is on All Saints' Day, November 1. ⚜

Austrian architect Hermann Bollé designed the neo-Renaissance arcade, now full of memorial statuary, in Zagreb's Miragoj Cemetery.

Šehidsko Mezarje Kovači

Between Jekovac and Sirokac Streets, Sarajevo, Bosnia and Herzegovina
http://www.sarajevo-tourism.com/cemetery-at-kovaci-(shahid-martyr-cemetery)

Sarajevo is unusual in Europe in that its old town neighborhood hosts a mosque, a synagogue, an Orthodox church, and a Catholic church in close proximity. Pope Francis called it the Jerusalem of Europe for its tolerance of many faiths, all of which are represented in the Kovaci Cemetery.

The large cemetery lies a five-minute walk from Sarajevo's old town. It has been called the Kovaci Cemetery, Martyrs' Memorial Cemetery, or Shahids' Cemetery at Kovaci. *Shahid* is Arabic for "martyr."

Around the main cemetery stand very old gravestones, some of which date to the 16th century. Some of the tombs go back as far as the 15th century. There were around 400 of these historic gravesites in the cemetery when the Austro-Hungarian monarchy decided to turn the graveyard into a park in the 19th century.

Unfortunately, the area was needed as a burial ground again in 1992 when Bosnia declared its independence from Yugoslavia. Kovaci is the main (but not only) cemetery where Bosnian Army soldiers were buried during the aggression against Bosnia and Herzegovina, which lasted from April 1992 until December 1995. Sarajevo itself suffered the longest siege in modern warfare, beginning on May 2, 1992, and dragging on for 1425 days. In addition to sniper fire, an average of 329 grenades struck the city each day. A total of 11,541 residents, 1500 of them children, died in the attacks. Most are buried here. In fact, the vast majority of people buried in the Kovaci Cemetery were killed during the siege of Sarajevo. Since the end of the violence, the cemetery serves as a war memorial.

The first president of the independent Bosnia and Herzegovina, Alija Izetbegovic, was buried here after his death in 2003. His grave marker is a perforated gray dome supported by twisting white pillars. ✣

This predominately Muslim cemetery holds an estimated 10,000 victims of the siege of Sarajevo, the longest siege in modern history.

166 Friedhof Jüdischer Chernivtsi

Zelena Street, 13, Chernivtsi, Ukraine

Tsarist Russia confined Jews to a geographical ghetto along its western border. In this so-called Pale of Settlement, 1.5 million Jews lived in some 700 towns and cities with Jewish majorities. Chernivtsi in the West Ukraine, near the borders with Romania and Moldova, was a major Jewish center in the 19th century.

Chernivtsi's large cemetery served as a resting place for poets, actors, scholars, and religious figures. Buried there are fabulist Eliezer Steinbarg and Eduard Reiss, the first Jewish mayor of Chernivtsi, as well as Jewish soldiers from the Austrian army who died in World War I. There is also a memorial for Jewish civilians from Chernivtsi who died in the Holocaust. Epitaphs in the graveyard appear in German, Hebrew, Yiddish, Romanian, Russian, and Ukrainian.

Jewish tombstones are considered sacred,

This jam-packed old Jewish graveyard—which dates from the second half of the 19th century—barely survived World War II and the Soviet era.

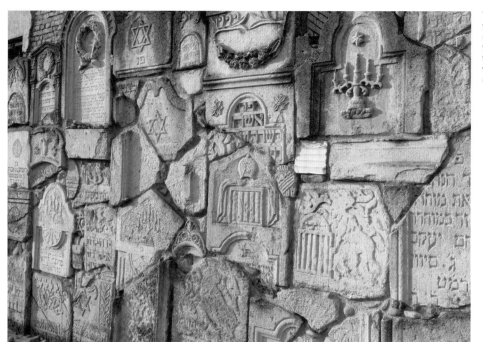

The Memorial Wall of the Jewish Cemetery of Chernivtsi holds fragments of broken tombstones decorated with lions, flowers, and candelabra.

manifesting the eternal essence of the deceased and linking the living and the dead. Traditionally, people would pray at the graves of relatives for protection.

The symbols engraved on the Chernivtsi stones speak across the years. A lighted menorah spans the front of a woman's grave from 1871. Several stones are decorated with pitchers, signifying the Levites, who perform the ritual hand-washing in the synagogue. A bird with leaves in its beak refers to the dove who returned to Noah after the Flood, carrying the promise that the bad times had ended. A sad-eyed lion gazes from one grave marker, while a flower droops over him.

Familiar graveyard motifs echo here as well. A disembodied hand plucks a branch starred with flowers, harkening back to the *Song of Songs*: "God's hand went down and plucked a flower." Broken flowers, particularly broken rosebuds, symbolize women or children who die in the bloom of youth.

Because this is one of the largest surviving Jewish cemeteries in all of Central and Eastern Europe, the Jewish Cemetery of Chernivtsi serves as a tourist destination. ⚜

The Church of the Holy Sepulchre is controlled by the Greek Orthodox, Roman Catholic, and Armenian Orthodox churches. The tomb is considered a common area of worship.

MIDDLE EAST

Church of the Holy Sepulchre

Via Dolorosa, Jerusalem, Israel
https://churchoftheholysepulchre.net

According to the gospels of Matthew, Mark, and John, Jesus Christ was crucified at Golgotha. "The place of the skull" has been identified as an area of stone quarries outside the old city wall. Christ was buried temporarily in a borrowed tomb dug out of the rock nearby.

Ten years after the crucifixion, the city walls of Jerusalem expanded to encompass the area of execution and burial—which is why the Church of the Holy Sepulchre now stands inside the Old City of Jerusalem.

In 326 AD, Roman Emperor Constantine ordered Jerusalem's Temple of Venus demolished to make room for a church. Eusebius, writing 200 years later, said the demolition uncovered an empty tomb. This was identified as having belonged to Jesus. Constantine's church was built around both the tomb and the Rock of Golgotha, believed to be where Christ's cross had been erected.

In 614, the Persian army destroyed the church. After it was rebuilt, Christian worship was tolerated there for 300 years, but anti-Christian riots in 966 burned away the church's dome. The Caliph al-Hakim commanded the church be demolished in 1009.

Byzantine Emperor Constantine Monomachus built a new church in 1042 in the same place, which drew pilgrims from all over Christendom. For the most part, they were welcomed by the Muslim rulers of Jerusalem, until the Seljuk Turks conquered the city in 1077. Rumors of mistreated Christian pilgrims—and a desire to "liberate" Christianity's holy places from Muslims—inspired the First Crusade in 1096.

The Crusaders recaptured the city in 1099. When they rebuilt the church again, the Rock of Golgotha was enclosed in its own chapel. The Church of the Holy Sepulchre was reconsecrated on July 15, 1149. That church is essentially the same as can be visited today.

Sometime in the Middle Ages, the tomb was covered with marble cladding to prevent pilgrims from chipping the rock away. The marble was removed in 2016 during restoration work, revealing the tomb's wall for the first time in centuries. ⚜

167

Mount of Olives Cemetery

Jericho Road 52, Jerusalem, Israel
http://mountofolives.co.il

The cemetery on the Mount of Olives has been used since antiquity. It's believed that anyone buried on the Mount of Olives is exempt from the ritual of atonement. Because of that, pilgrims have taken dirt from the Mount of Olives Cemetery to sprinkle on graveyards elsewhere in the world, hoping to improve their ancestors' chances of resurrection.

According to Jewish tradition, the Mount of Olives is where Elijah will sound the shofar to announce the resurrection of the dead on the final day. Those buried here will be the first to revive. They are buried with their feet pointing toward the site of the Temple.

Jews have sought burial here for the better part of 3000 years. The earliest tombs stand in the Kidron Valley at the foot of the mountain. One is believed to be the grave of Absalom, third son of the biblical King David. Another is dedicated to Zechariah, a priest in the First Temple. The inscription on a third mentions the sons of Hezir, a priestly family from two millennia ago.

168

This enormous graveyard on the Mount of Olives has been a burial place chosen by Jews since the days of antiquity.

More recent notables buried here include medieval sage Rabbi Ovadiah of Bartenura, who led the Jews of Jerusalem in the Middle Ages; Eliezer Ben-Yehuda, father of modern Hebrew as a written language; S. Y. Agnon, Israel's Nobel Prize winner in Literature; and former prime minister Menachem Begin and his wife, Aliza.

The enormous cemetery covers the entire western slope of the mountain and much of the southern slope. With approximately 70,000 gravestones, the Mount of Olives Cemetery is considered 80 percent full. The Visitor Center near Absalom's grave can direct visitors to specific tombs. ✤

169 The Rock-Cut Tombs of Petra

Petra Archaeological Park, Jordan
http://in.visitjordan.com/Wheretogo/
Petra.aspx

Between the Red Sea and the Dead Sea in southern Jordan stands Petra, ancient capital of the Nabateans. A natural fortress on a mountain pass, Petra grew wealthy in the 1st century BC as a crossroads for trade. Caravans hauling Arabian incense, Chinese silks, and Indian spices passed through for more than four centuries, until Rome grew so strong that it altered the trade route. Afterward, Petra withered, known only to the Bedouin until Johann Ludwig Burckhardt, a Swiss scholar traveling as a Muslim pilgrim, visited in 1812.

Petra, listed as a UNESCO World Heritage Site in 1985, is one of the world's richest archaeological sites. Jordan set aside 100 square miles as a national park in 1993, protecting temples, tombs, and theaters carved into the russet sandstone mountains.

Archaeologists aren't sure who was buried in the Urn Tomb, named for the small urn carved at its top. Since it dates to the middle of the 1st century AD, it's possible it was made for Malchus II or his father, Aretas IV, who died circa 40 AD. The tomb's three burial chambers have been empty since antiquity. During the Byzantine era, Bishop Jason converted the main chamber into a church.

Beside the Urn Tomb stands the smaller Silk Tomb, named for the dramatic color of its sandstone facade. It dates to the second half of the 1st century AD. Like the other tombs, it was looted centuries ago, so it's not clear whom it belonged to.

The ornate face of the Corinthian Tomb is badly eroded. Burckhardt named it for the decorations atop its pillars, but on closer inspection, the capitals are actually a Nabatean design. Some theorize that this was the true tomb of Malchus II.

The facade of the vast Palace Tomb originally stood three stories tall. Its design recalls the Golden House of Nero in Rome. Originally this tomb held four burial chambers. In front of it sprawls a large stage.

Separate from the others stands the tomb of Sextius Florentinus, the Roman governor of Petra around 126 AD. His tomb is marked with a Latin inscription. ❧

Nabatean and Greco-Roman architectural styles blend together in Petra's tombs, most of which were looted before the Roman-era trading city was rediscovered by the West.

Wadi Al-Salaam

Najaf, Iraq
http://whc.unesco.org/en/tentativelists/5578/

The biblical patriarch Abraham is said to have passed by where the holy city of Najaf now stands. Abraham, who appears in the texts of all three monotheist religions, predicted that one day a major shrine would stand here. He also promised that those buried in Najaf would be guaranteed to enter Paradise.

Centuries later, when Mohammed died in 632 AD, there was conflict over who should succeed him. Some believed that his cousin, adopted son, and son-in-law Ali ibn Abi Talib would have been the Prophet's choice. Those who revered Ali became known as Shi'at Ali, forebears of today's 150 million Shiites. Ali eventually became the fourth caliph of Islam, but he was assassinated five years later in his capital of Kufa, six miles from Najaf. Because of Abraham's promise, Ali wished to be buried in Najaf.

Caliph Harun al-Rashid ordered a grand mausoleum be constructed atop Ali's grave in 791 AD. Called the Shrine of Imam Ali, the tomb attracted pilgrims and clerics, who settled in the area. Now Najaf, which means "dry river," is one of the biggest cities in Iraq, with a population of around 600,000.

Also in Najaf lies the vast necropolis called Wadi Al-Salaam, the Valley of Peace. The graveyard stretches more than six miles, encompassing 1485.5 acres. It has been in continual use since the days of Ali, so no one can guess how many people have been buried there. Estimates run as high as 5 million. Both in size and in permanent residents, this is the largest graveyard in the world.

Sarcophagus comes by way of Latin from the Greek for "flesh-eating stone." Certain types of limestone speed decomposition, so it was believed that bodies laid to rest in limestone caskets were literally eaten.

Most of the graves are covered by sarcophagi built of baked bricks, some of which are sheathed in ceramic tiles. Among them stand room-size mausoleums, topped with domes. Beneath these lie underground burial vaults, reached by ladders. During the Iraq War, the Iraqi militia hid in the maze of tombs to ambush American soldiers.

The prophets Hud and Saleh rest in Wadi Al-Salaam, along with Ayatollah Sayyid Muhammad al-Sadr, a Shiite cleric murdered in 1999. Shiites from around the world wish to be buried here. ⚜

171 The Shrine of Hazrat Ali

The Blue Mosque, Great Masoud Street, Town Center, Mazar-e-Sharif, Afghanistan

Ali ibn Abi Talib—adopted son of the Prophet Mohammed—became the fourth caliph of Islam in 656 AD. Although it is widely believed that Ali was buried in Najaf after his assassination, Afghans disagree. They believe that Ali's body was secretly brought to Mazar-e-Sharif and buried shortly after his death.

The location of Ali's grave was forgotten until the 12th century, when a mullah's dream revealed it. When the hill was excavated, they discovered a steel door leading into a tomb. Inside lay Ali's body, with wounds as fresh as the day he received them.

Seljuk Sultan Ahmad Sanjar built a large shrine over the tomb, but it was destroyed by Genghis Khan in 1220 AD. The memory of Ali's tomb dimmed again until Sultan Baiqara built the present shrine in 1480.

The building fell into disrepair until the 1860s, when Sher Ali Khan restored it. He died in 1879 at the start of the Second Anglo-Afghan War. His tomb stands west of the main door to the shrine.

A larger tomb stands in memory of Wazir Akbar Khan, who drove the British Army out of Kabul in 1842.

Unfortunately, non-Muslims are not allowed into Ali's tomb, but the Blue Mosque is beautiful nonetheless. Its intricately painted polychrome tiles are replaced constantly, both because of the elements and because pilgrims break off pieces as mementos.

A tall pigeon tower stands on the east side of the shrine. It's said that this site is so holy that gray pigeons who come here will turn white within 40 days. Every seventh pigeon is believed to contain a spirit. ⚜

The exquisite Blue Mosque has tombs of several religious figures, including—perhaps—Ali, the son-in-law of the Prophet Mohammed.

Kart-e-Sakhi Cemetery

Mazar-e-Sakhi Road, Kabul, Afghanistan

Wrapped around the Kart-e-Sakhi Shrine—the second most holy Shia shrine in Afghanistan—lies the enormous Kart-e-Sakhi Cemetery. Most of its graves are marked with slabs of stone, but some have small shrines or roofed metal cages to protect the monuments inside. Modern gravestones sometimes have portraits etched into them. These always belong to men. In comparison, women's graves rarely acknowledge the deceased by name. Instead, she is remembered by the name of her son or father.

Children greet visitors to the cemetery, offering to wash headstones for money. Most make 10 afghanis—about 15 cents—for each gravestone they sprinkle with water. Afghanis believe that watering graves not only keeps the memory of the dead fresh but helps to wash away their sins. It also helps plants to grow in the arid soil.

After decades of war, many Afghan families visit the graveyard frequently. Hundreds of thousands of Afghanis died during the civil war, which spanned from 1979 to 2002. Others died in attacks on the nearby shrine or in the American war against the Taliban.

In Kabul, the cemetery is a part of life, not apart from it. Most Afghanis visit the cemetery on Thursday or Friday, when they celebrate the weekend. Young lovers come here to have private cell phone conversations, protected by the assumption of mourning. Some men bring in roosters for cockfights. Balloon sellers and cotton candy vendors roam between the gravestones. ✤

Victims of Afghanistan's civil war are buried in this enormous graveyard in Kabul.

172

Completed in 1963, the tomb of poet Omar Khayyám graces the town where he died in 1131.

Omar Khayyám Tomb Complex

Nishapur, Razavi Khorasan Province, Iran

During the Middle Ages, Nishapur served as a center for scholars. Omar Khayyám, arguably the greatest mathematician to live between Euclid and Copernicus, came to Nishapur around 1075 AD. He taught geometry, physics, and mechanics, but his astronomical observations challenged the earth as the center of the solar system. At his death at the age of 83 in 1131, Khayyám was respected as the greatest scientist of his age.

Seven hundred years after his death, Edward FitzGerald translated some of Khayyám's poetry into English. Since then, the *Rubáiyát of Omar Khayyám* is the second most popular work of Muslim literature after *The Thousand and One Nights*.

Khayyám's tomb is the most popular tourist destination in Nishapur, as well as one of the most visited burial sites in Iran. It sits in the Bagh-E Mahrugh, a lovely garden where visitors sip tea while being serenaded by caged birds. Khayyám's Islamic Revival tomb was designed in 1963 by Iranian architect Hooshang Seyhoun. The tomb has been described as an upended wine cup, an inverted hyperbolic cone, or an airy net of crisscross marble. Diamond-shaped tiles are inscribed with Khayyám's writing.

In the southern section of the same garden stands the 16th-century domed mausoleum of Imamzadeh Mohammed Mahruq, a descendent of the Prophet Mohammed who died a martyr. In another pretty garden nearby stands the domed octagonal mausoleum of 12th-century writer Farid Al-Din Attar and the grave of 19th-century painter Kamal-ol-Molk. ❧

Mevlana Museum

**Aziziye Mah., Mevlana Cd. No:1,
Konya, Turkey
http://www.kulturvarliklari.gov.tr/TR,44116/
konya-muze-mudurlugu.html**

Konya, in central Turkey, dates back to the Hittites nearly 4000 years ago. Saint Paul visited in Roman times. Since it straddled ancient trade routes, Konya flourished in the 12th and 13th centuries as the capital of the Seljuk Sultanate of Rum.

Son of an Islamic scholar, Jalal al-Din was born in 1207, near Mazar-e Sharif in what's now Afghanistan. Twelve years later, the family fled the Mongols, going first to Mecca. In 1228, they came to Rum.

Jalal al-Din was initiated into Sufism by a student of his father's. He became a Sufi teacher himself in 1240. In the West, he is known simply as Rumi, which means he came from Rum. In Turkey, he is called Mevlana: Our Master.

In 1244, Rumi left his students to follow Shams al-Din, a wandering mystic. His students wanted their teacher back, so they murdered the holy man in 1247. That drove Rumi to withdraw from the world to write poetry.

His masterwork was the *Masnavi*, a massive poem consisting of nearly 25,000 rhyming couplets. He dictated the ecstatic stanzas to his disciple wherever the poetry came to him: dancing, eating, night or day. Rumi believed in love as a spiritual path. He founded the order of the Whirling Dervishes in 1273 to express God's love.

The Sufi mystic known in the West as the poet Rumi founded the Order of the Whirling Dervishes in 1273. Their monastery—where the Master is buried—is now a museum.

When Rumi died on December 17, 1273, he was buried beside his father in a rose garden belonging to Sultan Ala al-Din Kayqubad. Husamettin Celebi, Rumi's successor, built a mausoleum over his master's grave. Turquoise faience tiles cover its conical dome.

In September 1925, Ataturk dissolved all the Sufi brotherhoods in Turkey. The following year, he decreed that Rumi's mausoleum and its adjacent monastery would become a museum. They opened on March 2, 1927.

Rumi's grave continues to attract pilgrims, especially on the anniversary of his death. His epitaph reads, "Do not seek our tombs on this earth. Our tombs are in the hearts of the enlightened." ❧

175 Divan Yolu Cemetery

**Divan Yolu and Babiali Street,
Cemberlitas, Istanbul, Turkey
http://www.turkeyfromtheinside.com/istanbul-guide/d/1007-stanbuldvanyolu.html**

Divan Yolu is an ancient street, laid out by Emperor Constantine in the 4th century AD, when Constantinople was capital of the Byzantine Empire. Divan Yolu was the main boulevard, leading from the palace at the center of the city through the Golden Gate in the city walls until it connected with Rome, a thousand miles away.

Divan Yolu remains the main street running through the historic quarter of Istanbul. At the corner of Babiali Street lies a small cemetery dominated by the octagonal tomb of Sultan Mahmud II. The domed building was funded by the Sultan's son Abdulmejid and designed by the Ottoman court architect Garabet Balyan. It was completed in 1840.

Sarcophagi draped with green cloths crowd the tomb's interior. In addition to the sarcophagus belonging to Sultan Mahmud II, both his son Sultan Abdulaziz and his grandson Sultan Abdulhamid II have monuments. Several female relatives are also buried inside. Overhead hangs a massive crystal chandelier. The tomb is open to the public and visitors are welcome to pray.

The last Ottoman prince, Sehzade Ertugrul Osman, was a student in Vienna when he received word that his family had been deposed. He lived modestly in exile in New York City until he was granted Turkish citizenship in 2004. He died five years later, at the age of 97, and was buried in the mausoleum beside his grandfather Abdulhamid II.

The cemetery holds the graves of dozens of other statesmen. Among them are Ziya Gokalp, the founder of Turkish sociology who inspired Ataturk's reforms. His grave has a lovely marble tablet filled with calligraphy.

While many of the graves have sarcophagi atop them, the people are actually buried beneath rather than inside them. ⚜

Divan Yolu, a small graveyard in Old Istanbul, holds the remains of three sultans and many other statesmen, including the last Ottoman prince.

Sehidler Khiyabani

Mehdi Hüseyn Street, Baku City, Azerbaijan

The people buried on this hill overlooking Baku City are heroes of the struggle for Azerbaijan's independence from Soviet Russia. Martyrs' Lane, the central avenue through the cemetery, is lined with polished black marble etched with photographic portraits. All of the dead buried along the lane share January 20, 1990, as their date of death. That was the day the Red Army fired into crowds gathered in support of Azerbaijan's independence.

Officials estimate 135 Azerbaijani civilians died, as many as 800 were injured, and 5 went missing. The unofficial death toll ranges as high as 300. Soviet President Mikhail Gorbachev later apologized to Azerbaijan by admitting: "The declaration of a state emergency in Baku was the biggest mistake of my political career."

The dead were brought to Kirov Park, where they were buried side by side in two long rows that culminate at a massive eternal flame. The flame burns in a round plaza at the edge of the hillside, overlooking Baku City below and the Caspian Sea beyond.

First among the black stones stands a double portrait of a young bride and groom. Ilham Allahverdiyev was shot and killed by Soviet troops on January 20. Ferize, his bride, committed suicide two days later. Their grave is celebrated as a monument to true love.

Parallel to the central avenue are more graves, casualties of the 1992 Nagorno-Karabakh War. Azerbaijian lost this war against Armenia.

176

Among the dead lie two journalists, both of whom have been declared national heroes.

Elsewhere in the cemetery, a monument commemorates British military personnel who died in Azerbaijan at the end of World War I. Because the British prevented a Turkish takeover that the Azerbaijanis welcomed, their monument is controversial. ⚜

Black marble tombstones etched with photographic portraits lining Martyrs' Lane remember the victims of the Soviet attack on Azerbaijan in January 1990.

AFRICA

The Great Pyramids

**Nazlet El-Semman, Al Haram,
Giza Governorate, Egypt
http://www.sca-egypt.org/eng/
SITE_GIZA_MP.htm**

The Egyptian pyramids are the only surviving Wonder of the Ancient World. Earth's most famous monuments to the dead were already old at the time of King Tut, who died in 1352 BC.

The Great Pyramid was the tomb of Khufu, whom the Greeks called Cheops. For 4000 years, Khufu's pyramid was the largest manmade structure on the planet. It was constructed between 2584 and 2561 BC. The entrance on its north face was made in the 9th century AD by Caliph al-Mamun, who was searching for treasure. Archaeologists think the pyramid may have been robbed as early as the First Intermediate Period, between 2181 and 2055 BC.

Inside the Great Pyramid lie three empty burial chambers. The one that had belonged to Khufu is built entirely of pink Aswan granite.

Outside the pyramid, archaeologists discovered three empty boat pits. In 1954, they uncovered a dismantled boat of Syrian cedar that had been used before it was buried. It is displayed in the Solar Boat Museum nearby. In 1987, while exploring a fifth pit with cameras, archaeologists found a perfectly preserved boat that is 4500 years old.

The other large pyramids—graves of Khafre (Chephren) and Menkaure (Mycerinus)—stand in descending order of age and size. Khafre's pyramid stands on a rise, so it appears as big as Khufu's. Some of its original limestone cladding is still in place.

Menkaure's pyramid, constructed at the end of the pyramid-building age, survived a sultan's attempt to dismantle it in 1215 AD. Workmen attacked the pyramid for eight months, before admitting defeat. It is so immense that the stones they removed are barely missed.

Only 300 tickets are sold to enter the pyramid of Khufu each day. There doesn't seem to be a limit on the Pyramid of Khafre. At the time of this writing, Menkaure's pyramid is closed. ⚜

One of the last surviving Wonders of the Ancient World served as the tomb of Pharaoh Khafre. The sphinx is the embodiment of Khafre.

Valley of the Kings

West Bank, Luxor, Egypt
http://www.sca-egypt.org/eng/site_vok.htm

Tomb entrances gape from the walls of the Valley of the Kings. None of the tombs hold bodies any longer, carried away by looters or archaeologists, but the remarkable mortuary decorations on the walls remain.

Thutmose I was likely the first pharaoh to be buried here, although there is some debate about when. Archaeologists disagree over the dates of his reign, which either spanned from 1506 to 1493 BC or 1526 to 1513 BC. Burials continued from the XVIII to the XX Dynasties. Sixty-three tombs have been discovered in the Valley of the Kings. Not all of them are open on any given date, because they close periodically for cleaning and conservation. Some tombs are only ever open to scholars. Most visitors concentrate on visiting only a handful of the rest.

Ptolemaic and Coptic graffiti hints at how long the tomb of Ramses IV has been open to tourists. The grave was robbed in antiquity; Ramses's body has never been found. His huge pink granite sarcophagus gapes beneath the goddess Nut painted on the ceiling. This tomb was the first to be electrified in 1983.

The tomb of Seti I is the longest tomb in the valley. It has wonderfully preserved reliefs, which recount the Egyptian version of the biblical flood.

The tomb of Thutmose III is more challenging to visit, since it has steep steps up to its doorway and a sharp descent inside. It also has a pit intended to thwart tomb raiders. Its illustrations are unusual: stars and papyrus and Thutmose's mother in the form of a tree. The mummy himself now rests in the Museum of Egyptian Antiquities in Cairo.

Of course, the most famous tomb in the valley belongs to Tutankhamun. It's on the smaller side and not as impressively painted as the others, since the boy king died in his late teens. When the tomb was discovered in 1922, it had not been opened since the ancients sealed it up 3300 years ago, so all its treasures remained in place. Now they are on display at the Cairo Museum.

In 2014, an exact replica of King Tut's tomb opened in Luxor, to ease the crush of visitors in the original. At some point, the original tomb will close to allow conservators to stabilize its murals. ⚜

The tomb of Ramesses VI in the Valley of Kings was robbed in antiquity, but the paintings covering its walls detail the origins of the sun and life itself.

Egypt's Valley of the Kings has 63 magnificent royal tombs, all different from each other. In this image, Anubis, the god of the dead, is opening the mummy's mouth so he can breathe and speak.

For 600 years, this cemetery—now in a neighborhood of Tunis—was used to bury children.

Tophet de Salammbo

Route de La Goulette, 7016, Tunis, Tunisia
http://www.gpsmycity.com/tours/
carthage-ruins-walking-tour-2987.html

This graveyard, a remnant of the North African city of Carthage, is one of the most bitterly debated finds in archaeology. The fact that there are no adult graves in this burial ground seems to underline both ancient texts and current archaeological evidence that the children buried here were intentionally sacrificed. Many of the grave stelae are dedicated to Baal and Tanit, patron gods of Carthage.

The word *tophet* comes from the Hebrew *topheth*, a place of burning or sacrifice. Both Jewish and Christian scriptures mention places where children were sacrificed. While the Bible doesn't specifically mention a tophet at Carthage, numerous tophets have been discovered around the eastern Mediterranean.

This cemetery was used between 730 BC and 146 BC, at which point ancient Carthage was destroyed by the Romans. Based on changes in the grave markings and forms of burial, there seem to have been three separate periods of use over the centuries.

The original layer contained burials of infants in small vaults with beads and amulets. Low stones marked the earliest graves.

Above the original layer, graves were marked with sandstone markers painted yellow, red, or blue. These feature the sigil of Tanit: a triangle with a disc at its apex, a symbol that looks to modern eyes like a child or a doll. These second-level graves held urns packed with tiny cremated bones. Some urns also contained bones from animals that had clearly been sacrificed.

Some archaeologists believe that the children's graveyard was merely segregated from the adults—the way our "Babyland" sections are separate in modern cemeteries. The inscriptions that reference sacrifice simply indicate that families hoped for new children to replace those who died.

Josephine Quinn, a lecturer in ancient history at Oxford University, disagrees. According to Quinn, the inscriptions do not hold out an offering for future favors but instead speak of fulfilling a promise already made. She suspects the sacrifices were philanthropic acts, made for the good of the whole community. ⚜

Avalon Cemetery

Region D, Zone 1, Tshabuse Street, Chiawelo, Soweto, South Africa
http://www.joburg.org.za/index.php?
option=com_content&view=article&id=
7319&catid=88&Itemid=266

When it opened at the height of apartheid in 1972, Avalon Cemetery was reserved exclusively for Blacks. It became the final resting place of many of South Africa's "struggle heroes." During the 1970s and 1980s, their funerals drew huge crowds in a powerful expression of defiance. Mourners—some dressed in fatigues and carrying wooden rifles—sang prohibited freedom songs and chanted banned slogans until security forces drove them away.

Just inside the cemetery's entrance stands a memorial to Lilian Ngoyi, who died in March 1980. She was the first president of the African National Congress's executive committee. She also served as first president of the Federation of South African Women.

At her side, sharing her headstone, is Helen Joseph, a white woman. Joseph, another founding member of the Federation of South African Women, spearheaded the march to protest the pass law in 1956. In 1962, she was the first person to be placed under house arrest. Her final banning order was lifted when she was 80.

Elsewhere in the cemetery lies Charlotte Maxeke, who organized an anti-pass protest in 1913. She went on to found the Bantu Women's League of South Africa, forerunner of the ANC, and the Industrial and Commercial Workers' Union in 1920.

In 2010, all three women's graves were declared national heritage sites.

Victims of the Soweto Student Uprising are buried here as well. Twelve-year-old Hector Pieterson was the first fatality, although fifteen-year-old Hastings Ndlovu was the first child to be shot that morning. Tsietsi Mashinini, who led the march, died in exile in 1990.

The *Mendi* Memorial remembers the 607 men who drowned when the *SS Mendi* sank in the English Channel during World War I. The men in the South African Native Labour Contingent were on their way to fight in France. In 1995, Queen Elizabeth II unveiled a plaque in their honor, inscribed with words supposedly spoken by the ship's chaplain as the ship went down: "I, a Xhosa, say you are all my brothers: Zulus, Swazis, Pondos, Basutos. We die like brothers. We are the sons of Africa."

At 425 acres, Avalon is the largest graveyard in South Africa and it is almost full. ⚜

An estimated 200 people are buried each weekend in Avalon. Most of them are second burials in graves. Some graves may hold three bodies.

Eastern European Jewish refugees were detained here by the British during World War II. When the survivors immigrated to Palestine, they left a pocket-size graveyard behind.

בית זרים
1940 BLESSED BE THE TRUE JUDGE 1945

Saint Martin's Jewish Cemetery

Raymond Rivet Street, Bambous, Mauritius
http://www.lemauricien.com/article/
jewish-cemetery-shalom

Five hundred miles off the coast of Madagascar lies the little tropical island of Mauritius. Bambous is a small village southwest of Port Louis, the tiny nation's capital. Three kilometers north of Bambous, a tiny Christian cemetery holds an even smaller Jewish section, where all the dates of death range between 1941 and 1945. Straight lines of tombstones record the places from which the deceased have come, along with their occupations.

In November 1940, 1700 Jewish refugees reached the port of Haifa aboard the steamer *Atlantic*. They'd fled their homes in Vienna, Gdansk, and Czechoslovakia, but because they arrived in Palestine without official immigration papers, the British government deported them to a detention camp in Mauritius.

Life in the underprovisioned camp, called Beau Bassin, was brutal. As many as 54 internees died in the first year of tropical diseases, inadequate clothing, and a shortage of food. The only free Mauritian Jew stepped in to aid the refugees. He purchased part of a Christian cemetery near the camp and sought aid for them around the world. In all, 128 refugees died in the camp and were buried on the island. Their graves were originally marked with local volcanic stone.

After the war, survivors were given a choice to emigrate legally to Palestine or to return to their home countries. None of them chose to stay behind to tend the tiny graveyard.

In 1999, the South African Jewish Congress replaced all the gravestones that had deteriorated over the years. The cemetery was finally consecrated. A small museum opened in the chapel nearby. ⚜

W. E. B. Du Bois Memorial Centre for Pan-African Culture

1, Circular Road–Cantonments, Accra, Ghana
http://webduboiscentreaccra.ghana-net.com

William Edward Burghardt Du Bois was born in Massachusetts only six years after emancipation. He was the first African-American to earn his doctorate from Harvard University.

In 1909, Du Bois co-founded the National Association for the Advancement of Colored People. For the next 14 years, he edited the NAACP's journal *The Crisis*. He resigned from the organization in 1934 and went to Atlanta University to chair the Department of Sociology.

In 1960, he moved to Accra, the capital of Ghana—a West African country bordered by Cote d'Ivoire, Burkina Faso, and Togo—to work on his *Encyclopedia Africana*. The masterwork was still unfinished at the time of his death at age 95 in 1963. He received a state funeral from his adopted country.

Du Bois's second wife, Dr. Shirley Graham Du Bois, was a political activist in her own right. She wrote an opera called *Tom Tom: An Epic of Music and the Negro* and authored biographies of Paul Robeson, Phillis Wheatley, Frederick Douglass, Booker T. Washington, and Pocahontas, as well as a memoir about her life with Du Bois. She was forced to leave Ghana in 1967 during a military takeover. She succumbed to breast cancer in 1977 in Beijing and her body was returned to Ghana for burial beside her husband.

The Du Bois home in Ghana is now the centerpiece of the W. E. B. Du Bois Centre for Pan-African Culture, dedicated on June 22, 1985. It contains a library of his books, a collection of his academic gowns, her bedroom with a collection of her books, a picture gallery of Pan-African leaders, African scholars, women freedom fighters, and African-American civil rights activists. Tours of the center culminate at their tombs. ❧

W. E. B. Du Bois was working on a Pan-African encyclopedia when he died. His home, where he is buried, has become a museum.

ASIA

Okunoin Cemetery

**Koyasan (Mount Koya), Ito District,
Wakayama Prefecture, Japan**
http://www.japan-guide.com/e/e4901.html

In Japan, the bodhisattva Jizō is venerated as the guardian of aborted, miscarried, and stillborn babies. Parents make offerings of clothing, especially bibs and caps, on his statues.

Kobo Daishi is one of the most revered people in Japan's religious history. He studied with Buddhist monks in China before founding a temple in a high valley between the eight peaks of Mount Koya in 816 AD. Since that time, the temple complex has expanded to 177 temples and monasteries. Mount Koya, headquarters of Shingon Buddhism in Japan, was named a UNESCO World Heritage Site in 2004.

Kobo Daishi entered eternal meditation in 835 and was entombed on Mount Koya. His followers believe he isn't dead, just "meditating without a sigh" as he awaits the Future Buddha. Twice a day, monks set food before the doors of his mausoleum.

Around the tomb, Okunoin Cemetery has grown to be the largest burial ground in Japan. More than 200,000 graves are marked with everything from traditional monuments to stupas to a rocket ship and even a giant cup. The thickness of the moss on some of the memorials hints at how long they have been standing.

The cemetery has two entrances. The traditional one starts with Ichinohashi Bridge. From

Japan's largest cemetery holds more than 200,000 graves. Lanterns around the mausoleum of the founder of Shingon Buddhism have been burning continuously for over a thousand years.

there, it's a two-kilometer walk through the graveyard to the lantern pavilion. Winding between towering cypress, hemlocks, and cedars, the path passes graves of prominent monks and feudal lords.

A shorter approach leads through the modern part of the graveyard, past corporate and association graves, including plots purchased by Nissan and Panasonic. One plot belongs to a pest control company that honors all the termites they've killed.

Both paths connect at the Gokusho Offering Hall. Here rows of statues depict Jizo, the popular Bodhisattva who protects children and travelers. Some statues wear vermillion bibs or knitted caps. These are offerings from parents who have lost a child, whether by accident, illness, miscarriage, or abortion.

Torodo Hall (the Hall of Lamps) stands in front of Kobo Daishi's mausoleum. The 10,000 lanterns there are kept perpetually lit. It's believed that some have burned for 1200 years. ⚜

The 47 Ronin are buried on the grounds of this Buddhist temple in Tokyo.

Sengakuji

2 Chome-11-1 Takanawa, Minato-ku, Tokyo, Japan
http://www.sengakuji.or.jp/
about_sengakuji_en

Sengakuji, a Buddhist temple complex near Shinagawa Station in Tokyo, was founded in 1612 by Tokugawa Ieyasu, first shogun of the Edo era. Sengakuji is considered one of the three principal temples of Old Tokyo, although it has been rebuilt several times due to fire and damage during wartime. The temple follows the teachings of Zen Master Dogen, who taught that zazen meditation was a realization of the Buddha. Young monks practice meditation at the temple to this day.

The temple's small cemetery holds the graves of the 47 Ronin, who participated in Japan's most famous act of vengeance and samurai loyalty. Their story began in the last years of the 17th century, when Asano Naganori was appointed by the shogunate to entertain imperial envoys traveling from Edo to the capital at Kyoto. His advisor, Kira Kozukenosuke, was supposed to train him, but Kira demanded payment for a service that Asano believed was merely the older man's duty. Kira continued to insult Asano

until finally Asano snapped. He attacked Kira in the Pine Gallery of Edo Castle, cutting him across the forehead and on his shoulder.

The wounds weren't fatal, but drawing a sword inside the palace was a capital crime. By law, both parties of the quarrel should have been punished, but Kira got off, while Asano was sentenced to commit seppuku—ritual suicide—in another lord's garden. The punishment was yet another insult: Asano should have been allowed to kill himself indoors. Only felons killed themselves in gardens.

Asano's lands were confiscated and his family stripped of their title. His retainers protested, but were dismissed. They went from being Asano's samurai to ronin, masterless warriors with no purpose in life.

Led by former chief retainer Oishi Kurano-suke, 47 of the former samurai vowed to avenge their lord. They knew if they attacked Kira immediately, he would be prepared, so they hid their armor and weapons and bided their time. Some of them took menial jobs. Oishi left his wife and went to live on the rough side of town, drinking too much in public and cavorting with prostitutes.

Two years after Asano's death, the 47 Ronin armed themselves and attacked Kira's castle. On December 14, 1702, they captured Kira in an outhouse and offered him the opportunity to kill himself. When he demurred, Oishi beheaded him. As a group, the ronin marched to Sengakuji to present the head of their enemy to Lord Asano's grave.

The following day, the warriors turned themselves into the shogunate. They were sentenced to commit seppuku together on February 4, 1703.

The story was popularized by the play *Chushin-gura* (*The Story of the Loyal Retainers*). Its themes of justice and loyalty still resonate with the Japanese after 300 years. Every December 14, a festival is held at Sengakuji to commemorate the ronin's vengeance. ⚜

Yokohama Gaijin Bochi

096, Yamate-cho, Naka-ku, Yokohama, Kanagawa, Japan
http://www.yokohamajapan.com/things-to-do/foreign-general-cemetery

Japan's isolation from the world ended in 1853, when Commodore Perry arrived in Tokyo Bay with four black-sailed ships. He delivered a letter from President Millard Fillmore demanding that the shogun government open Japanese ports to American vessels.

In 1859, Japanese nationalists killed Roman Mophet and Ivan Sokoloff, two Russian marines.

Sailors, brewers, inventors, businessmen, as well as diplomats and instigators of diplomatic incidents, are all buried on this hillside in Yokohama, representing a range of nationalities from around the world.

Their grave at the bottom of the bluff is the oldest remaining in the Yokohama Foreigners Cemetery. It was once magnificent, but only its pedestal remains.

Also buried here is Charles Lennox Richardson, a British merchant killed by escorts of Lord Satsuma on the Tokaido Road on September 14, 1862. Richardson and several Western friends, who had been sightseeing in Japan, refused to kneel when the Satsuma Daimyo rode by. The Japanese lord ordered his men to "chastise" the Westerners. Richardson was killed immediately, two of his friends were gravely wounded, and a third escaped to report what had happened. Richardson's death sparked the Anglo-Satsuma War. The British demanded the Daimyo punish the murderers. When he refused, the British Royal Navy bombarded his castle and sank three of his steamships. Satsuma's samurai climbed aboard the British ships and killed 13 sailors. Eventually, impressed by Western weaponry, the Daimyo executed Richardson's killers.

In 1864, the Foreigners' Cemetery expanded to 4.5 acres. After the Meiji government took power, the Ministry of Foreign Affairs wrote the American, British, Dutch, and Russian consulates, demanding that the consulates pay for the cemetery's upkeep. These consulates formed the Yokohama Foreign General Cemetery Foundation, which oversees the cemetery to this day.

Many cemetery records were destroyed by the Great Kanto Earthquake, so it's not known exactly how many people are buried here. The surviving list, added to those buried since 1923, numbers about 5000 names. Almost 3000 tombstones remain standing. Gravestones record forty-some different nationalities.

Among those buried here are Edmund Morel, father of the Japanese railways; William Copeland, who introduced beer to Japan; and Eliza Scidmore, who brought the cherry trees to Washington, DC. Also buried here are 120 Japanese wives of foreigners. ✿

186 Zoshigaya Reien

Toshima-ku, Minami Ikebukuro 4-25-1, Tokyo, Japan

The 25 acres in the heart of Tokyo occupied by Zoshigaya Cemetery was once an estate owned by the shogun, commander-in-chief of the Imperial Japanese armies. On this estate lived the shogun's falconers and his kennel keepers.

The idea of public graveyards was imported to Japan from the West during the Meiji era, which coincided with the Victorian age. After burial and cremations were banned in the center of the city, Tokyo claimed the Zoshigaya land for a graveyard in 1874. It became one of four nondenominational burial grounds owned by the city.

Originally, Zoshigaya Reien was called Zoshigaya-Asahidecho Bochi. Bochi, the traditional Japanese word for "graveyard," evolved to mean a graveyard associated with a shrine or temple. In 1935, this cemetery's name was changed to Reien, which connotes a spacious spiritual park, usually filled with trees and shrubbery.

In Japan, almost everyone is cremated. Afterward, any remaining bones are placed in an urn, which is added to a small crypt beneath the family monument. It is uncommon for people to have an individual gravestone.

During the Buddhist funeral, the dead are given a new name, a kaimyo. This is written in kanji on a large wooden blade called a sotoba, which is left in a rack behind the gravestone.

Most of the graves in Zoshigaya Reien are traditionally shaped: a couple of low stone steps topped by an upright stone marked with the family name in kanji. Often the upright also features a round family crest called a kamon. Every family in Japan has one of these heraldic crests. They range from leaves to birds to geometric symbols.

Many gravesites in Zoshigaya have private gardens, hedged by small bushes or surrounded by low curbs. Offerings of incense and flowers are common, but often bottles of water, beer, or sake are left behind as well. Some graves have what look like mailboxes with a slot where visitors can drop a business card.

Zoshigaya Reien contains the graves of several famous Japanese: Natsume Soseki, one of Japan's best-loved novelists and author of *I Am a Cat*; pre-war novelist and playwright Kyoka Izumi; poet and painter Yumeji Takehisa; and Ogino Ginko, the first woman physician to practice Western medicine in Japan. Nakahama "John" Manjiro, the first Japanese to visit the United States, is also buried here. He was shipwrecked while fishing at age 14. An American ship rescued him, taking him first to Hawaii, then to Boston. He returned to Japan just in time to serve as translator when Commodore Perry's Black Ships sailed into Yokohama Bay in 1853. Nakahama eventually became a professor at the Tokyo Imperial University.

Buried in Zoshigaya Reien is Koizumi Yakumo, known in the West as Lafcadio Hearn. His *Kwaidan: Stories and Studies of Strange Things*, a collection of Japanese ghost tales comparable to the work of the Brothers Grimm, was the basis of an Academy Award–nominated film.

187

Hiroshima Peace Memorial Park

**1-2 Nakajimama-cho, Naka-ku,
Hiroshima City, Japan
http://www.pcf.city.hiroshima.jp**

The *Genbaku Domu*—the Atomic Dome—caps the ruins of the Industrial Promotion Hall beside the Ota-gawa River. This was Ground Zero on August 6, 1945, when the *Enola Gay* dropped the world's first atomic weapon on Hiroshima. The bomb exploded in midair, leveling tens of thousands of buildings. Winds generated by the blast fanned a firestorm that destroyed 75 percent of all buildings between the mountains and the sea. Only the skeleton of the Industrial Promotion Hall, at the eye of the storm, survived.

The loss of life was staggering: 140,000 the first day. Children had been released from school that morning in order to create fire lanes through town. After the daily American flyover at 7 a.m., the all-clear siren sounded. Everyone who could be was outside that morning. Many of them were incinerated instantly, leaving behind nothing but shadows photographed by the explosion.

Peace Memorial Park holds a collection of monuments, but the simplest one is a grave. In the center of the park, a grassy mound rises like the barrows at Gamla Uppsala. This tumulus holds the remains of such victims as could be recovered, pried out of collapsed buildings or hauled from the river.

A plaque says that the barrow contains the remains of 70,000 people. In keeping with Buddhist tradition, they were cremated. The mound of ashes stands twelve feet high.

Nearby, a huge deep bell tolls. In Japan, temple bells are upended cups of bronze. They have no clappers. Instead, a baton—sometimes big as a tree trunk—is suspended outside the bell. Anyone can pull the striker back and let it swing forward to sound the bell. In this case, every peal is a prayer for the repose of the dead. ❧

The Cenotaph Memorial in the Hiroshima Peace Park stands in memory of all who disappeared in the firestorm after the world's first atomic bomb dropped on Japan.

The Atomic Dome was Ground Zero on August 6, 1945.

188 Museum of the Terra-cotta Warriors

Lintong District, Xi'an, Shaanxi province, China
https://www.travelchinaguide.com/
attraction/shaanxi/xian/terra_cotta_army/
mausoleum_1.htm

The burial site of China's first emperor has a circumference of almost four miles. The gravesite includes models of palaces, stables, a zoo, and riverbeds that once flowed with mercury between mountains of bronze. The layout of the burial site is modeled on the Qin capital of Xianyang. It was guarded by as many as 8000 terra-cotta warriors, along with statues of acrobats, jugglers, and horses.

The burial site was discovered in 1974 when farmers sank a shaft for a well. After 40 years, much of the site remains unexcavated. In fact, the emperor's actual tomb, which lies under a mound more than 140 feet high, has not yet been opened. The tomb is booby-trapped to dissuade grave robbers.

Thirteen-year-old Ying Zheng became king of Qin in 264 BC. By 221, he had unified the warring kingdoms of Ancient China and declared himself emperor. Among his achievements were the standardization of currency, a uniform system of writing, and a new legal code.

During his reign, thousands of artisans constructed the burial complex and its permanent denizens. They made molds for the warriors, cast them in orangish brown clay, baked them, and assembled the pieces. The workmen labored until the emperor's death in 210 AD, when the second emperor ordered them killed to protect the tomb's secrets.

In addition to the size and complexity of the burial site, the terra-cotta warriors themselves are works of art. Although elements of armor and dress recur, their faces were individually carved. Each figure was fully painted, but Chinese archaeologists were unable to stop the paint from flaking away when they unearthed the figures.

Up to 40,000 tourists a day visit the Terra-cotta Warriors each summer. ⚜

Larger than four football fields, the burial site of China's first emperor is guarded by 8,000 terra-cotta warriors.

Ming Tombs Scenic Area

Changchi Road, Changping Qu, China
http://www.visitourchina.com/beijing/
attraction/ming-tombs.html

In the fifth year of his reign, the third emperor of the Ming Dynasty—Zhu Di—began construction of a tomb in this area under Tianshou Shan (Heavenly Longevity Mountain). His tomb, called Changling ("long tomb"—*ling* means "tomb"), is larger than the 12 Ming tombs that followed. While Changling is not completely excavated, it is fully accessible.

The era in which Zhu Di ruled was named Yongle (Eternal Joy), which lasted from 1402 until 1422 AD. The tomb's construction was completed in 1427. Zhu Di is buried here with Empress Xu.

The most impressive part of Changling is the Hall of Eminent Favor, almost 2000 square meters in size. All its columns and beams are made of Chinese cedar, an easily carved softwood. This is the most magnificent cedarwood structure in China.

All 13 Ming tombs lie along the Sacred Way, a seven-kilometer-long avenue lined with monumental sculptures of camels, elephants, lions, and humans. Only Changling and two other tombs are open to visitors.

Dingling (Fixed Tomb) is the mausoleum of the 13th Ming emperor, Zhu Yijun, and his two empresses. He was known as Emperor Wanli (Much Experience). His reign, the longest in the dynasty, spanned 48 years. Inside Dingling's vast stone Underground Palace, the entrances of each burial hall are sculpted from jade. The halls contain white marble thrones and red caskets. More than 3000 precious articles, including jade and jewels, are on display.

189

Zhaoling belongs to the 12th emperor, Zhu Zaihou, and his three empresses. Its crescent-shaped Dumb Yard (built by mute workers, so they couldn't betray the tomb's entrance) houses the imperial coffins. Although much smaller than Changling, Zhaoling was the first Ming tomb to be excavated and restored. Past the Gate of Blessing and Grace stands a stone turtle. Touching the turtle's head frees one from worries for life.

The Ming Tomb Complex spans 30 acres full of trees and water, surrounded on three sides by mountains: perfect for nature walks or picnics. ❧

190 Shaolin Pagoda Forest

Shaolin Temple, Dengfeng, Zhengzhou, Henan, China
http://www.china.org.cn/english/TR-e/42673.htm

The Shaolin Temple on Song Mountain in China's Henan Province is the birthplace of Chinese Zen Buddhism as well as the cradle of Shaolin martial arts. It was added to UNESCO's World Cultural Heritage List in 2010.

Monks have practiced martial arts at the Shaolin Temple Wushu Training Center for 1500 years. The temple's founder, known as Dharma, taught martial arts exercises to improve the monks' health and as a way for them to defend themselves.

Not quite half a kilometer west of the Shao-lin Temple stands a Pagoda Forest, a graveyard of Buddhist dignitaries in use from 791 to 1803 AD. The pagodas were built during the Tang, Song, Jin, Yuan, Ming, and Qing dynasties. This is China's largest collection of tomb pagodas, about 250 in all, marking the graves of abbots and eminent monks.

The stone or brick pagodas average 49 feet high and range from one to seven stories. Mainly multi-tiered or pavilion-style, their shapes vary from three- to five-sided or cylindrical. Their shapes and number of layers indicate the deceased's Buddhist attainments. Each pagoda is marked with the year of its construction.

Other Buddhist practitioners are also buried here. In the eastern part of the forest stands a pagoda built in 1339 for a Japanese monk. A pagoda in the western part marks the grave of an Indian monk who died in 1564. ❧

Brick or stone tomb pagodas were built for eminent monks and abbots at the Shaolin Temple as early as 791 AD.

Monumental sculptures stand in the Longhua Revolutionary Martyrs' Cemetery, in memory of those who died to bring communism to China.

Longhua Revolutionary Martyrs' Cemetery

180 Longhua West Road, Xuhui, Shanghai, China
http://www.idealshanghai.com/venues/479

In the 1920s, Chiang Kai-shek's Kuomintang government believed that if it just executed all the Communists, Communism itself would die. Between 1928 and 1937, hundreds of members of the Communist Party and other political activists were rounded up and executed inside Longhua Prison. They were buried there, too.

After the Communists took power in 1949, the remains of the Longhua martyrs were exhumed. A design contest was held in 1957 to create a suitable monument, but nothing came of it. Longhua Park was fenced in 1963, but the project was interrupted by the Cultural Revolution. Xia Zhixu, wife of Zhao Shiyan—who had been killed in the prison—proposed a memorial in December 1983. Five years later, the State

Council authorized Longhua Revolutionary Martyrs Memorial Palace for the cultural relics under national protection. Construction began at last in May 1994.

The area became a monument to more than 500 martyrs who died to bring communism to China or were killed in the Anti-Japanese War (known in the West as World War II). The cemetery opened in July 1995 to serve as a patriotic educational base. Colossal sculptures of revolutionary figures—a surprising number of them topless—commemorate the heroes of New China.

In the center of the park stands a black marble wall lettered in gold that reads, "Red Heart Fresh Blood for the People," a quote from Jiang Zemin, former president of the Republic of China. It exhorts, "Sacrifice everything."

Behind the pyramidal memorial hall in the northwest of the park lie the graves of more revolutionaries, including Zhang Xiyuan, Deng Xiaoping's first wife, who died in childbirth.

Neither the memorial hall nor the revolutionary cadres memorial hall are open to the public, but visitors can tour the prison and visit its execution ground in addition to exploring the park. ⚜

Surrounded by high-rises, the Hong Kong Cemetery was originally called the Protestant Cemetery, then the Colonial Cemetery, then Happy Valley Cemetery. As many as 12,000 people are buried there.

Hong Kong Cemetery

Wong Nei Chung Road, Hong Kong
http://tgrfe88.wixsite.com/hong-kong-cemetery

This cemetery opened in 1845 to cope with the high mortality rates among British civilians stationed in Hong Kong. Cholera and dysentery killed hundreds. Even sunstroke could be deadly. The cemetery's 8000 graves hold more than 12,000 people.

The cruciform funeral chapel, built in 1845, is the oldest example of colonial architecture in Hong Kong. The cemetery's oldest graves surround the chapel. A pillar topped with an urn belongs to Lieutenant Benjamin Fox, who died in 1841 during the first Opium War after a cannonball shattered his leg.

The first Western woman to live in Hong Kong arrived as a newly married 17-year-old missionary from Virginia. Ten years later, Henrietta Shuck died of exhaustion after she'd borne five children, managed a household of 37 people, taught school, and wrote three memoirs. Most female missionaries survived only four years after coming to Hong Kong.

Daniel Richard Caldwell, Protector to the Chinese, went from working on an opium-smuggling ship to becoming Secretary of Chinese Affairs in the colonial government. He's a controversial figure: a Freemason who may have shielded brothels, pirates, and gambling dens for personal gain.

Also buried in the cemetery is Sir Kai Ho Kai, the first Chinese to qualify in medicine, the second to be admitted to the Supreme Court of Hong Kong, and third to join the Legislative Council. He pioneered Western medical training in Hong Kong.

Sir Robert Hotung, one of the first prominent Eurasians, faced down racism to integrate Hong Kong. The businessman and philanthropist was patriarch of a family who worked in business, government, and entertainment. Bruce Lee was his great-nephew.

Yeung Kui-wan, a prominent supporter of Sun Yat-sen's revolution against the Qing government, was assassinated on his doorstep in Gage Street by agents of the empress. For many years, Yeung's grave monument was left blank for fear of vandalism. In 2011, the Hong Kong government finally marked his grave with a plaque.

Others buried here include Police Constable Ernest Goucher, who was mauled by a tiger while on duty in 1915, and Colonel Cyril Wild, killed in a plane crash in 1946. As the only fluent Japanese speaker in the British army, Wild helped negotiate the Japanese surrender in Singapore. He had been en route to give evidence at the Tokyo War Crimes Tribunal. ⚜

Old Christian Cemetery

Fort Canning Green,
Singapore City, Singapore
https://www.nparks.gov.sg/gardens-parks-and-nature/parks-and-nature-reserves/fort-canning-park

After he negotiated the colonization of Singapore for the British Empire, Stamford Raffles built his home atop this hill. The British Army built a hospital, barracks, and an arms depot nearby, and called it Fort Canning.

Singapore became a major port of call for trade ships from around the world. To serve them, the Old Christian Cemetery opened in 1822. The southern half was used by the Anglican community, while the northern half served all other Christian denominations.

A high whitewashed gate—the earliest example of Gothic Revival style in Singapore—leads to the Fort Canning Green. The gateway was designed by Captain Charles Edward Faber, superintending engineer in the Straits.

By 1865, the year the cemetery closed, more than 600 people had been buried there. A third of them were Chinese Christians. Others came from around the world, as evidenced by surviving tombstones in German, Dutch, Thai, and other languages.

By the 20th century, the graveyard had become so dilapidated that its monuments were

removed. Legible tombstones were incorporated into a brick wall that now encircles the lawn where the cemetery used to stand.

Many of the dead remembered here were sailors. Twenty-year-old Peter Parks "fell from the fore topsail yard." His stone was "erected as a tribute to his worth by his shipmates." Others recorded here were spouses. One stone reads, "Sacred to the Memory of Elizabeth, the affectionate wife of Geo. Gray, M.M. who departed this life on board the *Allendale* in Singapore Harbor." Another remembers 22-year-old Lucy, "wife of Charles Hogg of Calcutta, Esquire," and their daughter Mary Ann "her infant child, who died on the evening of the same day."

The longest epitaphs hint at the most interesting stories: "William Scott Esquire of Singapore, eldest son of the late James

Scott Esq. of Penang, one of the first settlers of that island: born the 3rd day of May 1780 and died at Singapore, respected and beloved by all, the 18th day of December 1861." Penang, a state in Malaysia, was settled by Westerners prior to Singapore. With so much evidence of early death in the gravestones around him, it's remarkable that Scott survived 81 years. ⚜

Two cupolas stand in front of a brick wall that holds the headstones from Singapore's Old Christian Cemetery.

Baguio Public Cemetery

58 Naguilian Road, Baguio City, Luzon, Philippines

194

Baguio City was founded in 1900 as the American Summer Capital of the Philippines. Its name comes from the local Ibaloy word for "moss." Though humid, the summer temperature in the mountainous area was much cooler than in Manila.

Originally the only road that reached Baguio City was Naguilian Road, a so-called horse trail at high elevation. The American government opened this cemetery there in 1932. One of its oldest gravestones remembers Joseph Douglas, who died in December 1934. Joseph was one of six children of Samuel Jefferson Douglas, a Welshman who migrated to New York before becoming a soldier assigned to the Philippines. Samuel Douglas founded Suyoc Mines in Itogon.

Eusebius Julius Halsema, the last American mayor of Baguio, is buried here with his family. Halsema served as mayor from 1920 to 1937.

When the Japanese invaded the Philippines, Halsema and his children were interned in a prison camp. He died on March 15, 1945, when Americans bombed the hospital in which he was recovering from dysentery.

The most visited grave belongs to Ibaloy chieftain Mateo Carino and his son, Sioco. Before the American occupation, the Carino family owned the land on which Baguio City stands. Mateo Carino took his case to the U.S. Supreme Court and won a decision that has helped other native peoples regain land taken from them. Unfortunately, the Ibaloy did not get compensated for their land. Sioco Carino died of starvation during World War II.

The Public Cemetery is the largest cemetery on Luzon, the largest island in the Philippines. Twenty thousand graves are jammed into its 23-acre hilltop. Officials have been seeking a new cemetery site, but in the meantime, condo-type mausoleums maximize the remaining space.

In September 2009, Typhoon Pepeng was the second tropical storm to strike Luzon within a week. A landslide caused by the hurricane damaged a number of tombs. Despite that, *Business Insider* listed the cemetery as one of "The World's Most Stunning Cemeteries" in 2014. ⚜

The world's most famous tomb draws 3 million visitors a year. It is counted among the Wonders of the World.

195

The Taj Mahal

Agra, Uttar Pradesh, India
http://www.tajmahal.gov.in

The world's most famous burial place is the immense white marble mausoleum built by the Mughal emperor Shah Jahan in memory of his favorite wife.

When she lay on her deathbed in 1630, Empress Mumtaz Mahal requested that her husband build her the most magnificent tomb the world had ever known. The empress, reckoned to be so beautiful that the moon hid its face from her, died in childbirth.

Built by 20,000 workers at a cost of 32 million rupees, the mausoleum took nearly 20 years to be completed. The building employed craftsmen from Delhi, Qannauj, Lahore, and Multan, in addition to Muslim artisans from Baghdad, Shiraz, and Bukhara. The white marble walls are inlaid with scrolling calligraphic verses from the Koran done in agate and jasper.

The Taj stands on a raised platform 186 feet square. Its 58-foot-diameter dome rises to a height of 216 feet, flanked by four minarets. The vast burial complex also contains an elaborate garden, a mosque, a guesthouse, and several other palatial buildings. The Taj Mahal itself is surrounded by four reflecting pools and the Yamuna River flowing behind it. Inside the building, the sarcophagi of Mumtaz Majal and Shah Jahan stand together on one side of the tomb, throwing off its otherwise perfect symmetry.

In 1658, Shah Jahan was deposed by his son, who imprisoned him in the Agra Fort across the river, where he could look out on his wife's tomb. Shah Jahan died in 1666.

After Europeans flocked to India in the 18th century, the Taj Mahal inspired a fashion for building mausoleums back home.

When it was added to UNESCO's World Heritage List in 1983, the listing read, "The Taj Mahal is the jewel of Muslim art in India and one of the universally admired masterpieces of the world's heritage." Three million people visit it each year. ⚜

196

South Park Street Cemetery

184 Acharya Jagadish Chandra Bose Road,
Kolkata, West Bengal, India
http://www.christianburialboardkolkata.com/
archaeology.html

South Park Street Cemetery demonstrates that the idea behind modern cemeteries—unattached to a church, with individualized tombs and personalized epitaphs—originated not in Europe at all but in British India. The English opened the South Park Street Cemetery during the "sick season" of 1767, when the summer heat of Calcutta laid many Europeans low. The ways to die in the tropics were various and difficult to predict, as evidenced by the more than 1600 tombs here. Obelisks, pyramids, and mausoleums jam the little cemetery.

When Rose Aylmer died at age 20 in March 1800, it was believed she succumbed to eating too many pineapples. Cause of death was probably cholera. A lovely spiraling cone marks her grave. Her epitaph begins, "Long, long before her hour, death called her tender soul." Walter Savage Landor immortalized her in a poem.

The *Juno* Monument, a towering obelisk with reliefs of anchors, marks the grave of Captain William Mackay. The *Juno* left Rangoon in May 1795, loaded with timber. It ran partly aground and sprung a slow leak. As the ship slowly submerged, its cargo of timber kept it from completely sinking. Desperate passengers clung to its rigging, dropping one at a time into the sea. When the wreck finally drifted ashore two months later, only 14 people had survived. One of them was Mackay, who lived until 1805. His account of the wreck inspired Byron's *Don Juan*.

A copy of Caius Cestius's pyramid in the Protestant Cemetery of Rome marks the grave of Elizabeth Jane Barwell, who died at age 23. She'd been married for two years to Richard Barwell, Esq., a member of the Council of the Honorable East India Company. Her epitaph says more about him than it does about her.

Major General Charles "Hindoo" Stuart, who died in 1828, was an Irishman captivated by India. He unsuccessfully encouraged European ladies to cast off their corsets for saris. Eventually he married an Indian woman, which led to accusations he'd "gone native." He lies beneath an aedicule with an onion dome and tall, thin conical decorations, a combination of Indian and Islamic Revival.

Sir William Jones came to India as a Supreme Court judge and also fell in love. He had already mastered every European language, so he set about learning Sanskrit and translating the *Bhagavad Gita* into English. His whitewashed tomb is a broad obelisk, decorated with reliefs of urns. ❧

Opened in 1767, the South Park Street Cemetery was the largest Christian cemetery in Asia for more than a century. Some argue that it was even more influential than Père Lachaise in changing burial attitudes in Europe.

AUSTRALIA

197 Melbourne General Cemetery

College Crescent, Parkville, Victoria
https://mgc.smct.org.au

Founded in 1835 by free British settlers, Melbourne swelled in size during the gold rush of the 1850s. Melbourne General Cemetery opened in June 1852, two kilometers north of the city of Melbourne, in the suburb of Carlton North. The cemetery was organized under the direct control of four Christian trustees, who were empowered to make their own rules. Anglicans, Catholics, Presbyterians, Congregationalists, and Wesleyans received large portions of the graveyard, while Jews and Quakers were allowed much smaller areas. The Chinese, Afghan, and Aboriginal communities were consigned to the "Other Denominations" ground, but there they were allowed to pursue their own burial traditions.

Melbourne General was the first modern cemetery in Victoria, crossed by wide paths between its gazebos and chapels. Its oldest buildings are the Jewish chapel, completed in 1854, and the Catholic mortuary chapel, which dates to the 1870s.

Although the granite gravestones are packed together tightly, the cemetery has only 300,000 permanent residents. Among these are the following:

Native Chief Derrimut has a sandstone tombstone erected by colonists in gratitude for his warning in October 1835 when some up-country tribes planned a massacre. Because he didn't fit into the Western religions who controlled the cemetery, Derrimut was buried with the Chinese. Traditionally, the Koori people don't mark their graves.

Despite a lack of exploration experience, Irish-born Robert O'Hara Burke and Englishman William John Wills were chosen by the government in Victoria to walk across the continent from south to north. They starved to death on the return trip. In January 1863, their bodies were recovered and given state funerals, before being reburied in Melbourne General Cemetery.

Others buried here are Patrick Hannan, who discovered gold at Kalgoorlie in Western

Australia; British opera singer Frederick Federici, who created the title role of *The Mikado* in New York; Mendel Balberyszski, survivor of the destruction of the Vilnius Ghetto; and Sir Redmond Barry, the acting chief justice who sentenced outlaw Ned Kelly to hang.

The most unique monument in the cemetery celebrates billiards champion Walter Lindrum, who was so good that the rules of the game had to be changed to give his opponents a sporting chance. Lindrum lies beneath a full-size granite billiard table, complete with cue ball and stick. ✤

Rookwood Necropolis

Hawthorne Avenue,
Rookwood, New South Wales
http://www.rookwoodcemetery.com.au

In 1862, the government of New South Wales purchased 200 acres near the village of Haslam's Creek for a cemetery. It had sections for Roman Catholic, Anglican, Wesleyan, Presbyterian, Jewish, and Independent congregations, each portioned out according to the denomination's size in the 1861 census. The necropolis was dedicated in 1867. Burials began in January that year.

The cemetery was enlarged in 1878–79, when 577 acres were added. At 777 acres, the Rookwood Necropolis is the largest graveyard in the Southern Hemisphere. One million epitaphs have been recorded on 600,000 graves and 200,000 crematorium niches.

In fact, Rookwood's Spanish Mission-style crematorium is the oldest operating crematory in Australia. It opened in 1925.

When the cemetery was added to the National Trust of Australia in 1988, Rookwood was commended for being a "comprehensive and tangible manifestation of the social history of Sydney, documenting the cultural and religious diversity of the Australian community since 1867." In a more recent development, Rookwood acknowledges that the Dharug people—part of the oldest continuous culture in the world—are the traditional custodians of their land.

Rookwood serves as the largest public open space within urban Sydney. It provides a haven for birds and native fauna, including 19 species of frogs and reptiles. In addition to native brushtail possums and grey-headed flying foxes, the cemetery has colonies of imported rabbits, hares, and foxes. Several species of cuckoos and honey eaters breed in the cemetery. A large spectrum of birds migrates through each year.

While the cemetery is home to introduced plants including date palms, magnolias, and several species of pines, it also provides habitat for two endangered plant species: downy wattle and small-leaved dillwynias. ✤

This Garden of Remembrance at the Rookwood Necropolis honors Australians who fought in World War I.

Waverley Cemetery

**Saint Thomas Street, Bronte,
New South Wales**
http://www.waverleycemetery.com

The coast-side Municipality of Waverley began in 1859 as an isolated outpost east of Sydney. The area attracted industries such as soap making, candle making, shoe making, dairy farming, and even emu ranching.

Rather than trek 16 miles to Rookwood Necropolis to bury the dead, the Waverley Council agreed to manage a self-funding necropolis "as long as it incurred no cost" to do so. Forty gorgeous acres atop the headlands were purchased in 1875 and opened officially on August 1, 1877. The first burial took place three days later.

Among the artists and pioneers buried here are members of the Albert family, the music publishers who built the Boomerang mansion in Sydney; and poets Dorothea Mackellar (author of "My Country," which begins "I love a sunburnt country"), Henry Kendall, Henry Lawson (author of "The Drover's Wife"), Roderick Quinn, and Victor Daly. Other permanent residents include "Rum" Corp soldier and pioneer Major George Johnston; magician and conjurer Dante the Great, whose real name was Oscar Eliason; vaudeville actress "Queenie" Paul; author Ethel Pedley, who wrote *Dot and the Kangaroo*; as well as beer brewers, meat pie bakers, champion swimmers, theater owners, cricketeers, booksellers, at least one greeting card manufacturer,

The Waverley Cemetery in New South Wales stands atop cliffs overlooking the Tasman Sea.

former governors and chief justices of New South Wales, and 200 war dead.

Of course, any cemetery older than a century is going to have its darker tales as well. Sydney bookmaker and organized crime figure George Freeman was buried in Waverley in 1990 after he succumbed to an asthma attack. Murdered heiress and property activist Juanita Nielsen has a memorial at the Mark Foy family mausoleum. Her body was never found.

In the winter of 2016, severe weather damaged Waverley's coastal walk, which drew around a million visitors per year. After torrential rains, high winds, and king tides pounded the cliffs overlooking Bronte Beach, part of the cliff face collapsed. No graves were damaged, but crowd control barriers will block off the walkway until the cliff can be stabilized. ⚜

The Irish Monument stands above the grave of Michael Dwyer, a survivor of the Fenian Uprising, who was transported to the penal colony at Botany Bay. In addition, it remembers the 1798 martyrs, the Easter 1916 martyrs, and remains a site of pilgrimage for the Irish.

SPECIAL THANKS

Books are never written in a vacuum. Thank you to everyone who expanded my list of cemeteries for this book, especially Blair Apperson, David Bingham, Mary Jo Bole, Elizabeth Cleere, Deb Dauber, Jeff Dauber, Douglas Keister, Nancy Kilpatrick, Daniel Madar, Karin Peterson, Christine Quigley, Lydia M. Reid, Christine Sulewski, Sharon 444, Carole Tyrrell, and Rocky Wood.

Thank you to all the people who've poked around these graveyards with me, including Martha Allard, Paul Gault, R. Samuel Klatchko, Mason Jones and Lenore Rhoads, Daniel Malson, Timothy and Alison Renner, Roy and Kathleen Rhoads, Kim Richardson, Brian Thomas, Rage and Leslie, Tim and Wendy, the Ketchen family, and all those who've come to other cemeteries that I couldn't cram into this book. Thanks too to Terry Hamburg and the rest of the Cypress Lawn Heritage Foundation for the work they're doing.

I'm extremely grateful to Atlas Obscura and Findagrave for being such invaluable resources and to the community of cemetery bloggers who share my fascination. Special thanks to Bess Lovejoy and Colin Dickey for the perfect quotes.

Thank you to the publishers who've encouraged my curiosity about cemeteries over the years, from Darren Mckeeman and the crew at Gothic.Net to John Palisano at Western Legends to Lenore Gwynn and Steven Holiday at Gothic Beauty.

Thank you to the local members of Na-no-wri-mo and Shut Up and Write! They helped me get the book done by giving me a community of writers to work alongside. Thanks too to the staff of Borderlands Books and the Borderlands Café, especially Jude, Z'ev, and Jim, who knew just what I needed.

Thank you to Hannah Smith and Odette Fleming, who chased the details and made things lovely, and Melanie Gold for making sure my text was polished. I'm also grateful to Liz Driesbach for her amazing cover and interior design.

Finally, huge gratitude to Dinah Dunn, my editor at Black Dog & Leventhal, who gave me the freedom to write this book and whose suggestions were always exciting and on the mark. Dinah, I cannot thank you enough.

PHOTO CREDITS **123rf** funlovingvolvo p. 160; **Alamy Stock Photo** pp. 1, 3 Franck Fotos; p. 7 REUTERS p. 15 Randy Duchaine; p. 18 Danita Delimont; p. 19 Lee Snider; p. 31 Neal and Molly Jansen; p. 33 Franck Fotos; p. 34 Stephen Saks Photography; p. 45 incamerastock; p. 45 Will and Deni Mcintyre; p. 46 Pat Canova; p. 47 David Doubilet; p. 63 Allan Cash Picture Library; p. 64 Robert Mayne USA; p. 65 Greg Ryan; p. 68 Witold Skrypczak; p. 76 Daving Winger; p. 78 Gary Whitton; p. 84 Witold Skrypczak; p. 88 Mike Long; p. 90 INTERFOTO; p. 95 Chuck Pefley; p. 98 one image photography; p. 100 Ritaariyoshi; p. 101 Ian Dagnall; p. 102 Uwe Bergwitz; p. 104 David Hare; p. 106 niKreative; p. 107 Mgarfat; p. 111 JJM Stock Photography; p. 115 Des Conocido; p. 116 V. Dorosz; p. 117 Michael Dwyer; p. 118 Efrain Padro; p. 120 Geogphotos; p. 121 Liudmila Kotvitckaia; p. 123 Art Directors & Trip; p. 126 Peter Lane; p. 127 Agencja Fotograficzna; p. 129 David Kilpatrick; p. 130 Samc; p. 144 World Pictures; p. 148 Image Broker; p. 158 Luise Berg-Ehlers; p. 159 Radius Images; p. 160 Eddie Linssen; p. 165 Mauritius GmbH; p. 164 Alistair Scott; p. 166 Eamon O'Doherty; p. 170 Jill Schneider; p. 191 Martin Siepman; p. 193 Hackenberg-Photo-Cologne; p. 194 Kentkoberstein; p. 199 Nerissa D'Alton; p. 200 Dpa Picture Alliance Archive; p. 201 Michael Dwyer; p. 207 Jeremy Sutton Hibbert; p. 211 Best View Stock; p. 213 Henry Westheim; p. 214 Ahowden; p. 223 Ruben Martinez Barricate; **Associated Press** p. 114 Luis Porras; **David Bingham** p. 145; **Brian Brown/Vanishing Coastal Georgia** p. 39; **Cypress Lawn Heritage Foundation** p. 89; **Detroit Historical Society** p. 52; **Dianne Fallon** p. 1; **Flickr** p. 16 Ed Waste; p. 82 Pat Eftink; p. 113 Priscilla Burcher; p. 120 Flik47; **Kyle Green/The New York Times/Redux** p. 29; **Getty Images** p. 4 Buyenlarge; p. 8 John Greim; p. 56 Raymond Boyd; p. 59 Art Walaszek; p. 72 Robert Alexander; p. 108 Richard Ellis; **Carol M. Highsmith Archive, Library of Congress, Prints and Photographs Division** pp. 22, 24, 26, 27, 28, 40, 41, 68, 69, 70, 85, 87, 90; H Padleckas p. 57; **Bill Hillyer/The Natchez Democrat** p. 42; **Caitlyn Hopkins** p. 12; **Library of Congress** pp. 9, 11, 13, 20, 21, 32, 38, 48, 62, 92; **Les Parks** p. 76; **Loren Rhoads** p. 4, 14, 53, 60, 71, 79, 80, 85, 93, 99, 105, 125, 216; **Shutterstock.com** p. 2 Lee Snider; pp. 6, 7 Felix Lipov; p. 9 Marcio Jose Bastos Silva; p. 16 Joseph Sohm; pp. 20, 25 Daniel M. Silva; p. 25 Joseph Sohm; p. 28 Hang Dinh; p. 29 M. Dogan; p. 30 Lee Snider Photo Images; p. 33 Thomas Kelley; p. 35 Dvande; p. 36 Gerry Matthews; p. 37 Whytock; p. 40 Nagel Photography; p. 41 Leena Robinson; p. 44 Belen Bilgic Schneider; pp. 49, 50, 51 Ashen Felter; p. 51 Zack Frank; p. 54, 56 Nagel Photography; p. 56 Autumn H. Todd; pp. 65, 66 Nagel Photography; p. 73 Joseph Sohm; p. 74 Jeffrey M. Frank; p. 80 G Seeger; p. 81 Don Mammoser; p. 83 Dorn1530; p. 94 Robert Crum; p. 97 Nolleks86; p. 103 Josef Hanus; p. 111 Nessa Gnatoush; p. 119 Tupungato; p. 121 Flick47; p. 122 Liudmila Kotvitckaia; p. 124 Gary Perkin; p. 128 Tracilaw; p. 131 Elzbietasekowska; p. 132 Sertgejuslamanosovas; p. 134 Sean Wandzilak; p. 135 Restuccia Giancarlo; p. 136 Steven Bostock; p. 138 Nikitin Mikhail; p. 139 Anastasia Ness; p. 141 PHB Richard Semik; p. 142 Charlie Borden; p. 143 Fotokon; p. 143 Paula Sierra; p. 184 Fat Jackey; p. 186 Ivoha; p. 187 OPIS Zagreb; p. 189 Thomas Koch; p. 189 NicolasasFouri; p. 190 Hamed Yeganeh; p. 192 lighthunteralp; p. 195 Mohamed Hakem; p. 196 Vladamirmelnik; p. 197 Jakub Kync; p. 198 WitR; p. 202 Neale Cousland; p. 202 Cowardlilion; p. 203 Joaquin Ossorio Castillo; p. 204 KPGpayless2; p. 208 BlackRabbit3; p. 209 Suchart Boonyavech; p. 210 Blue Sky Studio; p. 212; seragayu; p. 216 Arndale; p. 217 Allen G.; p. 218 Saiko3p; p. 219 Radio Kafka; p. 220 Nilsversemann; p. 223 Annton Gorlin; **Thelmadette** p. 110; **Doug Wallick** p. 60; Walnut Hill Cemetery p. 58; **Jason Watson Photography** p. 18; **Bill Whittaker** p. 58; **Kenneth C Zirkel** p. 13.

INDEX

Page numbers in italics refer to photographs in the text.